THEOLOGICAL LIBERALISM

Creative and Critical

THEOLOGICAL LIBERALISM

Creative and Critical

Edited by

J'annine Jobling
and
Ian Markham

Published in Great Britain in 2000 by SPCK
Holy Trinity Church
Marylebone Road
London NW1 4DU

British Library Cataloguing-in-Publication Data
A catalogue record for this book is available from the British Library.

ISBN 0-281-05361-8

Typeset by Kenneth Burnley, Wirral, Cheshire.
Printed in Great Britain by
The Cromwell Press, Trowbridge, Wiltshire

Contents

Contributors

The Revd Prebendary Dr Paul Avis is General Secretary of the Council for Christian Unity of the Church of England, Sub-Dean of Exeter Cathedral and Director of the Centre for the Study of the Christian Church. He is a former External Examiner in Theology for Liverpool Hope University College.

Dr Lewis Ayres is a lecturer and Everton Fellow at Liverpool Hope University College. He is in the process of completing a study of Augustine and is well known for his work on theological method.

Hannah Bacon is a research assistant at Liverpool Hope University College, where she is undertaking a doctorate on 'Engendering the Symbolic in Christian Worship'. Working from a feminist perspective, this study seeks to revision the doctrine of the Trinity, pointing towards exciting new horizons in Christian worship.

Dr Mark Elliott is a lecturer in Christian studies at Liverpool Hope University College. His doctoral research was in the area of Patristic biblical interpretation, but his interests include the history of Christology, ecumenical theology and literature and theology. He has written work on Postmodernism and theological anthropology.

The Revd Leslie Houlden is Emeritus Professor of Theology at King's College, London. He has published widely on New Testament and doctrinal matters, and was co-editor of *A Dictionary of Biblical Interpretation* (SCM Press, London, 1990) and *Companion Encyclopedia of Theology* (Routledge, London, 1995).

Dr J'annine Jobling is a lecturer at Liverpool Hope University College. She has written on feminist biblical hermeneutics in theological and postmodern context, co-edited a book on *Theology and the Body* (Gracewing, Leominster, 1999) and is now preparing a more broadly focused work on liberalism and theological method.

Gareth Jones is the Professor of Christian Theology at Canterbury Christ Church University College. He is the author of a number of publications, including *Bultmann* (Polity, Cambridge, 1991), *Critical Theology* (Polity, Cambridge, 1995) and more recently *Christian Theology: A Brief Introduction* (Polity, Cambridge, 1999).

Shannon Ledbetter is a lecturer and Developments Officer for Church and Community Connections at Liverpool Hope University College. Her interests are wide and include pastoral theology, theologies of work, and religion and art.

The Revd Giles Legood is an Anglican priest working as a university chaplain in the diocese of London. He is interested in and writes about a range of issues relating to Christian life and thought, particularly those of pastoral care and ethics. His previous books include *Chaplaincy – the Church's Sector Ministries* (Cassell 1999).

Professor Ian Markham is the Foundation Dean and holder of the Liverpool Chair of Theology and Public Life at Liverpool Hope University Colleges. His publications include *Plurality and Christian Ethics* (Seven Bridges Press, New York, 1999) and *Truth and the Reality of God* (T&T Clark, Edinburgh, 1999).

Rachael Penketh is a research assistant at Liverpool Hope University College, where she is undertaking a doctorate on atheism and theological method. She has examined the Liverpool Statement and Radical Orthodoxy as part of this endeavour.

Dr Martyn Percy is Director of the Lincoln Theological Institute for the Study of Religion and Society at the University of Sheffield, where he is also a senior lecturer in theology and sociology. His recent research has focused on contemporary Anglican ecclesiology. Martyn is a Canon of Sheffield Cathedral, and an honorary curate in the City.

Dr Christine Pilkington is a Principal Lecturer in Religious Studies at Canterbury Christ Church University College, where she teaches Old Testament and Jewish studies. Her publications include *Teach Yourself Judaism* and teaching materials in the field of Jewish and Christian theology.

Professor Keith Ward is the Regius Professor of Divinity at Christchurch, Oxford. He is the author of numerous books, which include *A Vision to Pursue* (SCM Press, London, 1991) and his recent four-volume comparative theology published by Oxford University Press.

Preface:
The Liverpool Statement

A New Theological Vision: A Call to Join the Forum for Religion and Theology

On 26 and 27 September 1997, a group of theologians met at Liverpool Hope University College and reflected on the state of contemporary British theology. The following Statement was the result. This Statement was widely circulated, inviting colleagues throughout higher education to become signatories.

As we approach the new millennium, it is a good time to take stock theologically. For those of us in the West, this century has seen constant shift of emphasis between more 'conservative' and more 'liberal' approaches to theology. Emerging from the nineteenth century, a classical liberal theology was in the ascendant. The optimism and naiveté of such theology was challenged by conservative theologians. The late fifties and sixties saw a new liberalism emerge, one which suggested a new morality and a new theology for a newly self-confident age. Since the seventies, the conservatives have returned to the fray. In this battle there is no obvious winner. The agenda seems stale and the in-fighting futile. Theology seems too often a minority academic interest which has failed to keep pace with new scholarship and a rapidly changing world.

What sort of Theology and Religious Studies should shape our future?

All the signatories to this statement are sensitive to the problems involved with traditional liberal theology. In many ways it reflected the cultural dominance of European modes of thought; it linked itself too uncritically with individualism and progress and failed to perceive its own contingency. Perhaps its greatest failure was not to appreciate the richness of the Christian tradition, a tradition which was too often caricatured and misunderstood.

Granted that the conservative reaction to the failure of liberal theology has taken tradition much more seriously, but it has often done so by refusing to engage with contemporary culture. As new liberation movements, including feminist and gay movements, became more prominent, conservative theologies found themselves with little positive to say in a changing culture.

A future theology must learn from the past failures of both liberal and conservative approaches. For the Christian message to flourish a clear vision of the theological task is required, a vision that uses the tradition creatively yet critically to engage with our modern age. We need to encourage a positive, open vision of theology in the hope that it might once again influence the public sphere. To this end, we propose the following.

First, we must engage openly with our contemporary culture. We need to demonstrate that our tradition has the resources to engage in an ongoing dialogue with the social, cultural, and political problems and achievements of our age. In the university this will entail a critical openness to interdisciplinary work and the richness of much contemporary culture. It is no coincidence that recent church reports like *Unemployment and the Future of Work* have been written, almost entirely, without the assistance of mainstream theologians; it seemed so difficult to harness their talents and interests to the matters in hand.

Second, we need to be much more international in our vision. We need to look to the rest of Europe, the United States and the developing world for a sense of the theological options that are open to our age. Theological insularity has meant that many of the most vibrant contemporary theologies have been completely ignored.

Third, the neglect of other faith traditions is wilful. In a culture where religious choice has become a significant issue, the lack of interest in other religions is an abdication of responsibility. We need to engage in genuine dialogue in this area.

Fourth, a plurality of approaches in theological method and formulation needs to be encouraged, in order that, in a time of undeniable change, the better may be seen to stand out from the worse. Departments of Theology and Religious Studies should encourage a plurality of perspectives among the staff. All groups of human beings work out some core convictions and emphases, but living with plurality and working with difference is a sign of strength.

Fifth, there is a need for structural change. At present each of the main theological disciplines has its own learned society and there is in practice no common forum for interchange and discussion. We ought to move from this proliferation of small single subject societies to an all-embracing forum, which can embrace the separate individual societies. This is a necessary condition for the development of Theology and Religious Studies as comprehensible disciplines both in the academy and in society.

The Forum for Religion and Theology wants to encourage a spirit of openness and generous conversation. We want to encourage interdisciplinary study. We want to see theologians and scholars of religion enter into creative dialogue with those perspectives which have been marginalized – the perspectives of the laity, of women, of artists, writers and filmmakers, of the modern scientific spirit, of people of diverse ethnic backgrounds and sexual expression, and, in particular, of the great religious traditions. All these perspectives can provide a rich and vibrant resource with which theology should enter into dialogue openly and critically. We are a group which hopes that some sort of umbrella organization shall emerge that can encourage the creation of a British equivalent to the American Academy of Religion. Such structural change will help to open up theological and religious discourse in this country. We urge you to join and support us.

Introduction

THE PREMISE OF THIS VOLUME is the belief that a firm reasser-
tion of a liberal agenda is currently required. This is
understood to be an important contribution to the health and
diversity of British theology. British theology, internationally, is –
largely speaking – not considered to be relevant; British theology,
nationally, must open itself to societal needs, interests and
questions, if it is not to either fade away or retreat into the ghetto.
This volume articulates a counter-position to current conservative
tendencies, recently invigorated by the emergence of Radical
Orthodoxy as a significant movement. It takes its starting point
from the Liverpool Statement, with which this book is prefaced.
This was drafted and signed by a number of leading British theologians, and released to the press in January 1998. We had
before us some limited research data that suggested that British
theology was not considered important, even in the English-
speaking world. With the notable exception of Radical
Orthodoxy, our colleagues in the United States found British
theology parochial and uninteresting. It was as a result of our
musings that the Liverpool Statement was issued.

The Statement points to the need for a positive, open view of
theology, which might foster the contribution of theology to the
public sphere. Theology needs to be 'engaged' – to refuse the
temptation of sectarianism and take seriously the insights of
modernity. The principles of the Statement are fivefold: an open
engagement with contemporary culture; the need for an international vision; attention to other faiths; to embrace of plurality in
theological method; and the need for structural change. Yet we
must also recognize that the limitations of the Statement are
considerable. Almost inevitably the Statement reflects the

compromises of those who constructed it. Partly because we wanted the tone to be 'constructive', the Statement operates at a high level of generality.

In articulating our counter-position, we must also take care to give our colleagues who identify with Radical Orthodoxy some credit. In a world where the United States of America is the only superpower, the agenda in almost all areas tends to be set by our American friends. However, it is undoubtedly true that the movement started by John Milbank and ably assisted by Catherine Pickstock and Graham Ward, has attracted growing interest in the United States. This movement, called Radical Orthodoxy, advocates a distinctive blend of Augustinian theology and post-modernism. It is widely discussed both here and abroad: undoubtedly, it is good that British theology is being talked about.

Yet, for those of us in Britain not entirely persuaded of Milbank's vision, it is necessary to speak out. At every point there are difficulties with Radical Orthodoxy. It assumes a contentious epistemology: for Radical Orthodoxy the boundaries between tra-ditions are fixed; every tradition has a different rationality which evaluates issues in contrasting ways. It assumes a vision of the Church in opposition to other religions and secular expertise. This book is, then, an attempt to outline an alternative vision for theology.

Despite the limitations of the Liverpool Statement, it remains a useful hook for an alternative vision of theology to that offered by the Radical Orthodox. Granted, to be convincing there is a desperate need for a substantial 'manifesto' of the alternative, comparable to Milbank's magisterial *Theology and Social Theory*, and this book is not that. Instead it begins to set an agenda on which the subsequent manifesto could be built.

The greater part of this book is, then, an attempt to sketch out the nature of an engaged, liberal theology such as called for by the Liverpool Statement, with reference to a variety of themes and issues, and from a range of vantage points. Issues and topics examined include theological method, the role of New Testament scholarship, comparative theology and religious pluralism, feminism, Anglican unity, and Church and theological structures. An Appendix groups three chapters specifically generated in response to the Liverpool Statement (those of Rachael Penketh, Gareth Jones and Lewis Ayres). To round the volume off, Paul

Avis undertook to provide us with 'a crossbench response', approaching the question as an ecclesiologist interested in ecumenism. He too would place himself alongside those contributors critical of the liberal agenda; we welcome his voice in the debate. He is concerned that liberalism cannot fund a coherent ecclesiology, although notes with approval the advocacy in this volume of an enhanced role for the Church and Church Colleges in academic theology. He outlines his own vision of an ecclesiology driven by mission, engaging both with theology and socio-political contexts. Such engagement he does not see to be quintessentially 'liberal'. He concludes by arguing for the inadequacy of the language of 'liberalism' and 'orthodoxy', and calls for an evangelical catholicity with intellectual integrity. The best way of providing an introduction to the range and diversity of material is to survey the chapters comprising the body of the book. Prior to undertaking this task, we may briefly note some differences in perspective and approach.

The contributions of Paul Avis, Lewis Ayres and Mark Elliott run counter to the prevailing emphases of the book, in that they write from perspectives critical of the Liverpool Statement. Such counter-voices are important to the furtherance of the debate. With respect to the Statement itself, some contributors dialogue directly with its substance (such as Christine Pilkington and Martyn Percy); others write on themes of clear relevance and significance, but do not take their explicit points of departure from it (such as Keith Ward and Leslie Houlden). Thus the reader will encounter a range of ways in which the themes of the book are engaged.

To turn then to the individual chapters: Ian Markham provides the opening piece, mapping some of the key theological trends of the twentieth century which have carried us into the twenty-first. His argument is that, broadly speaking, we can discern a dominance of liberal perspectives for the first 70 or so years of the previous century, with a variety of conservative replies coming to prominence in the last 30. He locates the primary difference between 'liberal' and 'conservative' in methodology: the former holding that faith should be shaped in the light of culture, the latter maintaining a set of unchanging and authoritatively revealed core beliefs. He considers that the impact of these conservative trends, as exemplified by Barthians and the Radical

Orthodox, could be 'catastrophic', and calls for a revised and renewed liberalism to take us forward. He recognizes that the 'older' English liberalism did run into substantial difficulties, and that for anyone wanting to recover or revisit this tradition, such an understanding is important.

J'annine Jobling engages with one of the prime movers within the emerging Radical Orthodoxy, Catherine Pickstock. She uses the issue of feminist biblical hermeneutics as a test ground to unravel points at which Pickstock's eucharistic and liturgical model of theological meaning fails to provide an adequate framework, and offers suggestions for a model which takes seriously Christian tradition yet also fulfils the demand for an open, inclusive hermeneutics. She identifies the three horizons of eschatology, mysticism and the Other as key to this enterprise.

Leslie Houlden examines the role of New Testament scholarship, and its relationship to systematic theology. Humility is undoubtedly the theme, and Houlden argues that a critical understanding of the New Testament should induce such a humility in our attempts at any systematic theology. He highlights the difficulty, then and now, of distinguishing between matters of belief and theology which are peripheral and those which are important. The New Testament embodies a set of diverse voices emerging from a common devotion to Jesus, acting as a warning against totalizing attempts at theological systematization. The New Testament scholar can remind theologians of the value of placing their ideas in historical perspective – and also that the tendency to segregate theology into sub-disciplines is contextually driven, and alien to documents such as the Gospel of Mark. New Testament scholarship can – humbly – both criticize and contribute to theology.

Mark Elliott tries in his essay to show some historical connections between political liberalism and theological liberalism. He affirms the strengths of liberal forms of Christianity, but wants to defend and speak up in favour of the conservative version; according to his thesis, this preserves and re-vivifies the distinctive features of historical orthodoxy. He considers the theologies of both Radical Orthodoxy and liberalism as expressed in the Liverpool Statement to be forms of natural theology, and suggests that where there is an attempt to be constructive, theology has to be more 'orthodox' if it is to keep the 'saltiness' of radical Christianity.

Keith Ward intertwines a dominant theme of comparative theology with the motif of our heritage from Schleiermacher. Christian thinking about God, he demonstrates, was never self-contained, but comparative from the first, utilizing symbols and concepts from the available cultural stock. He argues that, given this, a creative encounter between Indian and Semitic traditions ought to be a possibility. Such a move would reflect the kind of thinking about revelation and experience undertaken by Schleiermacher. Within the contemporary world, a liberal attitude will reject the idea of rigid boundaries between traditions, and dialogue not only with global religious traditions but also with the experimental sciences and humanism.

Christine Pilkington tackles the issue of religious pluralism, seeing this as a keystone of the kind of liberal theology promoted in the Liverpool Statement. She argues that interfaith dialogue needs to proceed from the specificity and integrity of particular traditions. This she takes as the starting point for a consideration of Christian encounter with Jews; indeed one of her premises is that the distinctive natures of the traditions make issues of interfaith different in kind. She identifies preaching as an important context within which Christians can address pluralism; the task of Christian preaching remains the proclamation of the 'good news', but an appropriate question is whether this good news can genuinely permit a pluralistic outlook. This would enable Christians to engage with Jews both in society and in the Old and New Testaments on terms which are 'equal though not servile, open though not tame'.

Hannah Bacon and J'annine Jobling, working within a broadly postmodern context, argue that feminists should not dismiss the liberal heritage. They identify the relationship between feminism, liberalism and theology as complex and shifting, with liberalism, and liberal forms of feminism, subject to feminist critique. At the same time the typical concerns of feminist theology can be seen to share affinities with liberal projects. They argue that feminist theology can appropriately site itself in a suitably revisioned liberal framework. Their proposals take seriously a critical feminist theology of liberation on the one hand, and postmodern accounts of 'truth' and the (gendered) subject on the other. They begin to map ways in which the apparent consequent relativization of ethics can be addressed, ultimately to argue that liberalism, feminism and theology should remain in conversation.

Martyn Percy writes of the Anglican Communion and its fractured state. He asks whether Anglicans can re-learn the art of talking to one another, and advocates 'good manners' in theological disputes as a way of enabling the Anglican Communion to cohere. Liberalism, he argues, should keep the interests of communion close to its heart; this does not mean at the expense of the striving for truth, but that liberal campaigning should be marked by compassion, openness and thoughtfulness.

Giles Legood writes on Church structures in the light of liberal concern with cultural engagement. He suggests that theology and religious studies are actually gaining in interest and influence, and that the Church needs to consider how its ministerial structures can make meaningful connections with people's lives. He surveys the history of residential parochial ministry, arguing that this is no longer fully adequate to the twenty-first Century. Chaplaincies, more integrated into people's daily working and leisure lives, should be further established.

Shannon Ledbetter and Ian Markham explore the whole issue of structures for academic theological conversation. The Liverpool Statement proposed the creation of a British equivalent to the American Academy of Religion. In a rare discussion of these issues, the chapter explores the arguments for and against such an institution. In the process of doing so, the chapter moves out to look at other related issues that shape the quality of theology and religious studies on both sides of the Atlantic.

Rachael Penketh, in a candid exposé of the origins of the Statement, discusses the research project which set the agenda for the initial conversation. She documents the limited press coverage and outlines the difficulties we seemed to run into in the successor meeting a year later. She concludes, however, that there is an important methodological theme in the Statement which British theology needs to heed if it is going to have a long-term future.

Gareth Jones writes from a position supportive of the Liverpool Statement. He was indeed a signatory of it. The issue he identifies as key is that of the *status* of theological discourse and epistemology as related to other discourses and epistemologies. This chapter, slightly amended from an original publication in *Reviews in Religion and Theology* in August 1998, was intended to push forward the agenda of the Statement in an attempt to invigorate debate in and with British theology; he calls for a meeting at which the diverse voices in British theology can come together in a shared dialogue.

Lewis Ayres, like Mark Elliott, represents a dissenting voice in this book. Ayres is known as a sympathizer with Radical Orthodoxy. He criticizes both the Liverpool Statement, as neither clear nor straightforward, and Gareth Jones' elaboration of it. The exchange with Jones is highly illuminating. He argues, *contra* Jones, that the Christian account of reality ought indeed to be appropriately privileged. Jones believes we should have learnt from Kant and that this sort of judgement is impossible. For Ayres, the liberal call for pluralism, and for open and positive engagement, require the backing of a detailed theological account.

The editors would like to acknowledge the support of Professor Simon Lee and Liverpool Hope University College in the production of this volume. We must also make mention of Lesley Seery, our research assistant, whose work on it was of enormous value. We are grateful to the *Expository Times* for permission to reproduce Chapter 1, and to *Reviews in Religion and Theology* for Appendix 2. It is our hope that this collection of essays will contribute towards the aim of provoking debate about, and interest in, British theology.

J'ANNINE JOBLING AND IAN MARKHAM

CHAPTER ONE

The Liberal Tradition and its Conservative Successors

Ian Markham

THIS CHAPTER will set the scene for the Liverpool Statement. It will concentrate on systematic theology written from a philosophical vantage point. It will focus on particular trends in Britain, with occasional links made with the Continental and American scenes. The thesis will be simple and, perhaps, rather crude: the century has seen the 'liberals' dominating the first 70 years and the 'conservatives' responding in the last 30. Although the liberal strand ran into significant difficulties, the conservative response is equally problematic. Now the language of 'conservative' and 'liberal' is itself problematic. Without pre-judging the complexities, I am using the terms to stress a methodological difference. A 'liberal' believes that faith must be adapted in the light of the broad achievement of European thought and of contemporary culture, while a 'conservative' claims to hold an unchanging faith which is grounded in certain core beliefs that are authoritatively revealed.

Generalizations about British theology are very difficult. So, for example, it is often said that Scottish theologians are more interested in systematic theology than the English. Although it is true that Thomas Torrance's interesting use of Barthian theology shaped an entire generation of systematicians in Scotland,[1] it is also true that in the 1950s and 1960s the English had Eric Mascall, who developed a Thomist theology, and have recently provided a significant number of contemporary Barthians in our universities. So let us concede right at the outset that there are exceptions to all the generalizations that follow. I shall now develop the rise and fall of English liberalism (and it was largely an English phenomenon) and the conservative fightback by the Barthians and the Radical Orthodox.

1

The Rise and Fall of English Liberalism

It is difficult to date the start of almost any movement, especially one that never developed an overt structure and organization. Some suggest that Whateley, back in the 1820s at Oriel College, Oxford, is significant; others suggest that liberal theology came to prominence with *Essays and Reviews* (1860); I propose *Lux Mundi* (1890), especially the essay by Charles Gore, as a starting point for English Anglo-Catholic liberal theology (Gore, 1890). One of the ironies of the last century was the way in which the Tractarians gave birth to movements that they would have disapproved of strongly. Pusey *et al.* were utterly unsympathetic to the liberalism and Christian Socialism of F. D. Maurice, yet in 1877 Stewart Headlam brought the two traditions together in a very imaginative tension.[2] In the same way Pusey viewed with some horror developments in Higher Criticism in Germany, yet in *Lux Mundi* it was the Anglo-Catholics in the Church of England that pioneered a liberal approach to Christianity.

Lux Mundi is not a radical text. The strongest and most interesting essay in the volume is by Charles Gore. Here he introduces Britain to kenotic christology. The argument is simple: given that higher criticism has now shown that Jesus made mistakes when citing the Old Testament, then the Incarnate God must have laid aside his omniscience to become human.

The precise details of his argument need not concern us. His method is more important than his actual argument. Gore is here revisiting the tradition in the light of a critical understanding of the Bible; understanding of the faith needs to accommodate the discoveries of modernity. This approach then characterized the growing self-confidence of English liberalism.

One can trace a clear line from *Lux Mundi* through *Foundations* (1910) to *Essays Catholic and Critical* (Selwyn, 1926) to *Soundings* (Vidler, 1962) to *Honest to God* (Robertson, 1963) and *The Myth of God Incarnate* (Hick, 1977) and *The Myth of Christian Uniqueness* (Hick & Knitter, 1987). The extent of the radicalism grew and developed. Modernity made doctrines such as an objective source of evil, the reality of eternal damnation, and the traditional doctrines of the Trinity and the incarnation, increasingly implausible. Bultmann was an important influence in the later phase. His axiom that 'it is impossible to use electric light and the

wireless and to avail ourselves of modern medical and surgical discoveries, and at the same time to believe in the New Testament
world of spirits and miracles . . .' (Bultmann, 1953) persuaded
many. *Honest to God* was derived chiefly from the ideas of Tillich,
Bonhoeffer and Bultmann. Different arguments were used on
different occasions: but the following two were prominent. The
first was that Christianity must accommodate the epistemological,
scientific and historical insights of modernity. So Dennis
Nineham argued that the doctrines of the Trinity and incarnation
were originally formulated in a neo-Platonic setting using assumptions that are impossible for us to share. Indeed, in his opening
chapter of *The Use and Abuse of the Bible* he even suggested that
cultural variations make it an open question whether one can
claim that there is such a thing as a basic and uniform human
nature. The second was that Christianity must repent of its
oppressive past and create a genuine and open future. John
Hick's work on a pluralist theology of other religions is precisely
intended to create a model that transcends the traditional hostili-
ties and build constructive relationships with other faiths.

This tradition ran into three problems. The first two were
external to the liberal tradition, namely, the emergence of the
'postmodern', and second, the development of the New Physics.
The third was internal to the tradition; liberals found it harder to
justify their Christian commitment. Each of these will be briefly
discussed. On the first: Nineham's sensitivity to the different rationalities within different cultures was turned on his own position.
There is, explains Alasdair MacIntyre, a 'liberal' post-Enlightenment tradition that has its own rationality. There is no
tradition-transcendent reason for believing that this liberal
tradition is inherently better than any other. An Amish
community interprets the Bible according to the rules and rationality of the Amish community; Nineham is simply interpreting
the Bible according to the canons and rationality of his post-
Enlightenment community. It is simply unreasonable to insist that
this is better than the Amish one: they are simply different, or
perhaps Nineham's version is worse. MacIntyre believes that the
liberal claim to neutrality and objectivity is pernicious. Under this
guise, the liberal actually imparts values, for example the doctrine
of individualism, that are antagonistic to the cultivation of the
virtues, which need to be located within a community. Newbigin,

among others, has developed MacIntyre's argument and pointed out how the exclusion of religion from the secular agenda leaves the impression that religion is irrelevant and peripheral. On the second, the uncomplicated challenge from science was displaced by the New Physics. John Polkinghorne and others started to show that modern science could provide an account of providence, prayer, miracles and resurrection in ways that the traditional liberals thought impossible. Granted, the biologists still caused problems (see Dawkins), but physicists, certainly, were much more friendly towards theology. Science was becoming an ally of faith rather than an opponent.

The third problem was internal. Of the seven contributors to *The Myth of God Incarnate,* two found it difficult to remain Christian in any recognizable sense. Don Cupitt still used the language but eliminated the content. To his credit, he wanted to adapt the liberal tradition to the changing philosophical context. Inspired by Derrida *et al.*, he proposed to turn God into a poetic image that encourages commitment to a certain set of values. Meanwhile Michael Goulder described Don Cupitt's manoeuvres as 'paradoxical, and such paradoxes are only for the very clever' and resigned his orders after 40 years in the ministry (Goulder & Hick, 1983). Can you remain a Christian after you have rejected the main elements of the traditional story and doctrinal schema? Goulder's answer was a very clear 'No'. This seemed to many to cast doubt on the viability of the liberal tradition of theology as a workable way of seeing Christian faith or practising the Christian life.

Conservatives in the Past Century

For the first 60 years of the century, the conservatives were less prominent. The precise form that conservative theology took during the century changed considerably. While the Anglo-Catholic liberals developed momentum, other Anglo-Catholics were developing an interest in Thomism. Austin Farrer is probably the intellectual giant of this period; the combination of a scholar and a preacher attracted a significant following. Eric Mascall provided a defence of the Cosmological argument and Aquinas' view of religious language; Vigo Demant defended natural law and advocated a Christian Sociology – a significant influence on John Milbank. However, it was in the 1970s that a sophisticated conservative response began to appear.

Thomas Torrance's influence was starting to reach south of the border into England. As he influenced the work of scholars like Dan Hardy and Colin Gunton, a clear revival of interest in the work of Karl Barth started to emerge. Given the postmodern stress on community, Karl Barth's emphasis on the Church as the home of an enclosed and distinct thought-world as well as life-style made more sense. He became a popular postmodern option, because he acknowledges the impossibility of having knowledge of God without revelation and offered a robust response which could be seen as immune from secular critique. The Barthian argument runs thus: all speculation separate from revelation will end up being pure guesswork. Puny, sinful, human minds cannot get to know the divine, holy and transcendent. Therefore natural theology is always doomed to failure. The choice for Barth has always been between agnosticism and revelation. Apart from Christ, there is no knowledge of God. Trusting the Word, which is Christ, is the only way we can have knowledge of God. You encounter the Word in the preaching of the word, which takes place within the community of the Church.

The attraction of Barth is his real subtlety of mind and exposition. It is to Barth's credit that conservative evangelicals found him difficult to locate on the theological spectrum and viewed him with suspicion on a number of issues, not least for his view of Scripture.[3] Barth would not describe the Bible as inerrant, but a book that becomes the 'Word of God' as it witnesses to Christ – the Word of God. The task of theology, for Barth, was clear: located mid-way between the Church and the Bible, he set about an enormous task of making sense of what we can know about God through his revelation in Christ.

Colin Gunton and David Ford in England, and Trevor Hart in Scotland, are probably the clearest expositors of the Barthian position. They claim that an imaginative Trinitarian theology can solve the central theological difficulties of our age. To take one example, the dilemma of pluralism, inclusivism and exclusivism in Christian assessment of other faiths requires a sense that God the Father is creator of the whole world, who has made God known in the particular person of the Son, who will embrace the true insights of all traditions by the Spirit. The doctrine of the Trinity is a creative, imaginative resource for the Church.

The Barthians in our British universities operate in two distinctive ways. Those shaped more by Torrance are committed to the ultimate unity of truth and insist on demonstrating this unity by exploring the interaction of theology with other disciplines, especially science. Others fear such 'engagement' with other disciplines and insist that theology has its own methodology which confronts other disciplines. The latter way has much in common with the thought of John Milbank.

John Milbank and his advocacy of Radical Orthodoxy starts from the postmodern sensitivity that there is no traditionless basis for any position. So he deconstructs modernity by exposing its hidden assumptions. The natural and social sciences are exposed as manipulators of power. Natural science, explains Milbank, 'possesses no privileged access to truth and cannot, purely on its own account, build up a realist ontology. Its "truth" is merely that of instrumental control . . .' (Milbank, 1993, p. 259). The secular, on which the social sciences are parasitic, 'had to be invented as the space of "pure power"' (Milbank, 1993, p. 12). Therefore disciplines such as 'sociology of religion' ought to disappear because 'secular reason claims that there is a "social" vantage point from which it can locate and survey various "religious" phenomena. But it has turned out that assumptions about the nature of religion themselves help to define the perspective of this social vantage' (Milbank, 1993, p. 139). Sociology has no privilege over theology: insofar as sociology can continue, writes Milbank, 'it would have to redefine itself as a "faith"' (Milbank, 1993, p. 139).

Having deconstructed secularism, Milbank then constructs an account of Christianity as 'a true Christian metanarrative realism' (Milbank, 1993, p. 389). This, he believes, is the only adequate response to Nietzschian nihilism. Christianity is located in a community – the Church – and, unlike the secular, which is built on an ontology of violence, the Church is committed to an ontology of peace. He concludes the book: '[T]he absolute Christian vision of ontological peace now provides the only alternative to a nihilistic outlook' (Milbank, 1993, p. 434).

It is astonishing how captivated a significant number of theologians are with these two contrasting, yet both conservative, theological movements. It is proving difficult for the English liberal tradition to find exponents. George Newlands is an exception: he offered a thoughtful statement of a liberal theology in *Generosity and the Christian Future*. It is interesting to see how Newlands' sources are now almost entirely American: Gordon Kaufmann and David Tracy figure prominently. The only English text he draws upon is Gareth Jones' excellent study *Critical Theology*. Jones is robustly modernist: he is grounded in a Kantian epistemology. He is not given to the postmodern dismissal of liberal ideas. We cannot and do not have knowledge of God, however much we might wish otherwise. Instead the Christ event enables us to participate in the mystery of God. Jones is in many ways the great hope of the English liberal tradition: he provides the clearest challenge to the circular or introverted tendency of both the Barthian and the Radical Orthodox – a circle which involves a Christian community justifying the revelation, and the revelation justifying the Christian community.

Before moving on to examine some of the difficulties facing these conservative theologies, it is worth noting that Biblical Studies has not participated in this conservative reaction against 1960s liberalism. With the exception of Francis Watson at Aberdeen, the majority of those working in Biblical Studies continue to use a range of literary tools which is hostile to a high view of Scripture. The Bible remains an ancient text that should be examined in the same way as any other ancient text. The result is that biblical scholars are very unsympathetic to the Barthian and Radical Orthodox movements. Leslie Houlden has made this a theme of his work. He claims that assertions about the truth of the doctrine of the Trinity or a version of the classical pattern of Christology cannot be justified. Houlden writes

> In all cases, theological study yields the same cautions: these beliefs are not unchanging, stable rocks in a sea of shifting and developing human beliefs and notions. They are themselves, despite the continuing names by which they are identified, within the swirling waters, and the names are to a large degree convenient labels whereby a body of related but distinct ideas and institutions may be recognized. (Houlden, 1986, p. 36)

This significant gulf is a major difficulty for these conservative movements; however, due to the limitations of space, further discussion of this point is impossible.

Difficulties Facing the Future

The irony of our present position is that our postmodern sensitivities (a progressive tendency in other disciplines) have now entrenched conservative theologies in such a way that they have become untouchable. The Barthian refuses to deal with the obvious objection: alleged revelations abound in this world, so how do I know that the Christian one is the true one? The Barthian simply repeats that it is a matter of faith: a matter of trusting the Christian community that gives us Christ. And John Milbank turns everything into a matter of faith: sociology is a faith, as is Christianity. Traditions are largely incommensurable and incompatible. One cannot attack Christianity from outside; there is no vantage point that permits one to pass judgements on it. So again, one either 'sees' or fails to 'see'.

The impact of these conservative trends could be catastrophic. The problems operate on a number of different levels. First, the problem of the insider and outsider. For both the Barthians and the Radical Orthodox, theology is a task for the insider (i.e. for a Christian within the community of the Church). The outsider has no direct contribution or role; if you are outside and interested in theology, then all you need do is to come inside, enter into and understand the connections made by those within. Judgements from outside on those connections would be inappropriate – only the insider can 'see'. Graham Ward and John Milbank have both insisted that theologians must believe in God to do theology.[4] Our unchurched or uncommitted A-level students will find these assumptions difficult to appreciate; and our often very overt 'secular' institutions will find it difficult to justify the use of public funds to finance sectarian, seminary-type theology.

The second set of problems, which is linked to the first, is that the conservative boundaries of legitimate theological conversation make it difficult for all those who find the Christian discourse oppressive or even open to blatantly obvious legitimate questions. If theology can only be done within the Church, then a number of both intellectual and moral challenges to the Church will never be confronted. Many forms of feminist and gay theology become illegitimate. Daphne Hampson's 'post-Christian feminism' is important here (Hampson, 1990). It seems very odd to reject as methodologically inappropriate such an important moral challenge to the central tenets of Christianity.

The third set of problems surrounds the whole issue of 'justification'. The introduction to my book *Truth and the Reality of God* complains about the 'fideism' in this style of theology (Markham, 1998). The task of apologetics has been very attenuated, as assertion replaces argument. John Milbank simply wants to 'outnarrate', while the Barthians simply stress preaching. What this all amounts to is that Christianity becomes just another worldview, to be asserted, not justified. From astrology to tarot cards, Christianity is just one system that one chooses to opt into or to stay out of.

It is ironic that all these conservative Christians totally ignore the tradition of Natural Theology; even those (like Milbank) who have classical Catholic roots. From Paul in Romans 1 to Augustine and Aquinas and the whole Thomist tradition, Natural Theology is central. While conservative theologians ignore it, Anglo-American philosophers are excited about it. After the blind ally of linguistic philosophy and logical positivism, Anglo-American philosophers of religion defend the various arguments for God's existence with real enthusiasm. However, the worlds of theology and philosophy are now separated by a vast gulf. Philosophers find contemporary theologians muddled and confused, while theologians find philosophers unhistorical and crude in their doctrinal analysis. I am not entirely sure why this gulf has developed and been accepted so uncritically. Brian Hebblethwaite is virtually alone in challenging this gulf, in his highly significant presidential address to the Society for the Study of Theology in 1989. Perhaps it is because theology is an art (it constructs poems and paints pictures), while philosophy is more like a science (deducing a worldview from the evidence). Perhaps theologians model themselves on texts that at best are imperfectly coherent, at worst completely muddled (such as Paul's Epistle to the Romans), while the philosophers think their role is to turn Romans into something more coherent. Whatever the reason, the fact remains that theologians and Anglo-American philosophers are in a state of mutual antagonism and opposition. Encouraging dialogue between these two worlds is urgent. For theodicy reasons, God must have made some sort of 'natural' revelation available to those who think rightly about this world. A postmodern natural theology is urgently needed. A reasonable doctrine of creation forbids any readiness to do without it.

This gap has had one further deleterious consequence. Instead of grappling with the rigours of the Anglo-American philosophical tradition, we have seen an uncritical accommodation between theology and much continental philosophy. This needs to be challenged. Some theologians find continental philosophy conducive because it is equally woolly, from a more rigorous philosophical standpoint, to Romans. However, the most significant problem of them all is embedded in the language of postmodernism, which is the fourth and final area.

The fourth set of difficulties, then, surrounds the impact of the postmodern. Conservative theologians consider very important MacIntyre's talk of 'tradition-constituted' rationalities. However, what exactly they think this means is less clear. MacIntyre's illustrations stress the ways that different communities use texts and deduce truths from them. So, for example, the Qur'an is used by Muslims very differently from the way the Bible is used by even evangelical Christians. In this sense there is a different method of reasoning operating. But for many good reasons, it is difficult to imagine different traditions having a wholly different logic. If there were, translation and imaginative understanding of different traditions would become impossible. The basic laws of logic seem to be a condition for all language. Gavin D'Costa's suggestion that this is not the case and that in Buddhism contradictions are accommodated, is rightly criticized by Keith Ward in *Religion and Revelation*. The point is that 'tradition-constituted' rationality located in a community cannot and should not imply incommensurability or incommunicability – or a licence to give immunity from criticism. The basic laws of logic are shared, and it is this that makes conversation possible. It may be difficult, but it is not impossible. Once this is seen, encouraging the Church to rediscover that the God we worship is the God of the whole world – the God who has allowed diverse traditions to emerge – is a Christian obligation that is both possible and exciting.

The Way Forward

There is obviously considerable work to be done. To return to the liberal theology of the 1960s is not an option. Though it still does not lack adherents, its internal and external difficulties seemed to many to overwhelm the tradition: the internal drift to agnosticism was strong and, externally, modernity (or postmodernity) became more nuanced and apparently did not require a capitulation to secularism. The conservative reaction seemed to have much to commend it: but the philosophical confusions, combined with its lack of interest in culture, other faiths, and (for example) feminism will require adaptation for it to survive as a constructive position in the future.

The great hope, I suspect, is a rediscovery of the riches of our tradition. We ought to revisit Augustine and Aquinas. Milbank uses Augustine in such a way that I suspect Augustine would not recognize. Augustine does not believe that one cannot learn or engage with other traditions. This is important because it challenges the assumption that traditions are largely incommensurable. And I shall provide one illustration. Augustine has a highly positive view of non-Christian sources. Augustine has a love of wisdom wherever it is found. He writes in the *Confessions*:

> In Greek the word 'philosophy' means 'love of wisdom', and it was with this love that the *Hortensius* inflamed me. There are people for whom philosophy is a means of misleading others, for they misuse its great name, its attractions, and its integrity to give colour and gloss to their own errors. Most of these so-called philosophers who lived in Cicero's time and before are noted in the book [. . .] (T)he only thing that pleased me in Cicero's book was his advice not simply to admire one or another of the schools of philosophy, but to love wisdom itself, whatever it might be, and to search for it, pursue it, hold it, and embrace it firmly. (St Augustine, 1961, Book 3.4, p. 59)

Cicero's *Hortensius* is Augustine's way into philosophy. From it, Augustine learns the importance of seeking wisdom. As Augustine became disillusioned with Manichaeism, so he discovered neo-Platonism (probably the writings of Plotinus). He finds in these writings good arguments for the existence of God and his eternal word. Augustine explains:

> So you [i.e. God] made use of a man, one who was bloated with the most outrageous pride, to procure me some of the

books of the Platonists, translated from the Greek into Latin. In them I read – not, of course, word for word, though the sense was the same and it was supported by all kinds of different arguments – that *at the beginning of time the Word already was; and God had the Word abiding with him, and the Word was God* [. . .] In the same books I also read of the Word, God, that his *birth came not from human stock, not from nature's will or man's, but from God*. But I did not read in them that *the Word was made flesh and came to dwell among us*. (St Augustine, 1961, Book 7.9, pp. 144–5)

Augustine's readings in Neoplatonism persuade him of God and the eternal word, although there is nothing about the incarnation. He treats the illumination that these books provide him about God as intended by God. Although Cicero and Plotinus are non-Christians, he has no difficulty in acknowledging the truth about God he finds within their writing. This is an 'open orthodoxy' – an orthodoxy that can learn from other traditions.

A traditional methodology (i.e. one true to the theological method of Augustine and Aquinas) is one that will adapt, change and learn from other traditions.

Keith Ward has made this methodology central to his comparative theology. In addition he does try to live both in the philosophical and theological worlds. He attempts to create a system that acknowledges the sovereignty of God over the whole world, and tries to weave together science and other cultures into a defence of faith. Ward's methodology is traditional, yet his conclusions and analysis are often liberal. This sense that orthodoxy is liberal is one that we need to recover. It is with his vision of an 'open theology' that I conclude my chapter.

One might perhaps speak of an 'open theology', which can be characterised by six main features. It will seek a convergence of common core beliefs, clarifying the deep arguments which underlie diverse cultural traditions. It will seek to learn from complementary beliefs in other traditions, expecting that there are forms of revelation one's own tradition does not express. It will be prepared to reinterpret its beliefs in the light of new, well-established factual and moral beliefs. It will accept the full right of diverse belief-systems to exist, as long as they do not cause avoidable injury or harm to innocent sentient beings. It will encourage a dialogue with conflicting and dissenting views, being prepared to confront its own tradition with critical questions arising out of such views. And it will try to develop a sensitivity to the historical and cultural contexts of the formulation of its own beliefs, with a preparedness to continue developing new insights in new cultural situations. (Ward, 1994, pp. 339–40)

Notes

1 It is worth noting that lectureships in systematic theology in English Universities have only developed in the past 20 years. On the whole, writing in systematic theology came from those interested in Patristics. For Torrance on Barth see *Karl Barth: An Introduction to his Early Theology*, SCM Press, London, 1962. For a discussion see D. Hardy, 'Thomas F. Torrance' in D. Ford (ed.) *The Modern Theologians*, Volume 1, Blackwell, Oxford, 1989. This essay helpfully explains the significance of Torrance, although he is not happy to have Torrance simply dismissed as a Barthian. It is a pity that the second, one-volume edition did not retain this essay.

2 See for example Newman's views in *Sermons and Discourses 1825–1839* (new edition edited by Charles Frederick Harrold, Longmans, Green, 1949, pp. 44–53). Adrian Hastings rightly comments on the significance of Anglo-Catholic Christian Socialism when he writes, 'Almost all the movements of Christian socialism, and the groups of men at work in places like Oxford House in Bethnal Green, were Anglo-Catholic.' See Hastings, *A History of English Christianity, 1920–1985*, Collins, London, 1986. A significant exception, of course, was T. H. Green.

3 See for example, John Warwick Montgomery (ed.) *God's Inerrant Word*, Bethany Fellowship, Minnesota, 1974.

4 See the recent *Times Higher Education Supplement* controversy, 13 November 1998.

References

Bultmann, R., 'New Testament and Mythology' in Bartsch, H. W. (ed.) *Keryma and Myth*, SPCK, London, 1953, pp. 1–16.

Gore, C. (ed.), *Lux Mundi: A Series of Studies in the Religion of the Incarnation*, J. Murray, London, 1890.

Goulder, M. and Hick, J., *Why Believe in God*, SCM Press, London, 1983.

Hampson, D., *Theology and Feminism*, Blackwell, Oxford, 1990.

Hick, J. and Knitter, P. (eds), *The Myth of Christian Uniqueness*, SCM Press, London, 1987.

Hick, J. (ed.), *The Myth of God Incarnate*, SCM Press, London, 1977.

Houlden, J. L., *Connections*, SCM Press, London, 1986.

Jones, G., *Critical Theology*, Polity Press, Cambridge, 1995.

MacIntyre, A., *Whose Justice? Which Rationality?*, Duckworth, London, 1988.

Markham, I., *Truth and the Reality of God*, T&T Clark, Edinburgh, 1998.

Milbank, J., *Theology and Social Theory: Beyond Secular Reason*, Blackwell, Oxford, 1993.

Newlands, G., *Generosity and the Christian Future*, SPCK, London, 1997.

Nineham, D., *The Use and Abuse of the Bible*, Macmillan, London, 1976.

Robertson, J., *Honest to God*, SCM Press, London, 1963.

Selwyn, E. G. (ed.), *Essays Catholic and Critical*, 1926.

St Augustine, *Confessions*, trans. by R. S. Pine-Coffin, Penguin, Harmondsworth, 1961.

Streeter, B. H. *et al.*, *Foundations: A Statement of Christian Belief in Terms of Modern Thought*, Macmillan, London, 1912.

Temple, F. *et al.*, *Essays and Reviews*, J. W. Parker and Son, London, 1860.

Vidler, A. R. (ed.), *Soundings: Essays Concerning Christian Understanding*, Cambridge University Press, Cambridge, 1962.

Ward, K., *Religion and Revelation*, Oxford University Press, Oxford, 1994.

CHAPTER TWO

On the Liberal Consummation of Theology: A Dialogue with Catherine Pickstock

J'annine Jobling

ACCORDING TO CATHERINE PICKSTOCK, 'liturgical language is the only language that really makes sense'. A realistic account of the eucharistic event is the only possible site for an account of language as meaningful. Transubstantiation thus becomes the 'condition of possibility for all human meaning' (Pickstock, 1998, p. xv). This justifies her claim that philosophy is completed and surpassed through doxology: this constitutes, as per the sub-title of her major work *After Writing* (1998), 'the liturgical consummation of philosophy'. Pickstock's work, undoubtedly important, is an expression of Radical Orthodoxy: a movement which proceeds from a privileging of the Christian narrative as true and real, while yet acknowledging postmodern themes such as the indeterminacy of knowledge. Nihilism is avoided only through participating in the Christian ontological vision. As Pickstock puts this:

> Not only is the Eucharist invoked as an example of the coincidence of sign and body, death and life. It is also claimed that only a realistic construal of the event of the Eucharist allows us to ground a view of language which does not evacuate the body, and does not give way to necrophilia. Since such an evacuating and necrophiliac account of language also amounts to the claim that meaning is indeterminate and abyssal, my claims about the Eucharist also imply that it grounds meaningful language as such. (Pickstock, 1998, p. xv)

This chapter seeks to engage with aspects of Pickstock's thesis, within the 'test ground' of feminist biblical hermeneutics. It is argued that a eucharistic and liturgical model of theological meaning fails to provide an adequate framework, and suggestions are offered for a model which likewise takes seriously Christian tradition yet also fulfils the demand for an open, inclusive hermeneutics. Radical Orthodoxy does not seek to exclude the 'Other'; as Milbank expresses this:

> One way to try to secure peace is to draw boundaries around 'the same', and exclude 'the other'; to promote practices and disallow alternatives. Most polities, and most religions, characteristically do this. But the Church has misunderstood itself when it does likewise. [. . .] Christianity should not draw boundaries, and the Church is that paradox: a nomad city. (Milbank, 1997, p. 269)

And yet, it could be argued that this is precisely what Pickstock's model does; rich as it is theologically, it is also reductive. Even within the Christian theological family, space needs to be cleared for potentially multiple grounds of meaning. And what resources can such an account offer for dialogue in a pluralist world? Pickstock's argument is deep and wide-ranging: it is not possible to provide a sustained analysis and response in such a short chapter as this. Rather, what I attempt is to take one source of theological meaning – Christian Scripture – and consider how a doxological framework intersects with feminist perspectives. The latter are taken as examples of diversity and dissent within Christianity, and as such indicative of how well any given model can accommodate plurality. By 'accommodate' I do not mean 'uncritically take on board': but rather, take seriously, and provide genuine response.

Thus, I begin by raising the question of how might we interpret the Christian Bible in the light of philosophical developments loosely labelled 'postmodern' and the politicizing of interpretation by movements such as feminism? The underlying issue is hermeneutical: what understanding of theological writing provides a fruitful matrix for siting feminist biblical interpretation? As has been indicated, I take the view that Pickstock's account of meaning cannot well host feminist perspectives.

I argue instead that, writing within the horizons of eschatology and mysticism provides the resources to formulate an answer. This resonates with, but is not reducible to, Pickstock's eucharistic and liturgical model. Both theses can be distinguished from writings which (re)inscribe a metaphysics of presence.[1]

This initial section, then, sets out briefly the hermeneutical problematic for biblical interpretation as generated by postmodern and feminist critiques and which demand a theological recontextualization. Postmodern, poststructuralist and feminist destabilizations present challenges to the theologian and no less to the biblical interpreter. For religion, the postmodern condition would seem to offer an ambivalent promise. It is vaunted both as the saviour of theology from inhospitable modernity, and as the final nail in the coffin of God. Current trends in hermeneutics, often allied to postmodern critiques, highlight the mobility of meaning; meaning is not moored to a fixed anchorage, but forever adrift in the sea of signs. A recurrent motif of postmodernism is that of flux. Postmodernism runs counter to philosophies based on foundations and guarantors of truth, whether a Cartesian model of subjectivity or some other starting point.

On this understanding, postmodernism is a funeral procession. Man is dead; human nature, as such, does not exist. History is dead; as Man is a fiction, so is the History of Man; there is no progress, no possibility of fulfilling the Enlightenment quest for certain truth. Metaphysics is dead; 'Truth', indeed, is yet another fiction. Does this tale of disintegration require us also to eliminate God? How could a theology of Scripture be formulated in a postmodern context?

Feminism, no less, offers a deep-rooted challenge to theologies of Scripture. For religions such as Christianity, drawing on particular sedimented traditions, what is accorded the status of truth may well appear to the feminist ideologically oppressive. The stress on the Bible as theological source and arbiter may be especially problematic. Once the Bible is recognized as patriarchal, androcentric and misogynist, there is no simple answer to how it may be celebrated as an affirming resource for feminist spiritualities. As Mary Daly commented: 'It might be interesting to speculate upon the probable length of a "depatriarchalized Bible". Perhaps there would be enough salvageable material to comprise an interesting pamphlet' (Daly, 1973). There is a

certain commonality between feminist philosophy and poststructuralism as allied to postmodernism. Poststructuralism exposes
the constructed and falsely totalizing nature of ideological appa-
ratuses, and what else is feminism concerned with but the
constructed and falsely totalizing nature of patriarchy? Major
currents in both feminism and postmodernism seek to write differences and multiplicity.

Feminists approaching Scripture require a framework which
enables movement beyond the impasses of modernity with its
characteristic insistence upon authority and determinate
meanings and its frequent failure to delineate space through
which otherness and difference can peer. Feminists strive to write
the 'Other'; to brush history against the grain, to tell the tale *differently*. This is an act of resisting reading. This should not,
however, be reductively conceived in terms of a hermeneutic of
'redemption' or 'reclamation', set in false opposition to recognizing the text as 'sexist'. Rather, as is argued elsewhere (for
example, Jobling, 1999), a hermeneutic of destabilization is a
more useful concept. The notion of 'fixed meaning' in texts is
refuted, because textual valence is located in discursive communities. Destabilizing readings can be related to Derridaean *différence*,
in which meaning is differed and deferred, never coming to
closure. And yet this turn to the postmodern, as indicated, raises
in itself a host of pressing questions – not least of which is its
alleged nihilistic and relativistic tendencies, which scarcely accord
with a feminist account of the world. How do we locate theological meaning in such a framework?

This is where my encounter with Catherine Pickstock's *After
Writing* begins. She has produced a magisterial vision of a
different metaphysical order. Pickstock suggests that liturgical
writing offers a way past a modern metaphysics of presence or a
postmodern nihilism. Pickstock's liturgical consummation of philosophy is played out in the domain of language, which she
identifies as a key 'token of the postmodern' (Pickstock, 1998, p.
xiii). Recognizing language as liturgical (or doxological) is the
recognition that language exists for praise of the divine, and only
ultimately has meaning in this respect. This, she argues, avoids
both the over-spatialization of modernity (the domination of
presence) and the over-temporalization of postmodernity (the
domination of flux).

Pickstock traces a narrative in which the groundwork for shifts in early-modern mappings of space, time and knowledge was laid in late medieval times with the internal collapse of a liturgically and doxologically constituted *polis*. This disintegration she identifies as a 'disaster' (Pickstock, 1998, p. xiv). Space came to obliterate time, life was sundered from death, and language, now understood as 'the very opposite of liturgy', must in consequence cease to make sense (Pickstock, 1998, p. xiv). The unholy cities thus established pretend a clarity and knowledge, but are in truth the harbourers of a nihilism which is the 'inevitable outcome of a separation of ontology from theology' (Pickstock, 1998, p. 3). She locates a decisive moment in the expansion of the unliturgical world with Cartesianism: 'in the end, after Descartes, a spatialized written *polis*, a spatialized written being, and a spatialized written subject, cohere perfectly together, without priority or foundation, in a triadic mutual collusion, which sustains the "self-evidence" of the immanent, and its secular closure against the sun of the good only as a conspiracy . . .' (Pickstock, 1998, p. 74). Modernity then leaves the subject in a state of permanent suspension (Pickstock, 1998, p. 100).

On this account, postmodernism provides an apparent alternative to the spatiality of modernity but, according to Pickstock, it is simply spurious. Like modernity, postmodernity can only inhabit the necropolis. 'To the modern yoking of refusal of death with identical repetition, postmodern thought has responded with a gesture towards the void' (Pickstock, 1998, p. 106). This dissolution of identity privileges death, and 'the claim that there can be only death is identical with the claim that there can be only identical repetition' (Pickstock, 1998, p.106). For what could be more identical than nothing to nothing?

The way out of the city of death is through partaking in the liturgical journey. Liturgical language is the manifestation of the impossible possibility enabled by the resurrection; for while the human subject was rendered incapable of doxology through the Fall, this aporia is resolved through the person and resurrection of Christ (Pickstock, 1998, p. 177). Liturgy is then both gift from God and sacrifice to God. According to Pickstock's analysis, it provides for a renegotiation of not only space and time, but also of human subjectivity, which is only non-ironically central to itself in the 'dispossessing act of praise' (Pickstock, 1998, p. 177).

Where a liturgical order is held open, meaning can be restored to language at the site of the event of the Eucharist. The sign of the Eucharist, she argues, 'is able to outwit the distinction between both absence and presence, and death and life' (Pickstock, 1998, p. 252). Since all language is then understood to flow in time from eternity, which in the liturgical city is not obliterated, all signs can signify that which is beyond them without the efface-ment of the sign itself. Transubstantiation is the ultimate ground of meaning, for it dissolves the opposition between thing and sign, sense and referent; in Pickstock's words, 'the Eucharist underlies all language, since in carrying the secrecy, uncertainty, and discontinuity which characterize every sign to an extreme (no body appears in the bread), it also delivers a final disclosure, certainty and continuity (the bread is the Body) which alone makes it possible now to trust every sign (Pickstock, 1998, p. 262).

In what follows I shall mark out some of the points at which my own proposals run parallel with Pickstock's and where they diverge. There is a certain resonance between the two because, like Pickstock, I am concerned to delineate alternative models on which to think God, being and subjectivity which take different shapes from the hypostasized accounts of modernity and post-modernity. The site of my analysis, as already indicated, is feminist biblical hermeneutics. My aim is to mark out a meta-framework from which feminist theological interpretation of the Bible could proceed. I have already suggested that destabilizing tactics and practices can offer illuminating pathways for feminist interpreta-tion. However, as intimated, the question of how such a paradigm might relate to *theology* is not obvious. Within the Christian tradition, the Bible is, after all, supposed to function as Scripture. Providing ways in which feminists can relate to it as feminists does not explain what theological contexts and paradigms might enable a mutual hospitality between theology and feminism rather than disjunction and dissonance. This is especially so since a significant component of approaching Scripture as a feminist requires a deeply critical perspective.

How might a liturgical consummation of philosophy feed into this discussion? Essentially, the question is whether a doxologi-cally and eucharistically constituted theology of Scripture can accord us with an alternative vision of the relationship between God and truth which does not fall prey either to the logocentricism of modernity or to the dissolution of truth avowedly signalled by postmodernity. This question inevitably presses upon us, because questions about the theology of Scripture necessarily implicate the relationship between truth and God, since Scripture is on some understandings supposed to be paradigmatically the Word of God, the truth of God made text. And indeed, the question of the relationship between God and truth is one which, I would argue, is anyway demanded by all discourses of truth and meaning (or dissolution of truth and abandonment of meaning).

Pickstock seeks to ground meaning in the liturgical event of the Eucharist. To relate this to a theology of Scripture, let us consider, first, what promise there might be in a doxological framework for theological hermeneutics. If doxology is indeed the ultimate site of meaning, it should surely be postulated as constitutive of theological discourse. And certainly, a doxological matrix for biblical interpretation would answer not only a philosophical demand concerning the nature of language, but would also signal the community-constituted nature of interpretation. Interpretation is never simply interpretation *of*; it is interpretation *for*. The eminent New Testament scholar Elisabeth Schüssler Fiorenza, for example, has centralized this contention in her historiographical hermeneutic, and it is a key point (see Fiorenza, 1992). What it makes primary is the discursive context of readings. It moves away from any conception of meaning as mined from the semantic containers of texts, and stresses its contextual location at the point of production. As such, what comes to prominence is the register on which readings are undertaken. Thus doxology might be identified as the appropriate framework within which to site a theology of Scripture. It would subordinate interpretation of the Bible to the meta-hermeneutic of participation in an activity, the purpose of which being the encounter with God in a context of worship and praise. This widens the terrain in terms of the interpretative criteria which might possibly operate, rendering critical methods as one only of many possible approaches and opening up space for other types of readings, for imaginative reconstruals and bibliodrama.

And yet, it is arguable that such a matrix for interpretation fails to do justice to the richness of the Bible, homogenizing the multiplicity of texts under one reading paradigm. Are praise and worship always the responses most appropriately, or even

honestly, evoked by the biblical texts? Are not challenge, difficulty, puzzlement, even anger, sometimes called for – most
especially by the feminist reader? Reading the Bible in doxological key may for the feminist simply elicit a greater sense of
alienation from it, for it may not always lend itself to a response of
praise for the divine. It would be naïve to suggest that the matrix
of biblical discourses can ever be entirely welcoming to feminist
readers, precisely because interpretations take place in relationship with texts, and the biblical texts cast up androcentic and
patriarchal ideologies far more extensively than not. Friction
between the feminist and her religious matrix is not necessarily a
bad thing, for it is in friction that sparks can be generated and
sometimes the difficult path is the more fruitful. Yet we must
beware of glib answers which continue to legitimate discourses of
oppression. Feminist reappraisals may subvert, expose and creatively re-imagine biblical androcentricity and patriarchalism: the
latter are not thereby eliminated or redeemed. The very exten-
siveness of the need to subvert and re-imagine presents difficulties
which can seem insuperable.

If, then, as Pickstock argues, 'language exists primarily, and in
the end only has meaning as, the praise of the divine' (Pickstock,
1998, p. xiii), there is surely a theological difficulty here if the
primary religious text of a community resists such an account of
language. If it is only in the liturgical event of the Mass that
meaning can be doxologically grounded, and thus grounded at
all, what does that imply for a theology of Scripture? This point is
intensified by Pickstock's location of the repetition of Christ only
in the gift of the Eucharist. The Word was not only made flesh, but
made text also, and both Eucharist and Scripture could be viewed
as re-enactments of the enfleshment of the Word. But for
Pickstock, the writing of Christ is subordinated to the perpetual
realization of the eucharistic event; it is this which enables writing
to escape from spatialization, since it represents eternity, and
becomes a bodily event – not 'left behind in historical anteriority'
(Pickstock, 1998, p. 218).

This, it seems to me, does not do justice to the bodiliness and
repetition of textuality. If Scripture is understood as the site of
creative actualization of meaning, rather than a product from the
past for consumption, then this is a non-identical repetition
which is among the elements dynamically constitutive of

Christian identity and ontological formulations. According to Wyschogrod, 'it is only through narrative articulation that events are disclosed as such and take on the character of an ontological matrix' (Wyschogrod, 1990, p. 7). In the Christian poetic, the identity of God is placed within the narrative of the Hebrew Bible and of the life, death and resurrection of Jesus Christ; this narrative is enmeshed within the structure of the Christian ontological matrix. Narrative, however, is by its nature not static but a process; the tale comes into being in its telling. The ontological identity of God as posited in the Hebrew Bible is, in fact, verb: I am that I am, or, I am that I am becoming. Also, according to Blanchot, the movement of narrative is 'a movement towards a point [. . .] unknown, obscure, foreign . . .' This point is so imperious 'that the tale derives its power of attraction only from this point and cannot even "begin" before reaching it' (Wyschogrod, 1990, p. 7). Within the parameters of a Christian ontological matrix, such a statement could be conceived of eschatologically – if the eschaton is taken as the point towards which the Christian narratives move, in dialectical relation to the movement itself. Thus, a theology of Scripture could take its point of departure in narratology and eschatology. Furthermore, if we read Scripture in the frame, not of doxology, but of mystical theology, we may find more space opened up for a theology of Scripture to be the site, not only of praise, but also of struggle.

By mystical theology, I follow the lead of Mark McIntosh, and mean to denote an integration of spirituality and theology which does not render spirituality a privatized or paranormal affair. Rather, spirituality is here understood as 'the new and transformative pattern of life and thought engendered in people by their encounter with God' (McIntosh, 1998, p. 9). It is discernible in early Christian senses in this way, as something which is a quest for the inner self, but 'mutual, communal, practical and oriented towards the God who makes self known' in the whole pattern of the life of the Church (McIntosh, 1998, p. 7). The gain I see here in the move from doxology to mystical theology understood in this communal and God-orienting sense is that the stress is on encounter rather than praise. As such it carves out more space for traces of God to impinge and saturate world, life and language with meaning.

Interestingly, in the context of this discussion, there are some parallels here between the mystical tradition and the spiritual dimensions of postmodern philosophies. This is noted by Graham Ward, who finds common to Teresa of Avila and Hélène Cixous that 'the hallmarks of spiritual writing are absence and intense proximity, rich sensuality and the fierce discipline of self-emptying love, plenitude and intellectual darkness' (Ward, 1996, p. 230). Spirituality may be likened to the romantic idea of the sublime, something beyond our constructions but which 'nevertheless leaves its trace on them' (Ward, 1996, p. 231).

Within the horizons of mystical theology, biblical hermeneutics cannot be separated from theology and spirituality. The converse is also true. Neither can theology and spirituality be separated from text. According to Ward, spirituality is text, performed through writing and reading; in participation in the story, from the plenitude of the real is pulled 'a name, a thread, a note' (Ward, 1996, p. 232). This is the transcendent horizon impinging in the gap between signs: what is not written, what cannot be written, nevertheless leaving textual traces. Thus, Ward can assert that the vehicle for transfiguration is indeed Scripture, but Scripture as *scriptura*: writing, in the widest sense (Ward, 1996, p. 233).

Pickstock identifies textuality with vacuity, an endless deferral leading only to death. I want to argue that texuality is, rather, the playground of the Word of God and that not only Scripture but also Eucharist are textualized events of meaning. Text, here, is understood in the broader sense – not simply the written word, but the world itself as script for interpretation. This is where the eschatological imagination enters the discussion. Part of the problematic addressed by Pickstock was the need to renegotiate space and time, to find a way past what was characterized as the over-spatialization of modernity and the over-temporalization of postmodernity. A crucial part of Christian writing of time–space is its eschatological orientation. Eschatology points towards, not a singular and identifiable *telos* in time–space, but to the shattering open of finite writings of time–space. One reading of eschatology is to see it as marked by a dialectic of presence/absence and now/not yet. Thus the eschatological can be said to proceed with a dialectic of both spatialization and temporalization and to embody the promise of radical transformation of both. Eschatology disrupts a metaphysics of presence because God is not, in eschatological horizons, either present as such or absent as such. God gives God-self in traces: textuality. Here my account can be seen to overlap with Pickstock's, for she also stresses the eschatological context, but also to diverge, in its embrace of Derridaean categories of a disrupted presence/absence and the promulgation from that base of a theology of the trace. I want to site meaning in textuality, while agreeing with Pickstock that accounts of meaning are complicit in a theology. Therefore, God and truth also enter into the domain of textualization.

But this has profound impact upon the nature of the truth which can be told. Textuality, truth, and God: if the Word of God is in any sense addressed to the world, it can only do this by being immanent within the world. As such the Word of God is apprehended within the structures of the world. It is embodied. It is textualized. The Word made (literally) flesh is, of course, at the heart of classical Christology; the Word made (literally) text is the crux of orthodox understandings of Christian Scripture. Word as flesh, Word as text: this immanence of the Word of God can be deemed its textualization. There can then be no direct correspondence between the truth of God and the Word of God. Howsoever the truth of God is known to us, if at all, it is not through a self-presencing. The textualized Word of God does not denote a majestic presencing of guaranteed truth. It does not reveal 'the truth', but its ambiguity and partiality. The Word of God in these horizons is far removed from the Word of God as authoritative Word of the Father.

So truth is textualized; and if the truth of God is likewise textualized, it becomes subject to the differentiality of interpretation; truth in eschatological horizons is not present but undecidable. This does not, however, cut us loose into aimless wandering over relativistic plains. This is to lose sight of the eschatological as symbol of hope, as paradigmatic of hopes for transformation and the consummation of the passion for a just world. It is a call, not to passive resignation, but to transformative action. An eschatological metaphysics is one which is not grounded in 'presence', but it is oriented: towards horizons of hope, or alternatively one might say, of faith.

Theological thinking then takes its cues from *traces* of the divine. This plunges theology into the domains of the ethical, for if interpretation is inevitable and also differential, the criteria for judgements become a matter of profound ethical importance. But ethics, likewise, are not rooted in any transcendental domain. This does not equate to relativism: to assert the ungroundedness of meaning is not to hold the view that all interpretations are thereby equal (see Jobling, 1999; Bacon and Jobling in this volume). But transposed into the ethical realm, we may similarly talk of an orientation towards God rather than a grounding in God. Such an orientation walks the epistemological abyss: God may draw us on, but truth and meaning are not simply present to us as givens. There is a proleptically and partially discernible unfolding, from and towards a future we can never grasp.

This is a departure from Pickstock's identification of doxology as the mode of life which constitutes the 'supreme ethic' (Pickstock, 1998, p. 40), and a relocation of the ethical into diversely constituted human discourses. An orientation towards 'the good' does not depend upon praise of the divine, but may be articulated with reference to a number of different narratives which may or may not be theistically constituted. Pickstock is nevertheless correct to note the tendency of the 'mercantile city' to produce configurations of inside/outside and to identify the 'radicalization of boundaries' as an ethical goal (Pickstock, 1998, p. 46). Yet such a dissolution of boundaries does not, as per the implication of her argument, depend upon the ontological constitution of subjectivity within liturgy as the ground of possibility for other relationships.

Pickstock, in fact, argues that, without the liturgy, there is no subject (Pickstock, 1998, p. 196) – understanding subjectivity as oneness with God. While it may well be that Christian theological anthropology posits the fullness of subjectivity in these terms, liturgy cannot be the only arena for this without stripping the fingerprint of God from the ontology of creation. If there is any truth in this narrative, then we are constituted as subjects in and before God whether or not we are doxologically engaged.

Howsoever, my refiguration of meaning in eschatological rather than liturgical and doxological horizons does not entirely negate Pickstock's account of the Eucharist, but relocates its primary key from doxology into eschatology and resists its identification as sole ground of meaningful language. The close connection between the Eucharist and eschatology is oft-noted, and indeed figures in Pickstock's analysis. Eucharistic time is eschatological time.[2] It is also, and fittingly with respect to my hermeneutic model, time in which acts of remembrance of the past and hopeful anticipation of the future are central. Its horizons are not the present, set over against a non-present and irretrievable past and a non-present and unknowable future. It is the anamnestic re-enactment of the historical body of Christ within the context of a redemptive fulfilment which has both yet to come and already been given. This is a disruption of a secular conception of time as centred on the present. The eucharistic present emanates from both past and future, which converge within it; moreover, its completion is announced from both past and future, as the eschatological event inaugurated by Christ in the past unfolds from the future. In Zizioulas' words, the '*anamnesis* of Christ is realized not as a mere re-enactment of a past event but as an *anamnesis of the future*, as an eschatological event' (Zizioulas, 1985, p. 254). Remembrance, hope and an eschatological temporal perspective are thus profoundly diffused into the eucharistic imagination. As I argue elsewhere (Jobling, 1999), this dialectic between remembrance and hope within eschatological context can also be embodied within a feminist biblical hermeneutics.

Thus, let me return to the three horizons for a theology of Scripture with which I began this exploration. Eschatology, I have argued, should constitute the primary key and acts to disrupt both postmodern nihilism and a metaphysics of presence. Understood eschatologically, textuality can be the site of meaning as differed and deferred without thereby implying enclosure in the nihilistic tomb of the necropolis. Meaning is not grounded in the real presence of the Eucharist, but held proleptically open, with God giving Godself in traces. This is a presence which is yet absent and an absence which is yet present. It is the textualization of the Word of God. Within this textualization, Scripture is among the sets of discourses which structure Christian identity. It is discursively constituted by the communities within the praxis of mystical theology as communal, practical and oriented towards God. In the multiplicity of meanings this model can fund, the ethical constitution of meaning-making becomes paramount. For a feminist, it is writing the 'Other' which can preoccupy the hermeneutical agenda; in this way the repressed and silenced can drift back from the margins and enter once more theological discourses. This is not a recuperation of reading the Bible as an act of praise to the divine, but a problematization of it which makes it the ever-shifting site of encounter.

Now, let us return to the broader agenda with which I began this chapter. I claimed that the model I would put forward would answer more adequately the need for an inclusive and open hermeneutics. In what respects do I believe this has been achieved?

First, to begin with a negative: it has not been achieved by evacuation of the Christian tradition in favour of a loosely conceived, supposedly universal metaphysics. This hermeneutic model sites itself in an ontology of creation, incarnation and eschatological consummation. This is very appropriate to the sort of liberalism espoused by the Editors and a number of other contributors to this book. Liberalism does not equate to removing the specificities of a religious tradition. Why do I believe the framework outlined here to be more open and thus, in the context of this book, more 'liberal' than Pickstock's model?

This is my second point. Upholding the traditionally central 'truths' of the Christian tradition (such as incarnation and resurrection) does not require one to adopt an exclusivist epistemology in which truth and meaning are fundamentally only available to, and grounded in, a particular interpretation of the Christian narrative (for example, one which privileges the eucharistic event). On the contrary: a Christian ontological vision attentive to the pivotal points of creation, incarnation and Parousia can fund an epistemology in which truth and meaning are, on the one hand, disseminated into the world and, on the other, not 'givens' that we 'have' – something Pickstock likewise rejects as a position – but rather partial and provisional. The implications of this, however, are that we are all, Christian or not, in the same epistemological boat. No community possesses the 'truth' or 'ground of truth'. This engenders a certain humility about our claims, and should make us attentive to a multiplicity of discourses as potentially truth-bearing. Again, this is not to assert that 'all beliefs are equally true', but that no belief has an *a priori* epistemological privilege.

Third, and finally, if the nature of the Christian narrative (by which I comprehend texts, traditions, doctrine and practices) makes us aware of our epistemic limitations, then we need to recognize that the ontological and epistemological matrices we inhabit are one of a number. A Christian variety may be our preferred model. But it does not entitle us simply to dismiss other narratives because we consider them to be less appropriate, or 'wrong', or even – a Radical Orthodox manoeuvre – 'out-narrated'. Rather, we need to take part in the never-finished task of engagement. Engagement: the propensity of the Liverpool Statement writers to laud this activity as at the heart of liberalism has been criticized. For who does not 'engage'? It is not the preserve of liberals. Yet 'engagement' does not mean only to take note of and respond to, or to weave into one's own accounts of the world. Engagement is a meeting of equals, on a plain of differing commitments but no epistemological priority.

Pickstock's model fundamentally falls down in this respect. Her account of language cannot engage the 'Other', but only devour it. The bread and the body which feed become an event in which truth and meaning are consumed: sucked from a world which does not, however, operate only according to the logic of the Mass. Theological liberalism in eschatological horizons is a con-summation of theology precisely because it does not claim to complete it, perfect it, or raise it to its highest point. Theological liberalism in eschatological horizons aspires towards 'truth': but has no monopoly upon it.

Notes

1 The so-called 'metaphysics of presence' privileges immediacy and presence, manifest in the philosophical priority of being, essence, identity, permanence, subject, object, truth. It expresses itself in the craving for grounds and centres.

2 For an extensive elaboration of this, see Wainwright, 1971. See also Gerard Loughlin: 'The eucharistic gift includes the fundamental terms of the temporality of the gift. According to the order of the gift, the eucharistic present is temporalized not from the here and now, but from the past, the future and finally the present. From the past it is temporalized as memorial; from the future as eschatological announcement, and from the present as "dailyness and viaticum". This is not the metaphysical concept of time, which understands the whole from the present; rather it is a gifted concept of time, which under-stands the present from the whole' (Loughlin, 1996, p. 134).

References

Daly, M. 'Post-Christian Theology: Some Connections Between Idolatry and Methodolatry, Between Deicide and Methodicide?' (address given at the Annual Meeting of the American Academy of Religion, 1973).

Fiorenza, E. S., *But She Said: Feminist Practices of Biblical Interpretation*, Beacon Press, Boston, MA, 1992.

Jobling, J., *Restless Readings: Feminist Biblical Hermeneutics in Theological Context*. Unpub. Ph.D. thesis, Kent University, 1999.

Loughlin, G., 'Transubstantiation: Eucharist as Pure Gift', in Brown, D. and Loades, A. (eds), *Christ: The Sacramental Word*, SPCK, London, 1996, pp. 123–41.

McIntosh, M. A., *Mystical Theology*, Blackwell, Oxford, 1998.

Milbank, Ward, G., *The Postmodern God*, Blackwell, Oxford, 1997.

Pickstock, C., *After Writing: On the Liturgical Consummation of Philosophy*, Blackwell, Oxford, 1998.

Wainwright, G., *Eucharist and Eschatology*, Epworth Press, London, 1971.

Ward, G., 'Words of Life: Hosting Postmodern Plenitude', *The Way: Contemporary Christian Spirituality*, July 1996, pp. 225–35.

Wyschogrod, E., *Saints and Postmodernism*, The University of Chicago, USA, 1990.

Zizioulas, J. D., *Being as Communion*, Darton, Longman and Todd, London, 1985.

CHAPTER THREE

The Humble Role of New Testament Scholarship

Leslie Houlden

NEW TESTAMENT STUDIES and systematic theology ('theology' for short) are two worthy and established disciplines. They stand side by side, but do they (should they) converse, and on what terms? Or are they polite semi-strangers, like two business-men who wait on the platform for the same train daily, year after year, and occasionally comment on the weather? But if they do converse, what might be said? And are they equal partners and just distinct in their methods and interests, or is one of them the senior partner, entitled to the last word?

I

Consider a case. How did Christians of the first generation or two react to the Jews' rules about food, integral to their way of life under God? The topic is not untypical of the proceedings of students of the New Testament. Indeed, many student essays and many grown-up articles have been devoted to it. But students of theology in a general sense (i.e. interested in the truth about God) are not sure how to react to such cases. They may say this is a subject so lacking in modern relevance, so bound to the circum-stances of first-century Christianity, that it has no direct bearing on theology and even (to sing in another key) bespeaks the fatuity – from a theological standpoint – of current New Testament schol-arship. It is a discipline that has gone its own way, no doubt in the context of increased specialization of the academic world (I recall a visit years ago from the Professor of the Epistle to the Galatians at a university in the Congo) and the sheer impossibility of any longer being an expert in more than a narrow field. Or in a more engaged spirit, the theologians may say this is indeed a matter that belongs in the category of transient issues. It soon ceased to worry Christians in a serious way, and theology can leave it safely behind. True, preachers confronted with texts on the subject, may find modern parallels and make useful homiletic mileage: the problems have changed but the moral and spiritual issues of today make the old ones resonate still. This may not take the pursuit of the purest theology very far, but it can make a decent sermon and there may be useful theological repercussions. It is also true that in dialogue with Jews, even the old issues will figure in some shape or form, but scarcely precisely as they did in the early days. Anyway, Christian theology in its central pursuits does not organize itself round relations with Judaism; so interest is bound to be muted.

Our topic is an instance of a general truth: that Scripture contains both material of lasting import and material that belongs to a past era, hard though it may sometimes be to be sure where a given instance belongs – that itself may be a matter for anguished theological debate. However, we may say that the bearing upon theology of the New Testament in principle and in its great concerns is not affected. New Testament Christology and eschatology, for example, must still claim a vital role in modern discussion of these theological topics, and even determine its general lines, its basic directions and concerns, however precisely the connections between 'then' and 'now' turn out to be made. But while theology may find comfort and purpose along these lines, there may also be unease: can it be realistic or fair for us, now, so to discriminate among aspects of first-century Christianity – between those which now (and perhaps for centuries) strike us, in broad terms at the least, as crucial for Christian theology, and those that do not? Was early Christianity not a seamless whole? Well, surely not, surely New Testament writers are themselves capable of discriminating between trivial or uncertain matters and those that are important. Paul sometimes shows himself exercising this sort of judgement; though, it is true, not always where you would now expect or wish.

But how exactly is one to distinguish and, if hunch is not good enough, on what principle exactly may the line be drawn? Such decisions seem to be at the beck and call of chance, dependent on what happened to be of long-lasting interest or able to establish some kind of link with central theological topics. But down the years all kinds of subjects have, temporarily or over long periods, been felt to have such a link: from the date of Easter to the gender of clergy, from the language and shape of liturgy to marriage discipline. It is, it appears, a fickle link, compelling for a period and then dissolving, sometimes almost without much heed, so that its ever having existed at all comes to seem puzzling. It is no wonder that New Testament scholars are inclined often to follow the line of least resistance and leave theology alone. There is a kind of purity about sticking to one's discipline without feeling an obligation to move beyond into what may seem uncertain seas.

Certain topics (Christology, the nature of God, eschatology, ecclesiology) will always be central to theological discussion and formulation, but you can never be sure what will be felt, at a given time, to be their ramifications or their vital connections. What one cultural situation sees as a clear-cut ramification will seem to another no ramification at all.

So it was at the start with rules about food. To some Christians (Peter, James and others) it seemed (we assume) axiomatic that followers of Jesus should, like him, take on the manners of Jewish identity. To others (Paul for example) it seemed axiomatic that the role of Jesus was such as to undercut the necessity for his (Gentile) followers to take on Jewishness in becoming Christians. But for neither group was this a 'clip-on' extra, a matter indifferent, about which one might have a harmless preference, such as . . . such as what? One seeks with difficulty for an example now recognized by all as belonging plainly to that category, but silence is the better part, lest it turn out to be integral to faith for some group or other. In our present case, this was no detachable matter, but part and parcel of a theological whole that issued in a specific way of life. In the one case, the package of obedience to divinely ordained Torah which allegiance to Jesus by no means negated, in the other the implications of Christ's universal redemptive role.

It seems that an attempt to distinguish between important and peripheral matters of belief and of theology fails not simply when it is a question of comparing one period or cultural situation with another (those who hold to a particular set of beliefs are likely to include all sorts of items!); but also when contemporary groups are put alongside one another – like Paul and Peter in Antioch.

To generalize from that instance, and moving away from our limited example: it is now a common perception (and surely one that, once attained, cannot be lost) that the New Testament writers constitute a choir of voices, harmonious indeed in their devotion and witness to Jesus, but cacophonous on almost everything else – on how they perceive Jesus, what they think he stood for precisely, how he 'fits in', what really mattered about him, and how one should now proceed in the light of him. Not only is there the long-recognized case of Paul being apparently corrected by James in the interests of an older doctrine; but we must also believe that Matthew and Luke wrote their Gospels not just to tell more than Mark had done, but to correct what they saw as his inadequacies and errors (Luke virtually says so, perhaps referring to both Mark and Matthew, in 1.1–4). And while John makes no reference to predecessors in the guild of Gospel-writers, and it is not wholly clear whether he knew of their works or not, he transcends or bypasses them in the scope and manner of his thought. The point is that each brings to bear his own distinctive totality of mind and soul – has done his thing. And how illuminating and edifying this is once one sees it. Reading and entering into the minds of the various New Testament writers, each in turn, offers a richness and clarity comparable to that found in reading any other set of writers on a given subject, taking each in his or her individuality and valuing them for it. Now none of this was felt in this way by those responsible for gathering the writings together in the early Christian centuries. They saw some of the differences of course, and made attempts to reconcile some of the contradictions (in ways not always congenial to later generations or more bibliolatrously inclined Christians), but what they chiefly saw was evidence of a Spirit-given collaboration; if not unison then certainly harmony, for those with ears to hear – indeed perhaps for any honest reader. And, as for the discrepancies, they were isolated instances, not symptoms of diverse mentalities at work.

But to us who, once initiated, see differently, the New Testament itself is but the first set of examples of that vast array of overlapping but distinct Christian totalities which have been not only the bane of heresy-firemen of all generations, but also a kind of standard warning, even mockery, and certainly admonition to the theological systematizers of every age; especially of our age when there is no excuse for not seeing what has been going on! For the task of the systematizers is to write of Christian faith conceptually, as reasonably and as tidily as possible; and the New

Testament student will say (where appropriate), Well done, but recognize the limitations of your work – which is from, in, and of your time and place, and cannot enjoy the permanence that seems to belong to the genre to which you contribute.

Moreover (to shift ground a little), if that seems obvious – though who ever readily admitted it? – the writing of abstract theology raises also the matter of genre. In Christian history, this mode of theology has, for wholly explicable cultural reasons, enjoyed a position of privilege. (An interesting parallel concerns the way that traditionally music as a matter of abstract mathematical theory was regarded, until relatively recent times, as superior to the mere crafts of either performance or composition.) How can God best be spoken of by intelligent persons? Clearly in abstract language, philosophical in its affinities – with such modifications as to be appropriate to the case (for example, in the light of revelation). Of course, there is also the language of prayer and liturgy, too valued and venerable to be much objected to, but that too may be conformed to the language of theology: Aquinas probably wrote, beautifully and orthodoxly, the main liturgy for Corpus Christi.

But there is the Bible, hardly any of it coming anywhere near to such a mode of discourse; and the Bible is the foundation of theology. So how is it to be used in theology? In two ways, broadly, so theology has said. Certainly, some of the biblical writers used ideas that the theologian can, apparently without too much violence, take and develop: justification from Paul, the Father–Son–Spirit relationship from John. There might be the question whether, in acting thus, the theologian has quite seized the original character of the biblical 'idea'; whether he has not, for instance, over-easily drawn Johannine ideas, Jewish in provenance, into a Hellenistic philosophical sphere – even if those two be not so rigidly distinguishable as has been thought; or taken a Pauline surge of exegetical spirit, grounded in his apostolic vocation, to make of it a dogma capable of spawning its own dogmatic children, each marrying other dogmatic offspring, and so on for centuries (and tearing a continent apart in the process).

Secondly of course (and predominantly through Christian history), there is the way of decontextualized quotation of appropriate (as it seems) sacred words – in good times in the original tongue, more commonly in the version to hand; nearly always without reference to complexities and uncertainties in the manuscript tradition, and sometimes contributing to them in the process. There is no need now to argue the impropriety of this use of Scripture as a basis for theological argument, and biblical scholarship may claim credit for having at least made theology cautious (if not always perfectly behaved) in this respect. In fact, you do not have to look far to find examples of the guard being dropped and both theology and ethics reaching for what looks like the clinching text, as if we lived still in ancient Israel or first-century Greece. And liturgists, who work to different specifications, have not, in their reforms, been averse to the scriptural catena, resonant even where not all that appropriate or helpful.

Finally, identicality of words and forms can by no means guarantee identicality of thought and belief. To believe 'the same' in a new cultural setting is necessarily to believe 'differently', if only because, where one would have once been typical, one is now an oddity. Liturgy is perhaps the most obvious sphere for this to arise, but it is equally the case in that of theology – and apostles of postmodernism, hoping to make a virtue of their attempted traditionalism, display the baffling incongruity of the beached whale.

I do not know whether it properly takes the 'wisdom' of New Testament scholarship to make these points and adopt this stance, but they seem to stem from the sorts of reflection that New Testament students commonly generate. Now, of course, both New Testament scholarship and theology may exaggerate their tendencies, stick to them with tenacity in ways that do them no credit and make an unhelpful situation worse. For example: New Testament scholars, seeing Jesus as a Galilean holy man, may find it inappropriate that he came, very speedily, to be revered as God's saving agent, even 'God among us' – as if they could not accommodate a situation where a man comes to receive the wholehearted God-centred and God-related adulation of many. Indeed, the historian is almost bound to have a tendency to see such adulation as verging on madness. But have they never heard of pop stars or football heroes? That this adulation came to be expressed in philosophical terms, even rigidities, can certainly obscure the Galilean holy man, though in the terms of its fourth-century context it is as understandable as the enthusiasm of the Galilean disciples in theirs.

The Gospel of John may be seen as in some ways a helpful

balance. True, its Jesus acts sometimes in ways not easily assimi-
lated by scholarly portraitists of the Galilean healer and teacher
(water into wine perhaps, rising from the dead, making himself
fitfully visible), but he is nevertheless depicted as a person with an
identifiable life in the world – but also as one about whom great
things are said, the recipient of high honours, though probably
not going beyond what enthusiasm of thoughtful devotion in the
context might rise to: his followers simply experienced, as a result
of him, the reality of the creator-saviour God. And why should
they not? Who is to negate, in principle? To negate, that is, as
distinct from disagree or be surprised.

Spurred by the Johannine example, the New Testament scholar
may suggest to the theologian that he, the theologian, might
reflect that his trade, though naturally inclining to the minimiz-
ing of historical limitations and of the placing of ideas in
particular settings and seeing them as subject to constant
movement, and preferring to dwell on cohesive patterns and even
eternal verities, may grow in candour and commendability
through a more welcoming attention to the historical perspective
– so tentatively and humbly proposed.

II

Consider a case. Apart from the brief report in 1 Corinthians 7,
Mark 10.1–12 gives us the earliest testimony to the teaching of
Jesus on divorce. A plain reading tells us that Jesus was against it.
Its availability in Jewish Torah-based practice was a concession to
human frailty. In itself, divorce flies in the face of God's provision
in creation, his purpose for human bonding between the sexes.
There can be no mistaking, it seems, the severity, the uncompro-
mising quality of the teaching. Whether initiated by husband or
wife, divorce is out, marriage is for life.

But what kind of a passage is this, what kind of teaching? How
are we to 'place' it in our scheme of things? In our terms, it looks
like ethics, indeed a moral ruling for Jesus' followers, even for
humankind as a whole. What else can it be? That is how the
Christian Churches have taken it, and, when their institutional
life has led to such provision, they have, most of them, put it into
their rule books or canon law. Nearer to Mark himself, that is how
Matthew, perhaps 15 years later, took it – though he disagreed

with it and made his own modification to the rule ('except for
unchastity', Matthew 19.9) – and some Christian bodies have
followed his path. Either way, we are operating in the sphere of
moral rules, potentially of church law: this is how Christians must
govern themselves, and sanctions can be expected to operate
when there is infringement.

Were we right, however, to read Mark's passage as 'ethics', or at
least ethics of the kind that expresses itself in rules, community
law and discipline? Is that an outlook we see expressed in Mark's
Gospel as a whole? Well, certainly, as far as his vocabulary goes, he
emphasizes Jesus' teaching role – the relevant words of the *didasko*
family occur rather more frequently in Mark than in Matthew
(teacher *par excellence*) and slightly less frequently than in Luke
(John is well down in the score). And, contrary to first impressions
perhaps (by comparison with our intuitive sense of Matthew?), a
large proportion of Mark, up to one-third, is taken up with Jesus'
utterances, most naturally to be classified as 'teaching'. But what
sort of material is it? Chapter 13 tells us about the future cosmic
drama and, covertly, about the Passion that follows. Other
teaching (e.g. 7.1–23) is about what we see as ritual observance
questions (which get moralized) and conveys a liberal or even
radical attitude to crucial aspects of Jewish identity – food rules
and Sabbath. Mark seems to show himself as Pauline in tendency
and (leaving aside the historical question) to be Paulinizing Jesus.
Then there is the giving of primacy to love over 'all burnt
offerings and sacrifices' (12.28–34). And there is the passage on
divorce. Little of this lends itself easily to incorporation into the
bedside Christian rule book or the guide for canon lawyers; and
Mark makes no provision at all for the exercise of discipline in
Christian communities – what to do when Christians fail to obey
the teaching: no tariffs, no threats (in these ways, Matthew
helpfully made up the deficit).

No, Mark's teaching of Jesus is all, in one way or another, the
handmaid of Jesus' single and sufficient message, summarized in
Mark 1.15: 'The time is fulfilled and the kingdom of God has
drawn near; repent and believe in the gospel.' Thus and so will
life in the kingdom be; thus and so are the marks of community
life under the reign of God. If this is ethics, it is descriptive and
aspirational ethics, and it is wholly dependent on, an outcrop of, a
particular religious outlook, that is both intellectual and spiritual

in our terms. In the sphere that Jesus establishes and where he is joined by others and which will – one day – be creation's destiny, this is the shape and style of human life: including no divorce; but that alongside the perfection of love for God and neighbour. It is a state of affairs that will be, as 10.1–12 suggests, a renewal of Eden. It was a Pauline theme (Christ as new Adam and life 'in Christ' as 'new creation', 2 Corinthians 5.17, Galatians 6.15), and Mark had already laid it on his stall in the Temptation story, with Jesus, like Adam, in peaceful charge of the beasts. No help here, alas, for Christian rule-makers and discipline-keepers who must somehow speak and act; no help from Mark. But the inconvenience of rule-makers is perhaps a small price to pay for the enjoyment of the vision, as from Jesus, that Mark gives to us. Certainly, it makes ethics sing its song in a most particular key.

More important still for our discussion, this is an instance (among many others) where the New Testament scholar may lament the passing of a unified style of Christian awareness – in the academy most of all, but rubbing off elsewhere; where what we distinguish and segregate as theology, ethics and spirituality (including liturgy), each with its own academic apparatus and, in the churches, its own committees and boards, was once unified. It can be found in a document like the Gospel of Mark, there for us to read. New Testament scholarship may humbly suggest that to divide Christian awareness is to weaken and to falsify its character.

III

That 'humble role'. The purpose of this essay has been to suggest a few ways in which New Testament scholarship, as currently practised, might venture both to criticize and then to contribute to theology; that is, to thought concerning the truth about God. Theology may challenge the right of another discipline to do any such thing, especially where the idiom seems so alien, and so pass the essay by, even on the strength (weakness!) of its title alone.

There is indeed good reason for modesty. Whatever New Testament scholarship has any business to offer, it is indeed 'humble' – even in the proud sense that its glory lies elsewhere. New Testament scholarship has, after all, much to its credit, even (to take a practical example) when seen alongside theology as an academic discipline. In the UK universities, for good or ill, there are about three times as many posts in New Testament studies than in systematic theology. The reasons may be less to the credit of New Testament studies, viewed in a certain light, than one might hope: it is (the theory might go) a discipline free of dogmatic assumptions or ecclesiastical overtones, operating on the purest academic principles, able to stand alongside other historical and literary disciplines; one where ideology raises its threatening head only with difficulty and by running the risk of disgrace or marginalization. Yet, though a great deal of New Testament scholarship is 'objective' and ideology-free, and though those who bend it for doctrinal reasons are liable to be distrusted in the forum of their peers, this area of study is undoubtedly a special case. There are indeed other aspects of historical scholarship upon whose findings the self-understanding and pride of whole communities may depend, but none is so widely or urgently placed in such a situation as New Testament scholarship. After all, it holds within its hands the capacity to confirm or deny (or leave in suspense more likely) the validity and character of the events on which Christian faith has been held to rest, and to interpret, in the light of their historical origin or their literary import, the foundation documents of the theological edifice. To ignore this connection is bound to seem unrealistic – however strongly the pressures of the secular academy and the (now so distant) memories of ecclesiastical censors act as a deterrent. Western history has, in fact, had its share of warfare between biblical scholarship and authorities of one sort or another, and the subject has made headway in the public arena only with the greatest difficulty. And it has its largely unsung roll of martyrs (though not often with the shedding of blood).

Yet while New Testament scholarship may offer for scrutiny considerations of the kinds exemplified in the first two parts of this essay, New Testament scholarship in itself cannot go further. Its role towards theology is indeed humble, not in the sense of being obsequious or self-effacing, but in the sense of being ancillary – but also crucial. It is a Jeeves-like role: not dictatorial or determinative, but always ready to make helpful suggestions and even to be unobtrusively obstructive if they are not followed, and certainly to try to prevent the master making a fool of himself (yet again). Thus, it may put a brake on the absolutist pretensions of theological schemes, however venerable or magnificent in appearance: they are of the earth, earthy; of their time, timely; once maybe, but certainly not for ever, everywhere. It may draw attention, therefore, to the changing character of theological totalities in their various settings, from the manifest diversity of the first century itself and then afterwards. It has every reason to be sensitive to the movements of development, for it has experienced them in its own past as a discipline as well as in the small, intense compass of its own material. It is sensitive to the extraordinary range of uses, often now appearing misleading or foolish, to which its own texts, the New Testament writings, have been put, often for theological ends. In that way, there is an apposite eschatological instinct in New Testament scholarship – all is transient, the best has yet to be revealed. R. E. Brown, in the introduction to volume one of his great work, *The Death of the Messiah* (1994), answered those who said, having written on the birth and then the death of the Messiah, why not go on and write *The Resurrection of the Messiah*? 'I have no such plans. I would rather explore that area "face to face".' He was wise, not just in the sense that the time left to him would not, as it turned out, have sufficed or that the books are not in fact lacking from other hands, but also in the deeper sense that New Testament scholarship has an unfinished, open quality from which theology is inclined to shy away.

NT scholarship may also point to the 'lame' quality imposed upon theology by the boundaries which have come to be drawn around it, differentiating it not only from historical studies, with biblical scholarship among them, but also, as we have seen, from ethics and spirituality. The segregation would hardly have been felt in past Christian eras, but the explosion of knowledge has made it inevitable. The failure of theology often to perceive its limitations, regrettable though they may be, and then, on its own terms and from its own narrow base of method and ethos, to 'queen' it over the rest, is not thereby excused. People will now make their totalities of understanding in all kinds of different ways, on all kinds of bases, not necessarily conceptual in the traditional theological mode. New Testament scholarship may itself encourage, perhaps inadvertently, such constructions on narrative models – they served the evangelists powerfully, and echo across to us still. It is, when you consider it, a particular local Western difficulty and a minority taste to suppose that thought about God is most properly carried out by means of the conceptual constructions that (as we saw earlier) have happened to occupy the prestigious positions in the tradition of Christian reflection. In fact, a few biblical scholars have, from time to time, ventured into the theological field, from the base of their own work, trying to say 'how it looks to us'. One thinks, for example, of A. J. M. Wedderburn's *Beyond Resurrection*, working in an area that obviously lends itself to a dialogue of disciplines. Sadly, R. E. Brown, in *The Birth of the Messiah* (1993) and elsewhere, was inclined to steer clear.

No writing in the New Testament faces us with the question of such interdisciplinary dialogue more sharply than the Gospel of Mark. In much recent work, this long neglected Gospel has emerged as a book of great depth and subtlety – and never in its long centuries has it been so appreciated and, we trust, understood. It is a severe account of Jesus which faces us pitilessly with the starkness of his life and death, and which refrains from all cheap and cheerful answers. And it certainly refrains from subtle solutions too. There is just Mark's Jesus, who goes before us to the mysterious open 'Galilee' of our hopes. In an unpublished lecture, towards the end of his argument, John Fenton sums Mark up in these terms, which out of context reads a little too dramatically, yet the exaggeration is salutarily shocking:

Mark leaves us with nothing. No theology, no Christology, no ethics, no eschatology, no ministry and sacraments, no church history. Thank goodness. These are all things that divide us from one another. And Mark keeps them away. He just gives us a story, a story of disaster. Out of that we might have faith.

That is not a bad contribution for New Testament scholarship to make to theology for those who are clear-sighted in our present time.

References

Brown, R. E., *The Birth of the Messiah: A Commentary on the Infancy Narratives in Luke and Matthew*, Geoffrey Chapman, London, 1993.

Brown, R. E., *The Death of the Messiah: from Gethsemane to the Grave: A Commentary on the Passion Narratives in the Four Gospels*, Geoffrey Chapman, London, 1994.

Wedderburn, A. J. M., *Beyond Resurrection*, SCM Press, London, 1999.

CHAPTER FOUR

Authentic Conservatism: Accommodating the Liberal Critique

Mark Elliott

Political Liberalism

Political liberalism allows us many things. Although it is not perfect, not always knowing how to adjudicate, and often has to defer to pragmatism, nevertheless essential to its operation is the principle of collaboration, debate and consensus. The more views that are presented on an issue, the closer we get to truth, or rather the further we get from falsehood. Wisdom comes from outside, including spiritual wisdom. Although *laissez-faire* market economy need not mean democracy, still, as Giddens (1998) argues, the former has produced a fair amount of *Gleichschaltung* in this country (LEA, GLCs and now devolution, etc.). Democracy need not mean liberal democracy but it can, and is then at its best. Liberal democracy need not mean redistributive justice, but it can include it in a workable way by encouraging possession, even possessive individualism, and profit within an overarching strategy of benefiting all within the boundaries of the political nation. In fact, capitalists have a very strong view of what society should look like. As Nicholas Boyle has remarked, the development of a global market since 1945 has changed everything. 'Capitalism is an alibi for socialism. It is an imaginary object of hatred, whose function is to distract our attention from the will to power of socialists' (Boyle, 1998, p. 76).

In a consumer society desire is encouraged to be misdirected, and production has been replaced by seduction (Baudrillard) – the more targets and outlets, the better. For Tony Giddens, society is characterized by reflexivity as the:

constant monitoring and adjustment of ideas and practices
in the light of newly acquired information. This generates
uncertainty and instability [. . .] He (Giddens) argues that it
is now more difficult for individuals to cultivate a continuous
thread of self-identity in the face of the needless mutability
of time/space connections, the constant recombinations
of social relationships out of context and the perpetual
exposure of the self to fresh information about itself.
(Beckford, 1996, p. 34)

The lesson of the 1930s should make us uneasy about economic
and political quietism. True, liberalism has always had its values
and the things for which it would go to the stake. These, however,
are typically framed in negative terms: 'no' to racism or any other
form of blatant inequality; 'no' to the repression of freedom of
belief and expression, although qualified by the principle that any
clear harm at least to the principle of equality should be excepted.
It means treating people as 'adults', as responsible within their
own realm, until the exercise of their freedom infringes upon that
of others in an unacceptable way. Unfortunately this may lead to
scenarios of the 'bolting the door after the horse has bolted'
variety. We have a media which pretends to reflect in a value-
neutral way, in which everyone can have the spiritual solace of
fame on celluloid. In working practices, we find that the language
used is classically liberal – it is about 'freeing up', 'tapping human
resources', 'flat structures' as Richard Roberts has noted
(Roberts, 1995, p. 180).

The link between liberal political philosophy and liberal
theology can perhaps be traced to John Locke. Locke conceived
of freedom of conscience as something religious: as freedom of
worship rather than as either freedom of speech or freedom of
thought. Nicholas Wolterstorff has produced a good case for
seeing Locke as the one for whom the principle of the freedom of
subjectivity occupied centre stage (Wolterstorff, 1996). A secularized form of this appears with Voltaire's famous maxim: 'I oppose
what you say but defend to the death your right to say it.'

Theological Liberalism and the World

Liberal Christianity tends to be refreshing in its generosity of spirit, an ability to affirm the world, which means to affirm life. Liberalism is empathetic. It refuses to say that it knows another's experience to the extent of sympathy. (One could compare Edith Stein's critique of Max Scheler in her *On the Problem of Empathy* [Stein, 1989, pp. 27–35].) Liberal Christianity is not automatically suspicious of the rich diversity of human experience. But the corollary is the privatization of religion: you are allowed to believe what you like but are to keep reasonably quiet about it. In return, I shall not pester you. In times of alienation and loneliness, people look towards the private as the source of much meaning and thus tend to see the Church in terms of supply of personal needs when such meaning threatens to run out. As Robert Bellah put it, 'needs for personal intimacy in American religious life suggests why the local church, like other voluntary communities, indeed like the contemporary family, is so fragile, requires so much energy to keep it going, and has so faint a hold on commitment when such needs are not met' (Bellah, 1985, p. 232). Of course it would be churlish to lay the blame for these tendencies at the door of liberal theologians who, one senses, are only reflecting the currents within their churches: liberal theologians have usually been church theologians. But the prophetic aspect of theology in which the theologian seeks to be the mouthpiece of God to correct the wayward listing movements of the Church and wider society – this is somehow missing.

Natural theology is a liberal product, in that, taking its cue from Kant, it begins and ends with reflection on the human condition. It moves from apologetics to theology in suspiciously too easy a movement. God becomes that which it would be in the world's best interests to believe in, yet to say, as Markham does (Markham, 1996), that it is either Aquinas or Nietzsche, either God or nothing, is to raise the stakes artificially and unhelpfully too high, and falls into the same trap as some of the proofs for the existence of God: that the contingent requires the necessary to exist, that imperfection implies perfection, and so on. People can and do get by without reference to God; their lives are not meaningless or nihilistic, for all their lack of belief. Better to say that their 'reflexivity' often stands in need of a content; life as going somewhere rather than a cycle of choices.

Theological Conservatism and the World

T. S. Eliot wrote in 'Choruses from the Rock': 'Why should men love the Church? Why should they love her laws? She tells them of life and death and of all that they would forget. She is tender where they would be hard, and hard where they like to be soft. She tells them of Evil and Sin and other unpleasant facts' (Eliot, 1974).

Eliot's own life may be thought of as full of these 'unpleasant facts', a life which Antony Julius has declared to have been anti-Semitic and fascist in outlook (Julius, 1996). The neo-Augustinian Eliot, in his *Notes Towards Definition of Culture and Idea of a Christian Society* (Eliot, 1982) tended to privilege culture and tradition over civilization and society. C. Winquist has traced the cultural history of the last century as first, the death of God; second, the disappearance of the self; third, the end of history; and fourth, the closure of the book (Winquist, 1994). Barbarism and totalitarianism go together. Or, as Eliot wrote, culture is the incarnation of whatever religion a society has – in as much as it has any, we might now add. In this dark world, conservatism does not think that one can rely on the little light of the soul, but rather, through setting a compass darkly, on one's personal orientation to a truth who as Christ is Personal. Any inability to see the truth clearly is as much to do with the moral factor of choice and self-orientation as epistemological limitation. Jesus himself seems to have seen the world as a place where an amount of inner, moral struggle, as well as a struggle for survival, is required; in fact, life is available only through death. Rather than an ontology of peace or violence, he represented an ontology of renewal. Conservative Christians, far from what is commonly believed, see sin as something inner, and tend only to judge external behaviour when it is inconsistent with the statements of Christ (and Paul) and reveals a sinful disposition, one insufficiently focused on Christ as Master and Friend.

The twin aspects of God's holiness and love as emphasized by conservative evangelicals relate to the need to recognize discipleship and justification as standing under the 'rubric' of the presence of the resurrecting, renewing Spirit. (The last has been the particularly valuable contribution of the charismatic movement, whatever its excesses, as obsessively focused on by, for example, Martyn Percy *Words, Wonders and Power* and Andrew

Walker *Restoring the Kingdom.* The former uses an early Fou-
cauldian conception of 'power' as necessarily oppressive and
violent.) Both the conservative (Christianity sets us free from self-
ishness to obey the God of our fathers and mothers) and the
evangelical (there is forgiveness at the heart of Christianity,
offering a 'new chance', asserting God's intimate love *pro me*)
need to be tightly linked together. Of course, the principle of a
moral education, a Christian *paideia*, a *Bildung* which is painful,
can become corrupted into a misguided and neurotic disposition
in its sensed reasons for mortification: that I am sinful. The
Pauline teaching makes it clear that it is not so much 'I' the chief
of sinners who am the fount of all sin as that there are sinful
harmful situations already out there – a 'world of sin' – and also
operating inside 'me' to which I indeed may contribute. Thus any
self-hatred among believers is an accident and is not of the
essence of conservative evangelical Christianity.

Liberalism and Spiritual Freedom

In the present day, liberal Christianity is not about freedom to
think, express, but is typically 'freedom from' in the area of
behaviour: it is the freedom from rules which are externally given
in Torah or Christian teaching (*didache*, canon law) are meant to
work internally – the law of Christ through the mind of Christ (1
Corinthians 2.16). If such laws are external or simply belonging to
the past, then they are to be disregarded as outmoded – the stuff
of conservative Pharisees. Liberal theology makes a valuable contribution when it asserts that the gospel gives people at least the
illusion that they are free to take God or leave him: it shows
respect for persons at an existential level. It sees the gospel as persuasive and not to be enforced on people; that *didache* only follows
the freeing message of Jesus. Yet it must be reasserted that this
message carries the sense of 'freeing for' or 'to'. Freedom is not so
much found in no longer having guilt or despair but in creative
service. It includes power, which as the later Foucault agreed, is
not a dirty word or concept, but is part of human becoming
(Carette, 1999).

Coercive and manipulative love must indeed be rejected. But
other kinds of power are not only compatible with love but are

also essential to its meaning. For a start, love must have its own dynamic energy to will and to take initiatives, if it is to be truly relational and other-orientated. A merely passive attitude of 'love' which only waits on the other, rather than actively seeking his or her good, is fundamentally self-contained and ultimately self-orientated. (White, 1997, p. 157)

Christian ethics as Christian spirituality cannot be satisifed with the somewhat passive 'Other'-based ethics of a Levinas or of Tillich, who wrote 'But there is one limit to man's attempt to draw all content into himself – the other' (Tillich, 1963, p. 40). Unfortunately we have the illusion of being consumers making choices, being in control long before having to produce anything. Yet this kind of 'Heideggerian passivity' often sums up today's society quite well.

The negative side of conservatism is that it gives one further to fall; the image of God and the actual reality can have far more of an abyss between them. *Anfechtung* as anxiety and despair is not something too readily seen as an unhealthy, bad thing, to which healthy, liberating religion must be opposed. In its Schleiermacherian form, the liberal understanding of religion is already well on the road to Durkheim. Religion is understood as contributing to culture, which, as David Lyon has observed, is a dangerous route. From it we get the core experience of authentic humanity as the lowest common denominator of what religion is (Rahner); the presumed interchangeability of spirit and Spirit in Tillich is another example.

In an introduction to a recent Systematic Theology textbook we see Hodgson and King reiterating the approach of David Tracy: Christian doctrine in its true shape is 'classic'. Its rough edges get smoothed out, perhaps with time; it is also liberative, emancipatory. There is explicit resistance to Heppe's commonplace/topic style of theology, not least because it presupposes that theology can be ordered, coherent and might try to tie something down. Instead, a panel of experts sketches out impressionistic essays on various doctrines. Intellectual laziness gets excused on the grounds that 'personal experience' matters. There is a temptation among theologians to be 'almost contemporary': Scheler, Weber, Benjamin – they all seemed to live on the edge and to suffer for being intellectuals who were peripheral characters. The 'heroes of unbelief' become the sustainers of theology syllabuses.

The rise of feminism has meant further anthropologizing of theology and emancipatory anthropology at that. David Lodge's description of a college founded to train Free Church ministers applies generally to denominational institutions these days, as they bend over backwards to be inclusive and thereby (somehow) become more academically respectable. The syllabus contained:

> Phenomenology and faith, situational ethics, the theory and practice of charism, early Christian heresies, feminist theology, black theology, negative theology, hermeneutics, homiletics, church management, ecclesiastical architecture, sacred dance, and many other things [. . .] the discourse of much modern radical theology was just as implausible and unfounded as the orthodoxy it had displaced, but nobody had noticed because nobody read it except those with a professional stake in its continuation. (Lodge, 1992, p. 35–36)

With reference to the Bible, most liberal theologians will say that for most of the Bible, the theology is not explicit, and is to be better understood in terms of ideology and structures. Where there is any theology it is kept at arm's length as being 'theology for its own time' only.

Conservative Theology and Spiritual Freedom

It is a conservative virtue that one admits to one's *Anfechtung* and *Angst*: what is it about? To what are we directing it – we all have it, some more than others. 'How far does *Angst* about whiteness, maleness and middle classness, so typical of the middle class intelligentsia, really promote anyone else's liberation?' (Watson, 1995, p. 7). What is important is that by taking responsibility for one's own need for liberation, one is starting with a task that is a bit more self-contained than the liberal building the kingdom of God. As the negative energy is used to release us from moral paralysis, we become those with an earthly approach of becoming increasingly outward-looking. Martin Heidegger, as noted by Bryan Ingraffia in his book *Postmodern Theory and Biblical Theology* believed in earthly existence's supreme saving virtue in the acceptance of one's own death. Ingraffia challenges Heidegger's emphasis on guilt and conscience, as obscuring what in Christianity is faithful existence, something far more positive than authentic existence. (Although his diagnosis that it is 'originating in Hellenic not Hebraic thought' is none too helpful.) For Heidegger, according to Ingraffia, 'instead of God calling anthropos into relationship with him, into faithful existence, through the person of Jesus Christ (Romans 1.6). Dasein is called by its own (authentic) self, out of absorption in the world, out of the they-self, back to its own Self' (Ingraffia, 1995, p. 156). Heidegger also paints our situation too blackly and with too much generalization – surely to exist as a human does not mean anxiety and nothing else. On the other hand the good news according to Heidegger is that there is no place for a representative death and thus nothing but the eternal return of here-and-now repentance for oneself. This, for Ingraffia, is nothing but rebellious independence; and for Jacques Derrida it is laughable modernist ontologizing – as if there could be a 'free questioning of purely self-reliant Dasein' (Ingraffia, 1995, p. 164).

Liberalism and Uncertainty

In the account given by liberalism, theology is anti-ideology: it fosters pluralism (see Markham). Choice is a good thing, and reflexivity of a spiritual sort is the only way to maturity. This can be seen operating between religions but also within like communities and even within the maturation of the individual as moral agent. For Tillich, that doyen of Teutonic-become-Anglo-Saxon-theology, the personal centre is 'the subject of self-awareness as bearer of the spirit – dealing with drives, inclinations, desires, trends, moral experiences, ethical traditions and authorities, so that one can be said to have freedom in the sense of a total reaction of a centred self which deliberates and decides' (Tillich, 1963, p. 28).

According to Schleiermacher, religion was undergirded by religious affection which comes to self-consciousness and then communication or expression in words and doctrines. Behind this stands Kant and his anthropological turn, and the necessity of autonomy, but also the Romantic love of freedom through emancipation. Melanchthon, for whom God could be universally found in the conscience or the sense of the absolute undivided unity (no pantheism here) was also a strong influence (Schleiermacher, 1928, p. 132–4). Schleiermacher insisted on the need for human mediation in all religions, and held 'For there is only one source from which all Christian doctrine is derived, namely, the self-proclamation of Christ', who alone had 'true objective consciousness of the condition of men in general' (Schleiermacher, 1928, pp. 92; 80) but, of course, not of that of God, so that inspired revelation was not a source of timeless doctrine. We cannot have knowledge, only feeling, since no knowledge can contain the absolute – such limitation would make the unlimited and the infinite necessary. This is an aesthetic, as he had put it in his earlier *Speeches on Religion*, which seems to moderate between Knowing and Doing. We cannot know God but at least we can feel him. That is to say little new; what is new is that there is also little that we can say *about* God. That is what Hegel criticized, although his remedy poses its own problems: yet knowledge that God is, in Hegel, supplemented by the knowledge of the content of who or what God is, which is in turn supplied from without, by revelation.

Can faith not increase, if not the amount, then at least the quality of our knowledge, affording 'wisdom', 'spiritual insight' – into the same one reality (Hebrew Bible) not 'another world' – a spiritually infused world which needs us to receive it? By way of response to the Liverpool Statement, Gareth Jones, after spending time plotting the positions of five types of theology (cf. the obsession with methodology and preliminaries in, for example, the New Yale theology) calls for a Church theology. However, this is made with the caveat that it is bad for the Church to become divorced from society and *a fortiori* it is bad for theology to do the same. He adds:

> When a theological movement seeks to privilege its access to reality, or to claim that genuine reality is distinct from social reality, or, worst of all, to state that there is something immoral about not privileging theology's access to reality, then I think we are on the slippery slope towards prejudice and discrimination within a supposedly academic and intellectual discipline. (Jones, 1998, p. 89)

But what is social reality? It sounds all a bit naïvely modernist. Perhaps it is that which Berger and Luckmann pointed to in their

famous *The Social Construction of Reality* (1967). However, is it not
more plausible that there are a number of constructed worlds –
that we live life at one level in a world which everyone shares, but
perhaps through the private worlds of our own experience overlapping? Or, as John Searle has observed in his *The Construction of
Social Reality*, as linguistic beings, any reality we step out into has
already been shaped, or fitted to our own apprehension of it.

Jones also makes 'the point, which is rather that reality *per se* is
not something which knowledge *per accidens* can control in any
final or complete manner' (Jones, 1998, p. 89). This seems incon-
testable. In his book *Critical Theology* Jones had spoken of how God
is mystery, both present and absent in his creation. Now, the
meaning of 'mystery' in the New Testament is often neglected in
works on this theme, notably Andrew Louth's *Discerning the
Mystery* and Mark McIntosh's *Mystical Theology*. It is commonly
agreed by New Testament scholars of the relevant passage in
Ephesians that this is a secret (plan) that has now been revealed.
Jones' musings on the nature of knowledge and incompleteness –
we cannot know the past because it is 'complete' (Jones, 1995,
p. 154) – do not seem to me very convincing. Again, we agree with
Locke that religious knowledge is not certainty, certainly not
'Cartesian certainty', but rather the certainty that a conscience is
no longer as troubled as it was (Calvin's type). Meaning arises
from human responses to a symbol – various possibilities of
meanings.

> Mystery is the fundamental symbol of religion and the most
> meaningful analogy by which to interpret that symbol is time.
> (Jones, 1995, p. 162)

> For faith, Christians must proclaim the uniqueness of Christ
> as the revelation of the mystery; but for Christ, Christians
> must acknowledge the partiality of precisely this faith. Any
> other attitude would betray in human words the divine intent
> of the Word, and the kenotic character of that Word as it is
> revealed and concealed in Jesus Christ. (Jones, 1995, p. 201)

It is this two-layer opacity which is worrying: to speak of a veil over
our hearts/minds and of the figure of Christ as hiding more than
revealing is to focus negatively on the limitation rather than the

glory of Christ twice over. Once over would be enough. Furthermore, there is something problematic with his view that the cross,
as one more symbol open to interpretation, is about God's
'seeking at-one-ment with God's self' (Jones, 1995, p. 283), self-
limitation and fragmentation in search of an ultimate union. For
humanity to be left out of the picture in any theory of atonement
rather misses the point of who is needing to be made at one with
whom.

> Today critical theology acknowledges entirely its own rela-
> tivism because Jesus Christ took upon himself relativism in
> the incarnation and because that relativism expresses the
> most fundamental truth of the Christian image of God [. . .]
> if Christianity is in the business of drawing pictures of God in
> Christ (method), then it must understand the reasons why its
> own discourse can only be one amongst many (truth).
> (Jones, 1995, p. 245)

Eschatology becomes a symbol for 'provisionality' where it used
to stand for 'judgement', while remaining the judgement in itself.
Liberalism rejoices in phrases like 'openness to the future' – all
deliciously eschatological/theological sounding, but meaningless; in effect it means more like openness to next year. Yet, we are
who we have been (Boyle, 1998 p. 155). It matters that the theologian knows the biblical texts and what they (probably) meant, that
she be familiar with church history and its relationship to universal
history, and be aware that today's 'humanity' has been constructed
from layers of historical eras. Furthermore Christianity was once
thought of as ethics, but since Heidegger, the God of morality, of
'deals', is 'dead'. Yet a distinction has to be drawn between existential uncertainty and moral uncertainty. Christians (or human
beings for that matter) do have to live with the former, but not with
the latter. What is not of faith is sin, said Paul strongly: can we see a
way ahead of intended action, assuming God's help . . . ?

Conservatives and Uncertainty

Those with a keen interest in religious news may be aware that
there has, over the last decade or so, emerged some sort of a crisis
in evangelicalism. This is represented by works with titles such as

The Anglican Evangelical Crisis (Tinker, 1995) and *The Post Evangelical* (Tomlinson, 1995). Is it true that an evangelical is someone
who says to a liberal: 'I'll call you a Christian if you call me a
scholar'? Is evangelicalism simply one more tradition? Alister
McGrath and his view that the evangelical tradition is one among
others appears in stark contrast to Don Carson's position that
evangelicals of the present are in direct succession to the
orthodoxy from the apostles until now (as in Carson & Woodbridge (eds) *Scripture and Truth*). Admittedly, McGrath's
spirituality seems to owe more to a concoction of Luther's 'justification by faith' motto turned into a psychology of self-acceptance
with some colouring from the Christ-symbolism of the Ignatian
Spiritual Exercises than something redolent of the characteristics
of the spirituality of the Evangelical Awakening.

At the end of the 1980s, John Stott incurred some criticism
from certain fellow-evangelicals for his taking part in a dialogue
with the liberal David Edwards, published in a book called *Essentials* (Edwards & Stott, 1988), in which a remarkable amount of
common ground was found. What liberals and conservative evangelicals can agree on would include: love and forgiveness, the
priority of the indicatives of grace over the imperatives of law
(although evangelicals would probably want to make sure there is
a fairly tight connection between the two), and the beauty of the
Holy One of the Gospels.

They might also agree on a certain honesty in their account of
the Christian life. 'Honesty' was a buzzword in the camp of David
Watson, although intellectual honesty meant taking the trouble
to 'doubt one's doubts'. Watson began his book *I Believe in the
Church* with an account of Goethe's *bon mot* to a self-congratula-
tory doubting preacher: 'Give me some of your certainties. I have
enough doubts of my own.' Or, with Luther: 'The Holy Spirit is no
sceptic and it is not doubts or mere opinions that he has written
on our hearts, but assertions more sure and certain than life itself
and all our experiences and thus reason' (M. Luther, 1957,
p. 105). Sometimes in liberal circles there is something of a
'wannabe' atheism: yet this is playing with fire, in a truly
Promethean sense. 'Atheism is the rejection of God. Where it is
the rejection of God at the point of divine self-offering [. . .] it is
fundamentally a matter of the will' (Williams, 1996, p. 109).

And yet, inasmuch as humans in their 'spirituality' feel directionless, for that they need a directive God. What Barth wrote for the Christian may do for all such humans.

His deliverance from the ocean of apparently unlimited possibilities by transference to the rock of the one necessity which as such is his only possibility. It is really a matter of deliverance. That ocean spelled his destruction. The Christian as such is saved from this destruction. There can be no more question for him of an existence without horizon, contour or shape, open on all sides, exposed to every wind and thus a prey to disintegration. There can be no more question of the pride and misery of unrestricted thought and aspiration. He has awakened from the dream or nightmare of a freedom of choice in which he might always in all respects do different things, loving, choosing, grasping and executing now one thing and now another, according to fate or preference, chance or caprice. Called to be a witness of Jesus Christ, he finds a Lord and becomes his servant, and thus finds that he is given a definite task and definite orders. He may and will often forget or neglect these. He may and will misunderstand them and execute them in a wrong sense. But he has them. (Barth, 1962, p. 667)

Radical Orthodoxy

Tillich, focusing his theology on being (rather than God or Christ or the Church) called for the abandonment of any talk of 'levels' in describing the human condition, or indeed, all of being, taking a cue from Luther and Cusanus who challenged the hierarchical view of reality which dominated the Middle Ages. There is little place in liberalism (and, I shall argue below, this includes Radical Orthodoxy) for a nature–grace dialectic. Yet one problem with a creation-centred ethic, whether in Catholic *nouvelle theologie* or in the sort of thing Colin Gunton espouses in his recent work on 'creation theology', is that creativity is not everything: it ends with representing, not with helping to remedy. It has to become part of the drama of salvation.

There are similar problems with the movement or grouping of theologians which has come to be known as Radical Orthodoxy. It is apologetic and in that sense liberal in that it sets out its stall as defined by that which it opposes: it is no coincidence that Milbank finds clear water between himself and Barthianism – to which I think the framers of the Liverpool Statement have paid insufficient attention. Milbank views Barth as a denier of the inherent goodness in the world (Ward, 1995). However, Barth insisted that the covenant conferred goodness on creation which remains God's goodness and that the world is the more valuable because it is still valued even when it is fallen (e.g. CD III/1, 382: 'Must not creaturely being be good, and are we not called to admit its goodness, in view of the revealed fact that on our behalf God willed to make it His own being'). It is following this wide trajectory of Barthian thought that recent reformed theological treatments on creation have come – e.g., those of C. Gunton, D. Fergusson and F. Watson.

The endeavours of Radical Orthodoxy are characterized by four crucial claims:

1 Secular modernity is the creation of a perverse theology.
2 The opposition of reason to revelation is a modern corruption.
3 All thought which brackets out God is ultimately nihilistic.
4 All material and temporal realms of bodies, sex, art and sociality, which modernity claims to value, can truly be upheld only by acknowledgement of their participation in the transcendent.

There is not space here to deal with these points fully. Concerning (1), however, Hans Blumenberg made a lengthy case that the modern era did not arise as a corruption of theology but in an independent quest for discovery of the world (Blumenberg, 1985).

Points could be made on the subsequent items as follows:

• On (2). Maybe so, but the confusion between the two as sources of theology is not entirely helpful either.
• On (3). Why is that so? We get the same claim in, e.g., Markham.
• On (4). This is like (3). It claims far too much. Von Balthasar (who seems an influence here) did not speak in Platonic terms of participation in the transcendent.

Altogether, the movement's theology may be not radical enough (Graham Ward has tried to push it in the direction of 'critical theory'). Perhaps it would also not be too unkind to claim that it is not orthodox enough.

Postscript: Resurrection

Something which Leslie Houlden writes towards the end of his chapter in this collection strikes a chord. New Testament scholarship serves to correct Systematic Theology. Goodbye to Semler and Gabler and all that! He reminds us that, in terms of job opportunities, the ratio is 3 to 1 in favour of New Testament studies. The useful New Testament guild has helped us to remember that all theology is narrative. Specifically, Mark's Gospel gives us something literary and tragic. In this Houlden affirms the concluding argument of Sandy Wedderburn's *Beyond Resurrection.* 'It is a severe account of Jesus which faces us pitilessly with the starkness of his life and death, and which refrains from cheap and cheerful answers. And it certainly refrains from subtle solutions too. There is Mark's Jesus who goes before us to the mysterious open "Galilee" of our hopes' (Wedderburn, 1999).

Yet can Mark's Gospel seriously be called a tragedy? Even the shorter ending (Mark 16.1–8) contains a proclamation of Jesus' resurrection to the women at the tomb, telling them to remind the disciples of his post-resurrection appointment with them in Galilee (Mark 14.28). Why should this be allegorized into a 'Galilee of our hopes'? What is mysterious or open about 'Galilee'? God has the final say: just like the canonical end of Job, the resurrection is not a pious add-on but an eschatologically-to-be-fulfilled parabolic promise.

The evangelical belief in the resurrection, which is central to the New Testament confession of the Lordship of Christ, reminds us that Christianity is historically aware and informed but not nostalgic. Furthermore, evangelical belief is optimistic about humanity, albeit about a humanity which has suffered death and has risen in Christ, so that it admits but does not glory in human mortality, and will not see it as the last word about the human condition. The mystery of the resurrection warns us that while faith has to seek the world's understanding, it does not have to run after it like a bitch in heat, and should spend at least as much time attempting to understand itself.

References

Barth, K., *Church Dogmatics*, Volume IV/3, T&T Clark, Edinburgh, 1962.

Beckford, J., 'Post Modernity, High Modernity, Late Modernity', in Flanagan, K. and Jupp, P. (eds), *Postmodernity, Sociology and Religion*, Macmillan, Basingstoke, 1996.

Bellah, R., *Habits of the Heart, Individualism and Commitment in American Life*, University of California Press, London, 1985.

Berger, P. and Luckmann, T., *The Social Construction of Reality*, Penguin, London, 1967.

Blumenberg, H., *The Legitimacy of the Modern Age*, MIT Press, Boston, 1985.

Boyle, N., *Who Are We Now?* T&T Clark, Edinburgh, 1998.

Carrette, J., *Foucault and Religion: Spiritual Corporality and Political Spirituality*, Routledge, London, 1999.

Carson, D. and Woodbridge, J., *Scripture and Truth*, IVP, Leicester, 1983.

Edwards, D. L. and Stott, J., *Essentials: A Liberal – Evangelical Dialogue*, Hodder & Stoughton, London, 1988.

Eliot, T. S., *Notes Towards Definition of Culture*, Faber, London, 1948.

Eliot, T. S., *Collective Poems 1909–1962*, Faber, London, 1974.

Eliot, T. S., *The Idea of a Christian Society: And Other Writings*, Faber, London, 1982.

Giddens, A., *The Third Way: The Renewal of Social Democracy*, Polity Press, Cambridge, 1998.

Ingraffia, B., *Postmodern Theory and Biblical Theology*, CUP, Cambridge, 1995.

Jones, G., *Critical Theology*, Polity Press, Cambridge, 1995.

Jones, G., 'After Kant: The Liverpool Statement,' *Reviews in Religion and Theology*, August, (3), 1998.

Julius, A., *T. S. Eliot, Anti-Semitism and Literary Form*, CUP, Cambridge, 1996.

Lodge, D., *Paradise News*, Penguin, Harmondsworth, 1992.

Louth, A., *Discerning the Mystery*, Clarendon Paperbacks, Oxford, 1983.

Luther, M., *Bondage of Will*, J. Clarke, London, 1957.

Markham, I., *Truth and the Reality of God: An Essay on Natural Theology*, T & T Clark, Edinburgh, 1996.

McIntosh, M., *Mystical Theology*, Blackwells, Oxford, 1998.

Percy, M., *Words, Wonders and Power*, SPCK, London, 1996.

Roberts, R.H., 'Power and Empowerment: New Age Managers and the Dialectics of Modernity/Post-modernity' in R. H. Roberts (ed.) *Religion and the Transformations of Capitalism*, RKP 1995.

Schleiermacher, F., *The Christian Faith*, T&T Clark, Edinburgh, 1928.

Searle, J., *The Construction of Social Reality*, Penguin, Hammondsworth, 1996.

Stein, E., *On the Problem of Empathy*, ICS Publishers, Washington DC, 1989.

Tillich, P., *Systematic Theology III*, University of Chicago Press, Chicago, 1963.

Tinker, M., (ed.) *The Anglican Evangelical Crisis*, Christian Focus, Fearn, 1995.

Tomlinson, D., *The Post Evangelical*, SPCK, London, 1995.

Walker, A., *Restoring the Kingdom*, Hodder & Stoughton, London, 1985.

Ward, G., *Barth, Derrida and the Language of Theology*, Cambridge, Cambridge University Press, 1997.

Watson, D., *I Believe in the Church*, Hodder & Stoughton, London, 1989.

Watson, F., *Text and Truth*, T&T Clark, Edinburgh, 1995.

Wedderburn, A., *Beyond Resurrection*, SCM Press, London, 1999.

White, V., *Paying Attention to People*, SPCK, London, 1997.

Williams, S., *Revelation and Reconciliation, a Window of Modernity*, CUP, Cambridge, 1996.

Winquist, C., *Desiring Theology*, University of Chicago Press, Chicago, 1994.

Wolterstorff, N., *John Locke and the Ethics of Belief*, CUP, Cambridge, 1996.

CHAPTER FIVE

Comparative Theology: The Heritage of Schleiermacher

Keith Ward

Comparative Motifs in Early Christian Thought

Comparative theology is the elucidation and evaluation of traditions of thought about God in the context of the general history of religions. It may seem like a modern idea, produced by the globalization of culture and ideology in the age of the cybernet. But, though they would not have used the phrase, many religious traditions have been open to a development of their basic symbols in the light of what was known about human religious history as a whole. This is certainly true of the development of doctrines of God in early and medieval Judaism, Christianity and Islam. They were influenced especially by the thought of Plato and Aristotle, as well as by conversation with one another.

The Hebrew Bible does not specialize in critical reflection upon the nature of God. It presents a view of the God of Abraham, Isaac and Jacob, a God who acts in history to liberate the Israelites, who reveals commands and ordinances to Moses, and who makes a covenant with the descendants of Abraham, to protect them in return for obedience to the divine teaching. It is quite clear that the God so presented has knowledge of the hearts of men and women, has power to shape history to the divine will and is swift to punish sin, though no less ready to be merciful to those who repent and trust in the divine promises. There is one God, of knowledge, power, justice and mercy, who creates and has a purpose for human beings and ultimately for the whole universe.

Hebrew tradition is uninterested in the conceptions of God or the gods entertained by other nations. Sometimes it opposes particular conceptions like those of the Canaanites, but at other times it is content to accept that each nation will have its own God, or its own conception of God. But of course if there is in fact only one creator of the universe, all other conceptions of God will at least have to be compatible with the Hebrew conception of a merciful, powerful, wise and active creator.

Hebrew tradition has also been uninterested, on the whole, in developing theoretical concepts of God which might amplify the basic assertions on the subject made by the prophets. There is in the tradition a distrust of philosophers, as people who develop speculative schemes which may depart from the revealed tradition. So there is a strain of thought which insists on sticking to assertions that are revealed to the prophets and not presuming to go beyond them. There is a strong stress on remaining loyal to the revealed tradition, on the ground that it contains what has been reliably revealed to the patriarchs and prophets.

I do not wish to condemn that attitude, or to suggest that it is not justifiable to have such loyalty and trust in one's revealed tradition. But I do wish to suggest that there are strong reasons why many might wish to adopt a different attitude to belief in God. The strongest one is that it is very difficult to insist upon 'repetition without development' in a world in which knowledge in virtually all other fields is changing and developing rapidly. In physics, for example, the understanding of very basic laws like that of inertia has changed fundamentally since the fourteenth century, and knowledge is developing so rapidly that we can now not only theorize that all material things are made up of atoms, but we can actually identify those atoms empirically. What used to be a disputed speculation has become an experimentally established fact. This is not only a change; it is a growth in the understanding of the true nature of things. Similar things are true of almost every aspect of our knowledge of the physical world. So if the understanding of God is not to change, such understanding must be irrelevant to, and not be at all influenced by, knowledge of the nature of physical reality.

Obviously, many of those who insist on preserving revealed truth have thought that such revealed truth includes assertions which conflict with the findings of the natural sciences. The age of the earth and the origins of life and of the human species are the most obvious examples. If one takes the biblical accounts of these matters to be mythical, or non-factual, that is a change from the traditional interpretations, which took them to be literal. The Bible contains specific accounts of the early history of the world and of humanity which, in the light of modern science, must be taken as non-literal.

This is hardly a novel insight. All the great classical theologians realized that many statements about God in the Bible are not literal – that God rides on the clouds, or sits on a throne, or shoots arrows at the enemies of Israel, for example. The difficulty is to know when a statement contained in a revealed text is literal and when it is non-literal. When that difficulty is recognized, theology has begun. Even my characterization of the God of Israel as a merciful, wise and powerful creator is an abstraction from the very concrete poetic images which are used of God in the texts. It selects certain crucial texts – as that God is the creator of the heavens and the earth – and uses them to interpret the others (that God appears to live on top of a mountain, for example).

If one is to do more than simply repeat the texts, and refuse to provide any interpretation of them at all, the first theological task is to say what, if anything, may be said literally of the God to whom the prophets witness. And how is one to decide that, since there is no algorithm, no rule, given in the texts themselves, to help one decide? It seems very lame to suggest that statements must be non-literal only if they are contradicted by well-established conclusions in the natural sciences. That reinforces the accusation that believers give up their beliefs reluctantly, bit by bit, and only when they are forced to by the inexorable progress of science.

One needs a principle for interpreting revealed statements about God. That principle is not itself revealed, apparently (though I suppose it could have been). That is what I mean by saying that the Bible is not very concerned with theologically reflective thinking about the nature of God. The principle of interpretation must come from elsewhere. In Christian theology from the third century it came largely from Plato, who had developed ideas of one supreme being in a number of his Dialogues. Plato's concept was extremely apophatic, and embodied the view that the timeless is superior to the temporal, the universal is superior to the particular, and the simple is superior to the complex. So God is seen as a timeless, substantial universal form of absolute simplicity. Virtually all biblical statements are then interpreted as metaphors which point to such a being as the timeless source of temporal creation.

Patristic theology took the basic principle of theological interpretation from a Greek pagan philosopher, just for the reason that he was thought to give the best available account of what a God would be. Since it was a principle of interpretation, it was used to interpret the revealed metaphors in Scripture, not to erect a different doctrine. But there is no doubt that it contributed substantially to the concept of God upheld by the early Church. It was not understood to contradict the Bible, but it was used to interpret it, as the best available rational principle for interpreting revelation.

In a similar way, Greek philosophy was used by Jews and Muslims to develop concepts of God, so that one had a basic similarity in the fundamental concept, together with different sets of revealed metaphors, or different understandings of exactly what that God had revealed to human beings.

As well as having a common relation to Greek philosophy, these Abrahamic traditions also had complex relations with one another. Christians and Muslims accept that the Hebrew Bible is revealed, but Christians reinterpret it as prophesying the coming of Jesus as Messiah, while Muslims reinterpret it as a corruption of the original revelation which is corrected and completed in the Qur'an. These traditions are not completely self-contained traditions. Moreover, since they all offer differing interpretations of the Hebrew Bible, they are all aware that such diversity of interpretations is possible and thought justifiable by highly intelligent and pious believers. To some extent a comparative element is written into at least the Christian and Muslim faiths, as they seek to justify their reinterpretation of texts which primarily belong to a tradition they have rejected. One reason Christians cannot seek to begin theology simply from a presumed revelation of God in Jesus is that such a beginning presupposes the general validity of Hebrew faith, while yet that faith is rejected in its orthodox interpretation. The proper beginning must be a consideration of Jewish tradition and a justification of its reinterpretation in a Christian sense. Only then will one see what Jesus was claimed to be the – Messiah – and why this claim forced a reinterpretation of Jewish tradition.

The major Christian reinterpretation of Hebrew thought about

God is to see God as Trinity. In the New Testament, God is spoken of as Father, Jesus is spoken of as the Son, and the Church is inspired by the Spirit. But the relationship of these three to one another is not discussed. The complex doctrine of the Trinity as three equal *hypostases* in one *ousia* was only developed after much discussion and argument, and again uses terms drawn from Greek philosophy. It is much more than a simple interpretation of the text. It is a theoretical presentation of the nature of God, based on texts, but elaborated through discussion, and never completely agreed by believers – as the subsequent history of Trinitarian discussion shows.

The very terms in which the discussion is framed depend upon conceptual arguments and clarification. Resources are drawn from sources external to the Scriptures, and are then moulded into a distinctive form by reference to the Scriptures. Both the partial assimilation and partial rejection of external traditions feature largely in the development of Christian thinking about God. The Christian tradition is not self-contained: it grew by interaction with other currents of thought in its environment. Thus the Christian doctrine of God was comparative from the first, elucidating similarities and differences with analogous concepts, both in Hebrew and in Greek thought, and developing a distinctive view in interaction with those concepts.

Science and Religious Traditions – New Models of Revelation

For 1,500 years the Christian idea of God continued to work with Greek paradigmatic models – Platonism in the Byzantine (Orthodox) churches, and a 'baptized' Aristotelianism in the Latin. Then the scientific revolution brought about a huge change in human perceptions, both of the nature of the physical universe, and of attitudes to authority. Once Aristotle had been dethroned as the ultimate authority in science, the medieval picture of a world of real essences embodied in matter, of a perfectly self-contained, self-contemplating First Cause of all things, and of the superiority of the things of the intellect to the deliverances of feeling and sense, collapsed. Talk of real essences was replaced by talk of the laws of physics, sense-experience became the criterion of reality, and the things of time and history came to have an importance they could never have had for the ancient Greeks.

The idea of God came to be revised because the philosophical basis for thinking about the world was revised. Among theologians, one aspect of that revision is well expressed in the work of Schleiermacher, written in the consciousness that the Scholastic worldview had become obsolete, and that there was a real cultural problem in fitting the old theology into the new scientific world-picture. Schleiermacher's suggestion was both suggested by and reacted against the dominant scientific empirical method. It was suggested by it, because it took immediate experience – *Anschaung* – as its epistemic foundation. It reacted against it, by denying that sense-experience is the only reliable form of intuition or apprehension. There is also religious apprehension, which is *sui generis* and irreducible to anything else.

When it comes to describing what is apprehended, one must use concepts drawn from the culturally available stock, and at this point Schleiermacher elaborates the idea, present in various embryonic ways in Spinoza, Kant and Schelling, of one supreme reality expressing itself in an infinite variety of forms, and being apprehensible in and through those forms, when they are apprehended by the religious sense. This idea certainly has Christian roots, and in his fifth Speech, Schleiermacher refers to 'the God that has become flesh' as the root of this conception (Schleiermacher, 1958, p. 211). But his formulation of it embodies a new understanding of revelation, as rooted in privileged experience rather than in propositionally revealed truth, and a new way of thinking about God in terms of the infinite, essentially expressed in and through the finite rather than in terms of the supremely self-sufficient purely actual being, which is complete in itself even without any finite reality.

Schleiermacher was right to see, in his early work, that both these understandings open the field of possible revelation beyond the confines of the Christian tradition. It seems rather unlikely that just one religious teacher would have all inerrant experience of God, different in kind from any other – indeed, once inerrancy has been renounced in principle, it is implausible to take one teacher as having an exclusively correct apprehension of religious truth. And it seems rather unlikely that the infinite would only disclose its nature in one way and within one cultural tradition.

A propositional view of revelation tends to insist on one inerrant revelation, and exclude all others as false. But an experiential view of revelation will tend to see divine disclosures as matters of degree, which will be interpreted in differing conceptual frameworks. At this point the beginnings of a properly historical study of religions makes a difference to the perception of one's own religion. A view of religion which sees it as beginning from one primal revelation which must be guarded against error will differ from a view which sees all religions as developing from local tribal traditions towards a more universal rational and moral structure.

Nevertheless, there are various degrees and types of religious experience, and they are interpreted in very different cultural contexts. The drug-induced ecstasies of shamans are very different from the contemplative calm of Siddartha Gautama, and it is not implausible to hold that an experience which frees one from egoism, and seems to unite one to a wider reality of compassion, wisdom and bliss, is a more adequate form of religious experience than a narcotically stimulated encounter with fantastic dream-visions of demons and spirits. One might well hold that the founders of the great traditions had a rare quality and intensity of experience which enabled them to become authoritative guides to truth for millions of disciples.

In examining these great experients more closely, one will have to pay attention to the conceptual framework which governed the interpretation of their experiences, and to the historical context in which they lived. Differing conceptual frameworks cannot all be equally correct – though they may stress elements of reality which other traditions tend to overlook. If Gautama lived in a culture which lacked the concept of one active, personal God, and did not place a high value on individual personality, and if Jesus lived in a culture which made the idea of a personal God absolutely central, and gave human persons infinite value, the differing worldviews which result will express differing truth-claims which do not so much depend on the character or probity of the teachers or the inner quality of their experience, but on the reliability of the tradition itself.

The historical context will be important, too. The person of Jesus became interpreted in revised messianic terms, as the Saviour of the world and head of the community of a new covenant, the Church, which is to strive for the reconciliation of all things to God. Gautama, on the other hand, was the founder of an ascetic community which seeks to lead people away from worldly commitments to a contemplative life. These are different forms of religious community, focused on different symbols and originative stories – the founder of a community committed to justice and peace, and the exemplar of a way of non-attachment to the world, respectively. Thus not only the inner experience, but the belief system and the historical context in which religious teachers are born, shape the development of religious communities in distinctive ways. In the further development of religions towards a fully moral and rational global view, these differences have to be taken into account.

If one sees the exemplary experiences of the great religious teachers as authentic yet differing experiences of a supreme spiritual reality, interpreted in ways made possible by the conceptual framework of a particular culture, one might see the religions as different finite forms of the infinite, always described in fallible and developing human terms. Thus Schleiermacher says that each religion is one of the particular forms eternal and infinite religion necessarily had to assume (Schleiermacher, 1958, p. 216). Further, in each religion the infinite takes on an imperfect and limited form (1958, p. 216). All positive religions, on this view, will be partial and imperfectly apprehended perceptions of infinite Spirit.

It should be noted, however, that this idea – of the infinite expressing itself in the finite in circumscribed ways – is itself a product of European Romanticism. It is an idea with a history and a context. It arises out of reflection on the breakdown of medieval views of theology as a true and certain science, and out of a search for a more experiential foundation for belief in God. Indeed, if the view is correct, then it will itself be partial and imperfectly apprehended. So part of its self-understanding is that it will call for further self-critical analysis as new historical situations come into being, and it will recognize the need for complementary insights from outside its own tradition.

Schleiermacher expresses the critical spirit very well, in his acceptance of biblical scholarship and his readiness to place in question patristic formulations of doctrines. He is in principle ready to accept complementary insights – and of course he does use the philosophical insights of his Prussian colleagues. But, not

very surprisingly, his knowledge of Indian or Asian religious traditions was too scanty to allow any real encounter between Semitic
and non-Semitic religious traditions to happen very much.

The Indian and Semitic Traditions

One of the interesting possibilities for comparative religious
thought in the modern world is a genuine and deep encounter
between Semitic and Indian traditions, which has not seriously
occurred in the past. In the Indian traditions about Brahman,
one would find the idea of one supreme reality entering into,
indeed in some subtle sense actually becoming one with, the
subjects of finite experiences. And one would find, in the
doctrine of *karma*, an assertion of the responsibility of humans
for their own actions which leads to appropriate judgement.
These strands of belief might suggest new interpretations of
Christian tradition. Of course there is a tension in the very
statement of these two views side by side. If each finite self is the
supreme Reality in a finite self-manifestation, how can it also be
a free and responsible agent? Indian philosophers wrestled with
this tension in various ways, and perhaps one of the most satisfac-
tory resolutions of the tension is the view of Ramanuja, that each
finite self is an individual agent, responsible for its own acts, but
it is also part of the body, or self-expressive activity, of the
Supreme Lord, and will ultimately find its proper destiny only in
the conscious acceptance of its role as a vehicle of the manifestation of the Lord.

   Those in the Semitic religious traditions have often regarded
such Indian views as forms of unacceptable pantheism or
monism, which fatally confuse creator and creation, and fail to
recognize the transcendence of God. Such a judgement would be
too crude and premature, however. The best-known Indian
philosopher, Sankara, affirmed the utter transcendence of the
Real by calling it *nirguna Brahman*, or the Real without qualities,
utterly distinct from all finite things. The finite has the character
of *maya* or illusion, so that in the form in which it is perceived by
us, it is not at all identical with the Real as it truly is. For Ramanuja,
a very different philosopher who rejects the doctrine of *nirguna
Brahman*, the Supreme Lord is distinct from the finite selves which
form its body. Christians might recall that they are committed to

seeing at least part of the finite universe, the Church, as the body of the Supreme Lord, and to the hope that eventually Christ will be 'all in all', so that the cosmos will be some day, if it is not now, the body of the Lord. Perhaps the Indian traditions might offer something surprisingly nearer to biblical language about God than the Greek tradition did.

There are, at the very least, possibilities here for the sort of conceptual interaction which occurred with ancient Greek thought. Indeed, the idea of the divine as Absolute Spirit, which realizes itself in the forms of time, which is central to the Upanishads, was given paradigmatic formulation in Europe by Hegel. It cannot be said that he, any more than Schleiermacher, gave Indian thought much serious consideration, however, regarding Hinduism as an inferior and largely superstitious and backward form of religious life. In his *Lectures on the Philosophy of Religion* (Hegel, 1895), he says of Indian religious cosmology, 'we are attracted by its loveliness, and repelled by the confusion and nonsense in it' (vol. 2, p. 43). 'The people of India are sunk in the most complete immorality' (vol. 2, p. 47), since their religion is without reason, and is lost in fantasy. It cannot be said that nineteenth-century Prussians had a deeply empathetic view of Indian religions. The roots of their conceptual revision of theology were rather in European rationalism, which in one strand issued in the idea of one divine Substance emanating the world necessarily from itself (Leibniz and Spinoza), and in its transmutation into the Romantic vision of the intuition of that substance in and through the finite things which are capable of becoming symbols of the Real which transcends conceptual understanding.

Nevertheless it seems clear that Indian concepts of the supreme Reality could be used in the development of a Christian notion of God, though they belong to a revealed tradition which may seem to contradict that of Christianity. In Vedantic thought, for example, individual souls are part of Brahman, they reincarnate countless times, and in they end they are to transcend any individual personality in realizing a liberated, purely spiritual, form of existence. This seems to contradict the Christian idea that souls are distinct creations which have only one life on earth, and which will be resurrected in their own distinct individualities in the communion of saints. There is little in the Indian tradition about divine judgement, atonement and resurrection, or about the hope for a saviour who can liberate humans from oppression and sin. Can this tradition be a true vehicle of revelation?

Partly this depends upon how one construes revelation. If one thinks of it as a clear, precise communication from God, delivering information in divinely guaranteed concepts, then God could not both reveal the Upanishads and the Bible. But one might well hold that in the Upanishads, and in the teachings and practices of the sages which underlie them, one has a disclosure of a divine reality of bliss, wisdom and compassion, which is knowable by an experience resulting from detachment and meditation. The divine is revealed in forms of authoritative experience, the experience of those who, in attaining detachment and transcendence of ego, witness to the higher self they experience within. The Upanishads might be seen as partly reflective expositions of such experience, so that it is only for later generations that they become themselves the normative patterns for experience, as if they had been literally 'spoken' by the gods.

This is precisely the reversal that Schleiermacher asked for in Christianity, the reversal from seeing experience as wholly governed by an authoritative, propositionally revealed text, to seeing the text as itself the result of generations of reflection, imaginative elaboration and many personal experiences, especially those of enlightened – but not infallible – teachers. So the New Testament partly witnesses to the intense God-consciousness of Jesus, his sense of vocation and of the intensity of relationship to God which he was able vividly to convey to others. It partly witnesses the apostolic experiences of Jesus' resurrection and of the new reality of the Spirit in the community of disciples. It partly embodies the intellectual struggles of Paul and of early disciples to make sense of their new faith, in its relationship to Jewish tradition and to the new Gentile world in which they found themselves. These records become normative, not because they are dictated by God, but because they are taken to record authentic disclosures of God within human experience and reliable reflection upon its significance.

In a similar way the Upanishads can be taken to witness to the intense liberated experiences of great sages of the past, and to the possibility of such experiences for their disciples. They embody the intellectual struggles of sages and their disciples to make sense of those experiences, in the light of their existing traditions and beliefs. They become normative in the community because the basic experience of the unity of the Supreme Self and the human spirit is taken to be veridical, and because the general reflections upon it contain insights which are both fruitful and rare.

There are obvious differences between these traditions. The Christian view has an emphasis on historical particularity which is closely connected to the idea of God as historically purposing and active. The Indian view is relatively unconcerned with history, except as the stage whereon liberation is possible. But it is not hard to see experiences of a divine Self of power, intelligence, wisdom and bliss in both traditions, interpreted in their cultural contexts.

Theology in a Global Context

One might expect, that insofar as infallibilist claims to complete truth cease to be made, these and other faiths could take their place as co-existing paths to relationship with supreme Spirit. Islam, for instance, could be seen as testifying to the importance of moral law and to the hope of life with God. Judaism witnesses to the idea of world–historical vocation and of a moral goal of history. Christianity witnesses to the kenotic love of God, uniting creation to the divine through self-giving sacrifice. Buddhism calls for non-attachment and the calming of passion. Hinduism calls for realization of inner unity with the Supreme Self, and for progress through many forms of existence to final liberation from ego. Each historical faith, as Schleiermacher suggested, organizes its thought and symbolic life around one central idea or complex of ideas, but all of them offer paths from egoism to life in union with Spirit.

Non-exclusive interpretations of religious traditions make it possible for believers to reach wide areas of agreement and co-operation with many in other traditions. They make it possible for adherents of one tradition to share in the riches of other traditions. Yet in the end every reflective human being must believe that some views are more adequate than others. If one could list all possible religious assertions – the set of all possible religious views one might take – then one sub-set of them would have to be just true. It may seem rather unlikely that any human group could hit upon exactly that set. Nevertheless, at particular stages choices will have to be made which favour some traditions rather than others. For instance, either there is no personal God, or there is one. Either there is individual immortality or there is not. Either God is causally active with a purpose in history, or God is not. Because of human ignorance, frailty and partiality, disagreement and diversity seem ineliminable from human thought, and no set of beliefs commends itself overwhelmingly to all. So one might wish to preserve differing perspectives, which might serve to correct and amplify one another, yet seek to emphasize a very general, underlying unity at least in those faiths which seek a self-transcending orientation to Supreme Spirit.

All religious believers in the modern world have the problem of whether some form of their own faith is the most adequate form, or whether some faith yet to come may be, or whether a number of traditions are adequate in some respects and less so in others. Schleiermacher himself seemed to change his mind about that. In the *Speeches*, he denied that Christianity should ever claim to be the one true religion, but in the *Glaubenslehre* he argued that it would indeed take over the world because of its inherent superiority. One approach to this problem is to concentrate on developing one's own tradition by carefully attending to insights from other traditions and by being prepared to discard interpretations that do not measure up to critical strictures from expanding knowledge and moral insight. This might be said to define the liberal attitude to religious belief, rejecting interpretations of religious views which insist on rigid definitions of the boundaries between traditions and on preserving an unchanging truth which has nothing to learn from outside its own system.

In the contemporary world, the liberal attitude will mean paying special attention to the findings of the experimental sciences, to the voices of humanism, and to global traditions of religion. That is, after all, only a continuation of the Patristic tradition of paying attention to the voice of Greek science and humanism, and to the Hebrew Scriptures as sources of revelation. In that sense, Christianity has always had a liberal dimension, insofar as it has learned from Hebrew and Greek traditions, and critically examined and radically reinterpreted its own origins in Jewish Messianism. Unfortunately, it also quickly came to exhibit an anti-liberal dimension, as it appropriated the once new and radical Greek formulations as themselves unchanging tests of orthodoxy, and opposed and suppressed heretical and pagan faiths as dangerous and demonic.

In our day there are new anti-liberal movements in religion which wish to return to some supposedly original or primal and utterly distinctive Christian truth, and to oppose influences from cultural and broader strands of religious tradition. Such views are sometimes supported by a neo-conservative ideology which holds that the Christian tradition is in some way a self-contained language game, with its own quite distinctive ideas and even its own standard of rationality which cannot be compared with supposedly more general standards, and which has no concern with other language games, they being incommensurable with it and incomprehensible to it in any case. It is not surprising that some of the adherents of such a view hark back to Augustine, for in his most illiberal moods he does indeed mark a crucial point at which the radical intellectual and spiritual freedom of the early Church began to fall prey to the forces of authoritarian repression which led to the Holy Inquisition.

Why should such views be resisted? Basically, I think, because they misunderstand the radical dynamic of Christian faith, which embraced revision and conceptual development from the first. There could hardly be a greater change in a religious tradition than from Jewish Messianism to Hellenistic Trinitarianism. The thirteenth-century reception of Aristotelian science, after a short but sharp struggle, established Thomism as virtually the official philosophy of the Catholic Church. Revision and development, and therefore self-criticism and willingness to learn from others, have always been the hallmarks of orthodoxy, when it has not degenerated into the defence of the archaic. It is natural to suppose that this process of critical restatement and creative reconceptualization will continue. I have briefly sketched some ways in which empirical science and a knowledge of non-Semitic religious traditions can suggest new ways of modelling the divine nature and the modes of its self-disclosure in human experience. Schleiermacher envisaged, and partly began, this exposition of a consciously liberal orthodoxy in the context of what would properly be a comparative theology. We honour him best by continuing this project in a world in which, because of the vast explosion of accessible information and instant communication, it has become achievable for the first time.

References

Hegel, G. W. F., *Lectures on Philosophy Vol. II*, trans. Revd E. B. Speirs and J. B. Sanderson, ed. E. B. Speirs, Kegan Paul, London, 1895.

Schleiermacher, F., *On Religion. Speeches to its Cultural Despisers*, trans. J. Oman, Harper & Row, New York, 1958.

Schleiermacher, F., *Der christliche Glaube*, de Gruyter, Berlin, 1960.

CHAPTER SIX

Christians Meeting Jews: What Do They Think They Are Doing?

Christine Pilkington

O NE SIGNIFICANT WAY of interpreting 'liberal Christianity' is in terms of religious pluralism. Broadly speaking, this approach suggests that all religions are equally valid routes to the one divine reality. The crucial difference between this approach to 'other' faith traditions and that of 'conservative Christianity' lies in their respective attitudes to God's work in Christ. The conservative approach is either exclusivist, asserting that people are saved only by Christ as revealed in the Gospels, or inclusivist, asserting salvation is possible through religious traditions outside the Christian Church but, in the end, even after death, this salvation is always through or from Christ. Pluralism, by contrast, regards God's revelation in Christ as only one means of salvation (D'Costa, 1997, pp. 626–44).

The Liverpool Statement assumes a pluralistic view of the world's religious traditions. Although its use of the term 'theology' is not entirely appropriate to every single one of these traditions, nonetheless, the liberal theology of which it speaks is intended to encompass all of them. Indeed, its endeavour to 'engage with contemporary culture', to 'encourage a positive, open vision of theology' in the hope of influencing 'the public sphere' surely has pluralism not only as a corollary but as a keystone. It is hard to imagine 'an ongoing dialogue with the social, cultural, and political problems and achievements of our age' which does not take seriously the integrity of the great religions.

The question immediately arises, what are Christians doing when they adopt this pluralistic approach? Engagement, open vision, ongoing dialogue are such encouraging words, but what do they actually amount to in theory and in practice? The question is here addressed not only to professional theologians but to all Christians who are committed to their own faith tradition but who are unable to follow either an exclusivist or inclusivist approach. What are the implications for Christians of liberalism as religious pluralism?

Pluralism can, of course, take more than one form, even in its theoretical conception. In perhaps its most open form, it contends that no one faith system is in a position to claim superiority over another because historical and cultural relativism always plays its part in constructing such systems. This pluralistic model can surely be said to engage with other religions on equal terms and in genuine dialogue, as it takes seriously the 'truth' as constructed within the time, culture, historical circumstance and language system of each tradition. Popularly articulated, it says, 'If I had been born in a different time and place, I might have believed something very different from what I now believe.' Liberal Christians do so speak.

In another form, pluralism stresses a common core or essence of the great religions. Those who adopt this approach stress the spiritual, some would say 'mystical', experience of humankind. People of faith are united by an all-embracing reality, which transcends all specific creeds and historical manifestations. Popularly articulated, it says, 'What I experience is too deep to be contained by one religious tradition.' Liberal Christians do so speak.

A third pluralistic model emphasizes not so much what is shared by religions as what, theoretically at any rate, divides them. Rather than finding such division worrying and problematic, it delights in it for what the faith traditions can offer each other from their diversity. Dialogue depends on not pressing any one tradition into the mould of another. Nevertheless, this approach countenances a shared experience, not in its specifics, but in its overall religious nature and value. This 'experience' is often defined in terms of 'salvation' or 'liberation'. Popularly articulated, this brand of pluralism says, 'I do not pretend to know or understand fully what you experience of religious wholeness and freedom, but I trust that it somehow connects with what I experience.' Liberal Christians do so speak.

No matter how loosely or how comprehensively they may articulate it, what is it that Christians are doing when they 'meet' people of other religions? Observing a gathering of nine faith traditions in the Royal Gallery of the Houses of Parliament offered me some clues. In *Faith for the Millennium,* as broadcast on BBC 1 on 20 March 2000, I watched members of the various faith traditions represented in Britain meet for what was described as 'an act of reflection and commitment'. Religious leaders combined with 'ordinary' Jews, Christians, Muslims, Buddhists, Hindus, Sikhs, Jains, and Zoroastrians, in this act not of 'worship', but of 'reflection' and 'commitment'. Going through my mind as an observer was the recurrent question, 'commitment' to what? They were all clearly reflecting, at the turn of the millennium, on what was humankind's state and what was their particular contribution to this. Perhaps it was fortunate that we could only speculate on the content of the 'commitment' since it would probably be hard to express in consistent form. Indarjit Singh, editor of *The Sikh Messenger* and one of the very few non-Christians to be invited as a regular contributor to BBC Radio 4's *Thought for the Day,* acted as master of ceremonies – as perhaps only one so respected and trusted for his religious integrity could.

The Archbishop of Canterbury, Dr George Carey, introduced the first main speaker, the Chief Rabbi, Professor Jonathan Sacks. It is not for me to speak for the Archbishop of Canterbury, but I feel sure that he would not describe himself as a pluralist in any of the three ways outlined above. He is a president of CCJ, the Council of Christians and Jews, but it needs to be remembered that CCJ does not require a pluralist outlook among its members – the Archbishop of Canterbury included. It is for Christians of inclusivist persuasion themselves to work out how they operate within such a non-missionary organization. It should, however, be added that when CCJ was formed, against the backdrop of the Holocaust, one of its main purposes was to combat prejudice, intolerance and discrimination and to promote racial and social harmony. It is surely to this that the Archbishop was committed both on becoming a CCJ president and when taking part in the millennial 'act of reflection and commitment'.

This in itself indicates one of the 'things' Christians are doing when they meet Jews. They are doing what Jews also are doing when they meet Christians in the context of the Council of Christians and Jews. They are not necessarily involved in discussion of their respective faiths, at least not directly. They may be listening to a Jewish or a Christian speaker talking about some aspect of

social action, archaeology, language or culture. The quest is to
learn about each other, how faith is translated into action, or what
determines or feeds one's respective faith community. Both Jews
and Christians might be hard pressed to articulate any of the pluralistic positions adumbrated. What they are interested in is not
the philosophy of interfaith but the reality of interaction. They
seek social harmony based on mutual understanding.

In recent years initiatives have been taken in New York to
improve relations between Jews and Blacks. It is interesting that
one such venture, initiated by a rabbi and the mayor of New York,
calls itself an 'interfaith' group. Perhaps this reflects similarities
with the origins of CCJ. From the Jewish point of view, CCJ tends
to be not about religious dialogue, but about doing your social
duty for the Jewish community by dispelling anti-Semitism. Most
of its participants tend to be lay. Christian members of CCJ,
however, see the enterprise in quite different terms. They expect,
though probably seldom find, Jewish theological engagement
with Christianity. A mixture of lay and ordained, they tend to be
very much committed to their Christian faith. One of our central
questions as we encourage liberal pluralism should be, I contend,
how theological is the enterprise of interfaith dialogue?

A conference on 'God at 2000', co-ordinated by Dr Marcus
Borg, was held at Oregon State University in February 2000. One
of its aims was to offer Christians a broader view of the nature of
God than currently available in the more conservative churches.
Another was to build bridges between different religions, one
reason being that Christians are thereby helped in their own
spiritual development. At the very least, Christians who want to
meet people of other faiths at any level have got to think about
where they stand. They must address fundamental questions
about their tradition, if they are not to flounder or accept, uncritically, old attitudes and behaviour. True openness requires
security. It is sometimes evident in encounters between people of
different religions, especially where sensitive and controversial
matters are at stake, that they are talking past each other; indeed,
they are, even if unknowingly, talking about different things. If
people are instead truly to listen to each other and then to talk,
they need to have achieved an integrity about their own position.
Only then can each party expect the other to recognize this
integrity. Interfaith dialogue is surely about recognizing the need

and the benefit of such interchange. It is not about compelling a superficial sympathy or uniformity. That preaching may have a particular part to play in preparing Christians fully to enter into such dialogue will be argued towards the end of this chapter. In general terms, it is already clear that both the goals and methods of interfaith encounter will need to be constantly reassessed according to the time, the place and the constituency of each venture.

It may be instructive to ask at this point how the representative of British Jews, the Chief Rabbi, conceived of his 'act of commitment' from the Houses of Parliament. It was not a shared act of worship or he would not have been there. He could not have been there, since to worship God in terms of a faith tradition other than his own, especially Christianity, with Jesus as 'Lord and Messiah', is not possible for him. It is, of course, far easier for a Christian to worship in terms of the Jewish tradition. Though he or she may find the centrality of the Torah, its being ceremoniously removed from the Ark, carried round the synagogue with great reverence, and then placed on the desk from which it is read, 'different' from a Christian act of worship, it is surely not offensive in the same way as the ritual and liturgy of Christian worship offends Jewish belief and practice. I can speak for the Chief Rabbi even less than for the Archbishop of Canterbury, but he stated on this occasion succinctly what he intended by his presence. He was expressing his commitment to 'a society of diversity, peace, and mutual respect in which faith speaks to faith' and 'where our differences enlarge us all'. It is hard to better this summary of pluralism. Like the other speakers, he concentrated on the human need for community which he described as 'society with a human face'. Sacks defined religion, resting on its Latin root *religare*, as 'that which binds us' to our fellow human beings and to God. He was quite clear what he thought he was doing and that was appealing to all faiths to 'reach out to each other in love and generosity, faithfulness and trust'.

One of the past criticisms of liberalism has been its woolliness, the way in which its attempt to be healthily tolerant of other religious traditions has evacuated it of commitment to anything but cosy blandness. This is often the criticism levelled also at interfaith dialogue. It is easy for the uncommitted to meet people of other cultures and religious backgrounds who are equally uncommitted. Religious dialogue is no problem when you have no religion. Religious liberalism is no problem when you have no religion. Which model of pluralism best corresponds with interfaith encounter is perhaps for the reader to decide, but it is indisputable that such encounter requires the reality of different faiths. Once submerged or merged, faith as anything recognizable ceases to exist.

Specificity and concreteness are still the way in which human beings operate and communicate. That they do not have an absolutely coherent picture about the world and their participation in it does not mean that everything collapses into relativism. Recognizing that his or her interpretation of reality is culturally conditioned does not leave a person believing that someone else's interpretation is just as convincing. Religious people, however liberal in their pluralism, 'participate in the world according to the *realistic* claims of any one of a wide variety of different religions, attitudes and worldviews. These positions are certainly relative, understood hermeneutically; but this does not alter the fact they are all making important claims about reality' (Jones, 1995, p. 207). Again, it would seem that interfaith dialogue, far from being the pursuit of the theologically vacuous, may be important for the future of theology. So Jones contends, as he thinks of the common interest which religions have in matters of 'Spirit and eternity and the concomitant interpretation of time and history'. The Bishop of Bradford, the Rt Rev. David Smith, speaking at the 1998 Lambeth Conference in Canterbury about Christian–Muslim dialogue, said, 'Those who can best enter into this are those of a strong faith. Muslims do not want to enter into dialogue with those Christians who care little about their faith.'

I take as the heart of my consideration of pluralism the Christian encounter with Jews. The very particular relationship between the two religious traditions compels us to sharpen up what we mean by the unexceptional terms of our liberal statement as dialogue. By definition, this has to be open in the sense that it might lead someone away from his or her cherished position. It is not that Christians so engaged are planning on finding the Jewish faith so attractive as to convert. In my experience, the keenest dialogue-makers are sure that they intend to stand on the familiar ground of their own religious tradition before they interact with another. The long and often unsavoury history of Christian missionary activity towards Jews makes not only Jews but also liberal Christians themselves particularly sensitive to any perceived intention to convert. A new understanding has emerged in many Christian denominational statements in the last decade, one in which 'the mission of both Jews and Christians is to be understood as dialogue, mutual witness, and service to the world' (Phan, 1996, p. 91). The bottom line, as so well articulated by Jonathan Sacks quoted earlier, is respect not only for the 'other' tradition in theory but for its adherents in practice. Areas of behaviour and action where such shared mission might be worked out surely constitute one element of liberalism as promoted in this volume.

Because of their unique relationship, Christians meeting Jews may not be taken as representative of interfaith dialogue. The encounter with Judaism presents, however, a suitable focus for this volume on liberalism since the issues it raises for Christianity are particularly acute. Assuming that we are talking then about the religiously committed meeting the equally religiously committed, we may turn our attention more specifically to where Christians meet Jews, on what terms, and to what purpose.

Realistically, many Christians in Britain never meet Jews in such a way that their respective religious positions come to the fore. One could go further and say that, in most parts of the country, Christians never meet Jews at all. Indeed, some consider Judaism to be such a minority faith and the Jewish community to be in such decline numerically that we should not concern ourselves much with any interfaith agenda in which Jews loom large. Furthermore, there has been considerable discussion in recent years as to whether the Council of Christians and Jews should become the Council of Christians, Jews and Muslims.

It is not necessary to rehearse all the arguments for and against this proposal here. One point does need to be emphasized, however, in any agenda set largely by Christians. Sadly, past personal and religious experience shows us that disputes are always worse within the family (Read, 1996, p. 61). Christians so often make assumptions about the Jewish religion and assumptions usually spell the death of communication. A Christian point of view is being taken as the starting point of my consideration. This is not because it is thought that nothing is needed on the Jewish side in terms of efforts to understand the 'other'. But, in Britain at any rate, the partnership is often unequal in that, as the dominant religious tradition of the land, Christianity has at best regarded interfaith dialogue as a luxury and at worse been guilty of its wilful neglect.

For Christians, it is at the point of the relationship with Judaism that interfaith questions most impinge. For many Christians, especially in this country, the place where they meet the religion of Judaism, if not real, live representatives of it, is the Bible. This may be in private reading, but more often than not it will be in worship, where the Bible is read and expounded. What has liberalism got to say in this context, that is, the context of worship and the confession of one particular faith?

There is also a further consideration which, I would argue, has a bearing on the sort of pluralism being advocated here. If the 'meeting place' is a church service, then the setting is by definition 'confessional', in the sense that the people gathered there are explicitly and deliberately confessing the Christian faith. This, of course, is the major reason why interfaith worship is not feasible. In a Christian service, prayers are naturally said 'in the name of Jesus Christ our Lord'. Should this phrase be erased in deference to Jews who, after all, are not present? What about the content of the prayers which so conclude? Should they be emptied of all specifically Christian content so that Jews could join in the worship which, after all, they do not wish?

It is of deep significance that the gathering at the Houses of Parliament described earlier was 'an act of reflection and commitment'. For all that it had, among other specifically confessional activities, an imam chanting part of the Qur'an, it was not an 'act of worship'. The assembled crowd, whatever their commitment to interfaith relations and whatever their degree of religious pluralism, could hardly have been required to participate in Muslim prayers or, indeed, any other. Significantly, Christians could have 'joined in' Jewish prayers, as indeed any Christian who has visited a synagogue for Sabbath worship will have done. Prayers for the coming of the Messiah or the messianic age may carry a different significance for Christians, and they may feel unable to pray for the restoration of the Temple and of sacrifice, as in Orthodox Judaism, but there is nothing fundamental to Jewish prayer which would offend the Christian. Some Christians, it must be said, cannot understand why Jews cannot be similarly 'magnanimous', as they see it. The true liberal, so far as religious pluralism is concerned, can easily see it. From a Jewish perspective, Christianity, in which Jesus is 'more than' a human figure, is not truly monotheistic.

This rather general consideration about the participatory nature of worship becomes specific when examining the implications of liberalism for today's society. One need only recall the difficulties involved in the phrasing of the requirements for Collective Worship as in the Education Reform Act of 1988 to be further persuaded of the non-relativism of interfaith encounter. The requirement that 'the majority' of acts of collective worship in state schools be 'wholly or mainly of a broadly Christian character' was offensive to Jews, some of whom withdrew their children from what had been known as 'assemblies', and this for the first time. If their children were being compelled to 'worship', then clearly this activity was unacceptable to them. It became essentially exclusivist or, at the very least, non-pluralist, whatever the intention of the Act. The phrase 'wholly or mainly of a broadly Christian character', among others in the Act, seemed to need so much amplification (for example, Hull, 1989) that one began to wonder about its value as legislation or even as guidance. Worship is by its very nature confessional. A school hall is not a 'little church'. Muddying the waters or trying to compel unity between faiths by attempting to find some common denominator for a form of worship is at best unhelpful and at worst dishonest. The upshot of this may well be that schools, except for those explicitly belonging to one faith or denominational tradition, should have not acts of worship but acts of 'reflection and commitment', where no prayers or hymns which involve actual participation in any one faith tradition, feature.

When in church as distinct from school, however, Christians turn their attention to the Bible, what are they doing? An initial question at issue is, which Bible is it that is being read and/or expounded? This is not simply a matter of what you call the shared Scriptures of the Jewish and Christian communities. It is a matter of how the respective faith communities interpret these texts. Those of the Old Testament/Hebrew Bible are shared in a way in which the New Testament texts are not. The term 'Old Testament' is being used advisedly in this chapter. In the first place, it is the term with which Christians are familiar. In the second place, what Christians hear in church is not the Bible in

Hebrew. There may be a different argument for using the term 'Hebrew Bible' in a professional society where academics, be they Jewish, Christian, or of other or no religious affiliation, all have a knowledge of Hebrew and read learned papers. Such is the Society for Old Testament Study, as currently named, in Britain. Yet, Christians meeting Jews in this academic setting can hardly be described as typical, however significant it may be, not only for scholarship but for either or both of the faith communities. In the third place, it is my contention that terminology is nowhere near being the main point at issue. It is often argued that the term 'old' suggests something outmoded, superseded, or in some other way inferior to the 'new'. I am not convinced that, in reality, this is what is conceived by Christians when they use the term. For those Christians who view the Old Testament in this way, simply changing the terminology will not achieve a change in attitude to the Old Testament or to Jews and Judaism. And for those Christians who do not regard the Old Testament in this negative way, a change in terminology is not necessary.

It is no good just renaming, especially in such a way as may alienate Christian worshippers. After all, why should they use the terminology of 'Hebrew Bible' for their Scriptures any more than Jews should use the Christian terminology of 'Old Testament' for their Scriptures? What Christians must ensure is that they do not make derogatory references to these Scriptures. It is, it should be noted, from the churches that society gets these references and with them a distorted picture of the Old Testament. The contrast between an 'Old Testament God of wrath and law' and a 'New Testament God of love and grace', still heard from Christian pulpits, allows people at large to speak of 'the God of the Old Testament' as a rather nasty piece of work, best grown out of.

Similarly, it is not what a Christian calls the Old Testament or whether he or she erases bits found to be unpalatable that matters in Christian worship. In a church setting, the Christian preacher, however committed to liberalism as pluralism, remains a Christian addressing Christians. The task, as I have argued elsewhere, is to represent this Old Testament, in its richness and diversity, as accurately as possible and to draw on it for spiritual and moral resources (Pilkington, 2000). This is where integrity, as advocated in the Liverpool Statement and in the interfaith gathering at Westminster, can truly be cultivated. Within a

Christian congregation many philosophies, if this is not too sophisticated a term, may underlie attitudes to other faiths and their adherents. What I would like among Christians is not just a sensitivity to other faiths and a consideration of phrasing and possible causes of offence on occasions when Jews are present, but an ethos in Christian worship which values the 'shared Scripture' of Christians and Jews. This valuing needs to be in a way which is consonant with the Church's accepting and retaining the Old Testament as part of its Bible and in a way in which the central common ground, namely God, is allowed to be God. When we do this as Christians we are not evacuating our worship of Christian content in order to please Jews, nor are we emasculating our faith to please those Christians who seem to concentrate on Jesus, sometimes at the expense of God. We are endeavouring to be Christian, gaining from our rich Jewish heritage. In this way, honest encounter and dialogue which goes on outside of worship may be encouraged. Moreover, the wider society may then have more time for this sort of liberalism than it has had for the liberalism of the past which it has found to be too vague and accommodating.

What do Christians think they are doing when they 'meet' Jews in the Bible? So far as the New Testament is concerned, they are probably exploring the roots of their own religion, Christianity. They may have eventually got the message of the Jewishness of Jesus and the pharisaic thought-forms of Paul, and they want to understand these roots. They are essentially trying to understand a faith which developed from Judaism, and whose first adherents were all Jews. From a Jewish perspective, however, the New Testament is considered, if at all, in an attempt to understand Christianity in its non-Jewishness. What strikes Jewish readers of the New Testament, even more forcefully than it strikes Christian readers, is the writers' polemic against Jews, whether explicit or implicit. These 'hard sayings' (for example, John 8.31, 44; Matthew 27.24–25; Acts 2.22–23) are hardly aids to mutual understanding and tolerance.

What are Christians hearing when such passages are read in a church service? I feel that there are limits to how much erasing of material from the New Testament is possible. Much attention has been paid to this in recent years, with the highly desirable removal from Christian liturgy of the so-called 'teaching of contempt' against Jews. But does one then also start removing chunks of the New Testament on the ground that they may otherwise damage Christian–Jewish relations? Such dictation to Christians, by those passionately against anti-Judaism, could well backfire. After all, the purpose of Christian worship is not exclusively or even primarily to encourage interfaith dialogue. Far more important is what is said about these New Testament passages, the elucidation of the context of the words which convey anti-Judaism, and the general tone in which Jews, be they of the first or the twenty-first century (of the pluralistically named Common Era), are spoken of.

It is when texts are actually expounded, that is preached on, that real opportunities, whether for good or for ill, open up. Again, possible encounter, with its challenge to explore theological issues, is not the same for Jews as it is for Christians. Jewish preaching need not, of course, concern itself with another faith. Why should it? Christian preaching, by virtue of the fact that the Old Testament became and has remained part of the canon of Christian Scripture, inevitably does need to. Our perspective, within the framework of this volume, has been predominantly Christian. But asking what Christians think they are doing when 'meeting' Jews inevitably involves some awareness of what Jews think Christians are doing when meeting them.

Increasingly in the last decade, Christians involved in dialogue with Jews, whether through CCJ, other interfaith networks, or on an academic programme (such as the taught masters degrees in Jewish–Christian Relations at Bangor, Cambridge or Canterbury) have engaged in joint readings of the Hebrew Bible. (The nomenclature is adopted on these occasions as a unifying factor, directing Christians to the origins of these Scriptures and reassuring Jews that their fellow-readers are not engaged in some essentially non-pluralist enterprise of offering them a 'New Testament'.) An example of this is a weekend at Aylesford Friary, Kent, in May 1995. It was jointly led by Rabbi Sylvia Rothschild of the Reform Synagogues of Great Britain and Sr Margaret Shepherd of the Sisters of Zion. The weekend was entitled 'Reading the Book of Psalms'. It drew heavily on Rabbi Dr Jonathan Magonet's work (1994). It could well be argued that it is comparatively easy for Christians and Jews to find common ground in their reading of the Psalms. They both think they are doing the same thing, namely drawing on this wealth of theological literature in order to enrich either their public or their private devotions. Nevertheless, there are contributions from Jewish interpretation which Christians seldom come across except through a Jewish speaker or biblical commentator. A comprehensive and much-needed survey of Christian and Jewish usage of the Psalms through history has been offered by William Holladay (1993).

When it comes to other parts of the Old Testament, however, the readings may well diverge more sharply and indeed raise issues of division. Rabbi Jacob Neusner, for example, has argued that very careful consideration needs to be given to any assertion that what Christians and Jews share is the same Bible (1991). He further reminds us that what Christians encounter in their Old Testament is not Judaism as such. The rabbinic writings, supremely the Babylonian Talmud, constitute the Scriptures of Judaism alongside Tenakh, the usual Jewish term for the Hebrew Bible. Neusner compares this dual Torah, comprising Bible and Talmud, to the Christian combination of Old and later New Testament. To say that in the Old Testament what Christians encounter is the Judaism of Jesus is also oversimplified, for the writings which later formed Tenakh were already being interpreted by Jews of Jesus' day.

Accepting these caveats, we may still argue for the desirability of 'a common theological reading of the Bible', noting that today is 'the first time in history that Jews and Christians have had the opportunity to meet on an equal level, without being dependent on any political or religious institution or authority, and to meet as individuals, each with his or her own commitment to a religious tradition and community' (Rendtorff, 1994, pp. 34–5). Ever since Christianity developed a separate history from Judaism, the two communities have been linked in their respective uses of their common Bible. Ignorance of each other's tradition among so many representatives has been regrettable and need not continue. Not only symposia but also joint publications by Jewish and Christian scholars are now increasing.

Comparatively few Christians, however, even of liberal/pluralist outlook, are engaged in such joint readings. As argued earlier, the theological health and vivacity of Christians may depend more on such genuine interchange than is generally recognized.

Meantime, we must accept that if Christians hear anything that might challenge their attitudes to other faiths it will be in the form of sermons. That sermons played a major role in promoting the anti-Judaism of the second to fourth centuries CE is well known (Saperstein, 1989, pp. 5–13). Ways in which sermons may have an equally strong influence in a positive direction surely deserve attention in the present climate. Now it is not the task of Christian preaching to make non-pluralists pluralist, or even to make pluralists' dominant concern be their relation with a religion other than their own. The purpose of Christian preaching is surely to proclaim the 'good news'. This is bound to be in Christian terms. This is the integrity of the Christian religion and Christians need not be apologetic about it. Indeed, as we have already seen, such confessionalism is much to be preferred to weak or hazy pseudo-dialogue. The question now arises, does this good news conceived in Christian terms genuinely permit a pluralistic outlook, along the lines of any of the models with which we began?

Remembering earlier anti-Judaism, the question can be asked in relation to the New Testament, can there be preaching of the good news which is good news for Jews as well as for Christians? I believe that this question should be asked far more frequently than it is of the Old Testament. It is not that Jews will actually be present in Christian worship to hear this version of the good news, but the Christians who hear it may then be able to engage with Jews on terms which are equal though not servile, open though not tame. Within the context of living out a faith in a God of justice and love, Christians may then meet Jews in a way that speaks to modern society both verbally and in action. Progress has been made in the second half of the twentieth century in the Church's trying to formulate its attitude to Judaism, but unless 'education, preaching, and worship in local congregations are appropriate to the good news of God's all-inclusive love and God's command that justice be done to all those whom God loves, none of the church's fine theological pronouncements on relations between Christians and Jews will, in the end, be worth a fig' (Williamson, 1993, p. 47).

Jews and Christians do handle their shared traditions in different ways. This has something crucial to say about the way in which differences between religions should be squeezed of their potential to enrich rather than be politely ironed out or, worse still, ignored. If ever there was a religion which was concerned with doing God's will, it was – and still is – the Jewish religion. Key terms in this religion appear in the Bible as covenant and kingship. There is a sense in which these two religions display both their diversity and their common ground in relation to how these essentially theological ideas get translated in action. Clearly Christians and Jews are never going to agree Christologically. It is, therefore, a pity when Judaism gets defined by Christians in terms of what it does not believe, that is, that Jesus is not the Messiah. More crucially, we should be asking how both religions conceive of God's kingly rule and of the human response in promoting it. Attention should now be focused not only on the impact of the New Testament on Christian–Jewish dialogue but also on the Old Testament. From this biblical basis, there is much exploration to be done in terms of the common aims and purposes of human life as perceived by members of both faith communities.

References

D'Costa, G., 'Theology of religions', in Ford, D., (ed.), *The Modern Theologians: An Introduction to Christian Theology in the Twentieth Century*, second edition, Blackwell Publishers Ltd, Oxford, 1997.

Holladay, W. L., *The Psalms through Three Thousand Years*, Fortress Press, Minneapolis, 1993.

Hull, J. M., *The Act Unpacked*, The University of Birmingham Press, Birmingham, 1989.

Jones, G., *Critical Theology*, Polity Press, Cambridge, 1995.

Magonet, J., *A Rabbi Reads the Psalms*, SCM Press Ltd, London, 1994.

Neusner, J., *Jews and Christians: The Myth of a Common Tradition*, SCM Press, London, 1991.

Phan, P. C., 'Preaching Jews and Judaism in Light of the New Catechism', in Kee, H. C. and Borowsky, I. J. (eds), *Removing Anti-Judaism from the Pulpit*, The Continuum Publishing Company, New York, 1996.

Pilkington, C., *Preaching on the Old Testament*, Foundery Press, Peterborough, 2000.

Read, D. H. C., 'Reflections of an Imported WASP', in Kee, H. C. and Borowsky, I. J. (eds), *Removing Anti-Judaism from the Pulpit*, The Continuum Publishing Company, New York, 1996.

Rendtorff, R., *Canon and Theology*, T&T Clark, Edinburgh, 1994.

Saperstein, M., *Moments of Crisis in Jewish–Christian Relations*, SCM Press, London, 1989.

Williamson, C. M., *A Guest in the House of Israel: Post-Holocaust Church Theology*, Westminster/John Knox, Louisville, 1993.

CHAPTER SEVEN

Why Feminists Should Still Be Liberals

Hannah Bacon and J'annine Jobling

FEMINIST THEOLOGY owes a double debt to liberal traditions. One philosophical mandate for the liberation of women came from liberal demands for justice, freedom and equality; feminist theology might also be appropriately seen in some respects as an expression of a liberal theology, inasmuch as it is a critique of theological traditions and authorities in the light of social and cultural concerns. Liberalism, in both its political and philosophical guises, clearly has connotations for both theology and feminism. Within both these arenas, liberal perspectives – never monolithic – have changed and developed, and continue to do so.

In this chapter, we argue that feminism should continue to dialogue with liberalism. To this end, we explore aspects of the relationship between liberalism and feminist theology. We begin by mapping briefly the impact of liberalism upon theology, identifying how liberal perspectives led to the promotion of a rational, autonomous faith, incorporating scientific and sociological developments as reflexive of its commitment to making theology relevant to the contemporary world. We then note how liberal theology not only had a tendency to reproduce the flaws of earlier liberal positions, but more specifically seemed to reproduce 'male' values and ideals. Liberal feminism acts as an examplar of how liberal philosophies and ideals may actually undermine rather than promote the causes of feminism.

However, we wish to argue that a reframed liberalism still has much to offer feminist theology. Our sites of recontextualization are: on the one hand, liberation theology, more particularly the critical feminist theology of liberation of Elisabeth Schüssler Fiorenza; further to this, we seek to marry a postmodern account of the (gendered) subject with liberal ideals. This dual theoretical position pushes us towards a brand of postmodern feminist theology committed to openness, plurality and inclusiveness, in a framework affirming the validity of justice and equality as sociopolitical goals. One methodological issue entailed by this position is that of the ethical foundation for emancipatory ideals within a postmodern context. This question we also begin to address.

Liberal Theology: Features and Developments

It is of course important to note that the term 'liberalism' does not refer to a homogeneous school of thought; when considering 'liberal' theology, we do so with such an understanding in mind. This initial section aims, however, to outline briefly and in general terms the main features and themes of liberal theology.

Reason

Liberal theology became dominant at the turn of the late nineteenth/early twentieth centuries. Originating in Germany, liberal theology was greatly influenced by the Enlightenment principles of reason, autonomy and independence, placing great emphasis on the individual subject. Within this framework, human reason became the primary judge of truth and religious beliefs. External authority and tradition were, therefore, rejected, and religious beliefs were instead called to answer to the criteria of reason and experience. Thus, early liberal religion promoted values such as freedom and tolerance, rejecting uniformity in worship, strict adherence to creeds, and blind reliance on authority and tradition. Reason was the central driving force for all moral decision-making.

This emphasis on reason provided a clear challenge to central Christian doctrines such as the incarnation, Trinity and resurrection; the need for revelation was obviated in favour of a rational, personal religion which did not make metaphysical claims about God. Friedrich Schleiermacher was fundamental in influencing such understandings, presenting a view of religion as a deep personal conviction, as an inward emotion and disposition (Schleiermacher, 1958).

However, such a stress on autonomy, reason and personal faith tended to reinforce the liberal assumption that the subject preceded society and so presented a notion of the self as abstract and disembodied. Salvation was viewed as totally personal, and competing notions of the 'good life' were seen as equally valuable and authentic. Moreover, as there was such a stress on the omnicompetence of reason, Christian heritage became relatively insignificant.

Cultural and Contemporary Relevance

Such a focus on reason also means that theological ideas have to be coherent within a modern context, incorporating the intellectual challenges circulating within educational environments. For example, Darwinism came to be embodied within theological perspectives in such a way that God was seen as acting in history, transforming humanity from a primitive state towards maturity. Such an evolutionary worldview provided a new context for religious belief. The crucial consequences of engaging seriously with contemporary culture are threefold: one, an imperative to relate theology to the shifting ground of cultural knowledge to maintain its plausibility and perceived coherence; two, a commitment to making theology relevant and meaningful in light of cultural concerns and situations; three, a recognition that as knowledge of God is reconstituted with relation to cultural and historical contexts, it is thus inherently contingent. This insight contributes to the role and status of history in liberal theology.

History

The rise of liberalism intertwined with a growing historical consciousness, and an awareness that religious texts, dogmas and traditions were human products, dynamically evolving in history, rather than timeless, divinely revealed truths. The authority of the Bible as the infallible word of God was challenged and replaced by a focus on its historical content, identifying the historical Jesus as a man providing an insight into the characteristics of God. Historical critical methods were employed to find the 'real' Jesus, stripped of the veils of dogma and tradition. Early religious liberalism, then, tended to lose sight of the christological doctrines of the early medieval and Reformation churches, presenting Jesus as an ethical guide: one of perhaps many who have revealed God in history (Niebuhr, 1996, p. 6). The focus on history was coupled with a withdrawal from metaphysical speculation – a move influenced by Kantian restriction of the limits of knowledge.

Religious Plurality and Diversity

Liberal theology was also influenced by a rising awareness of other religions. The expansion of Christian missions, trade, travel and military contact meant that Christians became increasingly aware that non-Christian faiths had coherent moral and religious systems of their own. Comparative religion arose as a sphere of academic study in its own right. For liberals, this awareness of other religions led to two typical consequences: the relativization of the authority and truth of any one tradition, and an advocacy of tolerance as a key ethical principle. Liberal theologians characteristically emphasize the significance of religious plurality and diversity.

Ethics

Liberal theology, then, does not simply envelope a political viewpoint, but also points towards an ethical paradigm, at the heart of which must be the concept of liberty. This typically takes on two forms within liberal thought: positive liberty insists that the individual must be free to follow whatever path he or she may choose and so defines liberty as free from the coercion of others; negative freedom, on the other hand, suggests that coercion – or at least infringement of personal liberty – might, in fact, be necessary in order to prevent the individual from acting in ways that might compromise his or her autonomy (for example drug taking). Despite this debate, most liberal theologians stress the goodness of developing one's own individual capacities, viewing this as fundamental to the construction of the well-developed human being. Given this, there is a definite stress on the co-existence of equality and difference as each individual demands the freedom to develop uniquely – but this must not pose a threat to the subjectivity of others. Religious tolerance then comes to be of specific value. The relationship between respect for individual liberties and the broader humanitarian ethics of liberalism is disputed. What can be stated is that liberalism usually entails a concern with equality, justice and freedom and a strong interest in human rights.

Liberal theology can then be seen to centralize the themes of reason, cultural and contemporary relevance, history and religious plurality, within a humanitarian ethical framework. Among its dominant principles are freedom, justice, tolerance, and the questioning of authorities.

Let us turn now to some of the criticisms of liberal theology, many of which go in tandem with criticisms of liberalism more generally. This is certainly the case with respect to a dependence – at the very least often implied – on liberal individualism. Here the subject is placed within an imaginary sphere, detached from the situation and networks of social formation, and stripped of preconception and interest (Damico, 1986, p. 203). Religious belief is then judged from a stance of impartiality and neutrality. Such accounts of the subject have been criticized from the points of view of the sociology of knowledge, communitarian philosophies and postmodern deconstruction of the Self as stable. Furthermore, liberal individualism not only furnishes an inadequate account of the subject: it also risks perpetuating the relegation of religion to the private sphere – as something housed in the sphere of an individual's personal freedoms, and not able to offer a significant collective voice within the public, political domain.

There is a sense in which liberal theology's uneasy negotiation of the private/public distinction reflects a more deep-rooted liberal contradiction. On the one hand it wants to accept culture, making theological discourse both constituted by and relevant to the contemporary world; yet, on the other, calls for social reform, implying that society is in fact in need of transformation. The disjunction between God and world which characterize 'conservative' theologies offers a more obvious home for the prophetic voice than the seamless continuities of liberal ontologies and epistemologies. Of course, it could also be argued that liberalism has been too eager to reject tradition, placing too great an emphasis on the future of theology at the expense of Christian heritage. From a feminist point of view, liberal theology must also be criticized for maintaining the 'male-stream' framework provided by liberalism, thus continuing to exclude the voices of the marginalized and oppressed. It is this central difficulty that will now be explored.

Liberalism and Gender

Liberalism has been criticized as functioning to sacralize the Victorian ideals of female fragility and male supremacy within the public domain. Feminism has exposed liberal theory as gendered, highlighting a central contradiction in the liberal principles of neutrality and equality. The liberal citizen was assumed male, possessing the 'masculine' traits of reason, autonomy and individuality, pushing women to the margins of agency, thus reinforcing her 'natural' position within the private domain.

As Kate Nash puts this: 'Women [then] cannot be the free and equal individuals of liberalism because of their position in the private sphere and their association with values *opposed* to the public sphere in which liberal individuals have their place' (Nash, 1998, p. 31).

Indeed, as liberalism encouraged the ownership of private property by individual citizens (men), and viewed women as belonging within the private domain, women came to be justly regarded as the property of men. Liberal feminism, therefore, emerged as a critique of such an ideology, attempting to extend the rights of citizenship equally to women.

Liberal Feminism

Central to the thesis of liberal feminism was the notion that gender could be transcended and, therefore, was not biological. Women were not bound to an inferior status, but should be free to compete equally with men in the public domain. Mary Wollstonecraft, in *A Vindication of the Rights of Women*, sought to promote the equality of women through identifying their identical capacity for reason. She wanted to extend all the prerequisites of citizenship to women so that they might at last be perceived as fully human. For Wollstonecraft such equality was only to be grasped through access to education and the employment market. Reason was not a male biological 'given', it was simply that women had been socialized into certain personality traits, making them 'appear' less rational. However, Wollstonecraft did not want to dispose of the importance of women's unique capacity to bear children; thus, she asserts that women should have the right to choose motherhood and still be able to work within the public sphere (Eisenstein, 1984, p. 200). However, Wollstonecraft does not achieve much for women's liberation. She maintains the division between the private and public domains, viewing women as primarily wives and mothers, yet encouraging all to take up a position within the public sphere through work and education. Wollstonecraft provides no insight as to how such a 'double-shift' is to operate in reality.

Betty Friedan demonstrates similar difficulties. In *The Feminine Mystique*, Friedan encourages women to seek equality with men through education and employment (Friedan, 1965, pp. 244, 357). Believing such moves will displace the 'false consciousness' of the feminine mystique, she calls all women to compete equally with men in the public domain. However, realizing that such an agenda simply encourages women to become like men and therefore to reject their 'womanhood', Friedan later modifies her views and suggests that women should be free to choose motherhood as well as a professional career (Eisenstein, 1984, p. 189). Once again though, it is unclear as to how Friedan envisages women to perform such dual tasks. Indeed, Zillah Eisenstein states that it is difficult to see how a professional woman might choose motherhood, given that she may risk loss of earnings and other repercussions (Eisenstein, 1984, p. 189). Surely sexual inequality is the very reason why women cannot make such a choice in the first place.

Critique
From this brief discussion, it should be clear that liberal feminism does not extricate itself from the difficulties of liberal thought. The distinction between the private and public domain continues to be upheld to such an extent that it is difficult to see how 'equality' is in fact to be achieved. Encouraging women into the public domain is all well and good, but if they are going to be disadvantaged by their sex when they arrive, it seems that the journey may be rather unworthwhile. Moreover, it is unclear how in fact women are to make such a step into the public domain given that such feminists as Wollstonecraft and Friedan do not free them first from their 'private' responsibilities. Indeed, even if women do manage to fulfil their dual commitments, it seems they will still enter the public arena as primarily concerned with the private, still viewed as dependants concerned with the unpaid care of others (Nash, 1998, p. 34).

Thus liberal feminism tends to overlook sexual difference, reverting to the liberal idea that all individuals share a neutral position and so should be entitled to the same opportunities. Such a naïve view seems rather unhelpful, given our inescapable embodiment. Furthermore, presenting the notion of an individual, autonomous, rational subject who makes decisions outside the influence of society and thus from a completely neutral position tends to place everyone within the same position, denying the perspectival and contextual nature of all knowledge and, more importantly, the diversity which exists within this. Liberal feminism in fact tends to group all women together, ignoring the differences in 'women's experience'. Liberal feminism then does not seem to fulfil its own goals of recognizing and valuing diversity. For to do so would mean a recognition of the impact of positionality upon epistemology, something not readily discernible on the agenda of most liberal feminists. Indeed, it can be argued that structural change is a necessity and something liberal feminism fails to address in any sufficient way. The liberal ideal of equality, for feminism to be played out in gender relations, will never be achieved if liberal feminism continues to simply bandage the wound of patriarchy without attempting to deal with the disease directly.

Beyond Liberal Feminism

Let us then summarize the case so far: it has been stated that liberal theology focuses around the central themes of reason, cultural and contemporary relevance, history and religious plurality, seeking to present a theology which is open, practical and applicable to the present day. However, despite such ideals, it has been demonstrated that liberal theology tends to contradict such values through a failure to incorporate marginalized groups, of which we considered women. A parallel case can be made against liberal feminism: its adoption of a neutral subject and failure to address inequalities embedded in material structures likewise point towards the need for a feminism more constituted by considerations of systemic oppressions, and proceeding from contextual understandings of identity and knowledge. In mapping the way forward, liberation theology thus constitutes a key framework for discussion.

Liberation Theology
Whereas liberal theology often tends to be restricted to the confines of academia, often difficult to apply in any meaningful way to broader fields of existence, liberation theology alterna-tively seeks to reverse this situation – making theology not only

relevant, but contextual and practical, grounded in the experiences of the oppressed. Indeed, 'Latin America liberation theology speaks of God as manifest in the poor of history' and is dependent on God choosing to reveal himself as poor (Chopp, 1997, p. 409). Liberation theology is, then, first and foremost, a practical theology, primarily concerned with living out the Christian message within a particular historical context.

The meaning of what it is to be poor and marginalized is stressed through an emphasis on praxis. Liberation theology is always striving to link religious beliefs and actions to the real world and so always provides a practical ground for theological claims. Rebecca Chopp states that praxis has three main meanings: first, it asserts that human beings are constructed from political–historical reality; second, it states that human reality is inter-subjective, arising through contact with other people; and third, it states that human beings can create history and that the transformation of society is, therefore, both possible and desirable in order for humanity to flourish (Chopp, 1997, p. 412). The notion of praxis, therefore, disposes of liberal individualism, viewing the individual as part of a community to the extent that transformation is only possible through such solidarity. Christian communities that practise solidarity and gratuitous love anticipate the communion in the eschaton and therefore go about establishing the kingdom of God on earth (Murray, 1998, p. 53). Liberation theology tends to focus on the ecclesial community as the driving force for change and salvation.

Of course such an emphasis on contextuality means that the liberal conceptions of epistemological neutrality and 'objectivity' are challenged. Knowledge is not asocial, obtainable from a position outside society, but is, instead, contextual, arising within a particular culture and environment and therefore taking its place within the web of human experience. Such a view is obviously helpful within a feminist framework, for it allows space for diversity within women's experience of oppression.

It is evident by this point that liberation theology places much weight on structural oppression. For liberation theology, oppression is a sociopolitical system which operates within a complex web of relations within society as a whole. There is, therefore, often an emphasis on structural sin as opposed to personal sin. Oppression stems from oppressive social structures and so redemption comes to be filtered through an identification with Jesus as *for* the poor and oppressed; as liberator and as the one through whom transformation is brought and new ways of being are signalled (Chopp, 1999, p. 413). Indeed, there is an awareness within liberation theology that the poor do not simply occur but are, in fact, created. Such an awareness means that oppression is denaturalized and consequently seen as unstable, and therefore open for change. Within liberation theology therefore, human life enters the realm of the political, rejecting the liberal notion that human conduct, within a framework guaranteeing certain rights and freedoms, should be left entirely up to the individual. For most liberation theologians, politics extends to the question of how individuals are enabled to fulfil their subjectivity. Liberation theology, then, begins to deconstruct the line between private and public domains, recognizing that such a separation too easily can be used to reinforce the *status quo* and to ensure the continuing oppression of marginalized groups.

Critique

Elisabeth Schüssler Fiorenza suggests that the main inadequacy with liberation theology is that (like liberalism) it is 'male-stream', being based on the assumption that the subject is male and thus denying the diversity that exists between women's experiences (Fiorenza, 1996, p. 5). However, incorporating women into this model must always take place in light of the recognition that all oppression is structural. Thus, women's liberation cannot simply mean liberation from men as the oppressors, but must instead constitute liberation from all social structures which marginalize women, poor and indigenous people (Pena, 1995, p. 82). Given this, women's liberation cannot and should not be seen outside the wider context of (for example) class, race and ethnicity. Indeed, separating the issue of gender from the thesis of liberation theology simply assumes that gender does not affect experience, thereby forcing women into a realm of insignificance.

Beyond Liberation Theology

Where, then, do we move from here? The task is to delineate a methodological framework which fulfils the (in our view) laudable aims of liberalism: open, inclusive, culturally relevant, at home in pluralist society and capable of hosting varieties of opinion within a structure which seeks to guarantee freedoms. At the same time, we must strive to avoid presuppositions which in effect perpetuate marginality and oppression through insufficient acknowledgement of structurally differentiated positionalities, the sociology of knowledge, and variably constituted subjectivities.

The framework we propose takes its jumping-off point in Elisabeth Schüssler Fiorenza's revisioning of liberation theology into a critical feminist theology of liberation. This provides an analysis of interlocking oppressions which creates space at the centre for the marginalized, neither excluding them nor obliterating their specificities. Within these complex and shifting sociopolitical configurations, the voice calling for justice is located not with autonomous individuals but with coalitions of individuals-in-community (the *ekklesia*), which is a congress of decision-making citizens identified with the oppressed and seeking justice. Developing Fiorenza's concept, we argue that this provides an appropriate platform for feminists espousing liberally oriented principles. Sensitive to typical critiques of liberalism, we interrogate the question of what models of identity and the (gendered) subject might underpin the *ekklesia*. We then raise the question of ethical foundations for the *ekklesia* in light of a postmodern rejection of external guarantors of truth.

Fiorenza's Critical Feminist Theology of Liberation

Fiorenza firmly rejects radical tendencies to take women's oppression as the primary form of oppression, challenging the assertion that *all* men are oppressors and *all* women are oppressed (Fiorenza, 1996, p. 62). Placing women and men so easily within two separate camps simply risks lapsing into an essentialist framework, failing to take account of differences between women and their experiences of oppression. Fiorenza goes about redefining patriarchy with this in mind. She states that patriarchy is 'a complex, pyramidal political system of dominance and submission, stratified by gender, race, class, religious and cultural taxonomies and other historical discursive formations of domination' (Fiorenza, 1996, p. 62).

Patriarchy, for Fiorenza, does not simply refer to the oppression of women by men, but points to a more sophisticated paradigm in which the components of race, class, religion and ethnicity all play their parts. In fact Fiorenza goes one step further to say that such components are not only multiple, but also multiplicative (Fiorenza, 1996, p. 55). Thus, sexual oppression does not simply exist alongside racial oppression, but actually multiplies that oppression. Given this, Fiorenza suggests that the term 'patriarchy' be replaced by the word 'kyriarchy', taking the emphasis away from *male* domination, and placing oppression within the broader context of sociopolitical structures of oppression and dehumanization (Fiorenza, 1996, p. 63). Within this framework, the marginalized come to play a central role in the doing of theology. Sin is, once more, seen within a structural context of kyriarchal systems of domination and oppression. Theology thus seems to be in need of desperate reform – to the extent that solidarity is desired and sought after, it must begin to incorporate the voices of the marginalized, for it is only through such measures that equality and liberation might truly be achieved. The driving force for such structural change is, for Fiorenza, situated within the *ekklesia* of wo/men.[1] The *ekklesia*, as a vision of a congress of full decision-making citizens, is both a sociopolitical vision and a Christian one; for it is not only the means by which transformation will occur, but is consequently the tool by which God's kingdom may be established on earth (Fiorenza, 1996).

The Ekklesia *and Identity*

Given the criticisms of liberalism as insufficiently attentive to differences and as based on an inadequate model of the subject, the question arises: what model of identity underpins the concept of the *ekklesia*? Related to this is the question of how specificity and particularity relate to community, in a context where solidarity has been identified as a goal. Is diversity inevitably flattened into uniformity with a communitarian ethic?

Tackling the latter point first, Jobling has suggested that it is helpful to consider the *ekklesia* in the light of Lionnet's concept of the 'métissage'.[2] This is the 'braiding together of cultural forms'. Lionnet uses it to denote a sheltering site, in which differences can be nurtured (see *Bible and Culture Collective*, 1995, p. 243). Thus, it can be usefully deployed to refer to a 'knotted bridge' of feminist community. It signifies hybridity, and so can convey a sense of a community of communities, with many diverse elements brought together but not reduced to one thing or the other. It is a crossbreed community, multi-parented, composed of differences which are nevertheless gathered together into a shared but differentiated space. Thus if we read the *ekklesia* in the light of the métissage, we can understand a space which is anything but monolithic. An imagined community of communities, designating a positioning and a commitment towards justice, it expresses solidarity between feminism, womanism, the Hispanic *mujerista* movement, and other varieties of groupings countering kyriarchy and gender oppression; but it is a solidarity which is loosely woven together and made up of differences. It provides for an overlapping of 'communities of resistance and solidarity' (see Welch, 1985) in a space oriented towards polyphony, dialogue and inquiry. Thus community, as well as diversity and particularity, are all embraced.

For Fiorenza, the *ekklesia* is the church of wo/men. She positions it in the logic of democracy or equality, rather than in so-called logic of identity characteristic of kyriarchy. We may note at this point a *caveat* with respect to Fiorenza's terminology. The political flavour of the term 'democracy' is on the one hand a positive thing, for it highlights the public and political character of the *ekklesia*. However, against this, historical sociopolitical investments in democracy are inextricably bound up with kyriarchal structures and worldviews, as Fiorenza's own analysis actually demonstrates. Similarly, in feminist circles the language of equality can resonate with liberal sociopolitical programmes which, it is argued, end up by equating equality with sameness within perduring kyriarchal structures. We shall, hence, employ the language of equity rather than either equality or democracy. This is intended both to retain a sociopolitical force and to avoid a liberalistic reduction to sameness connoted by the language of equality.

What are the crucial defining features which might distinguish a logic of equity from a logic of identity? The most significant of these is indubitably a hospitality towards differences. We use the plural advisedly. If we speak of difference in the singular, it can raise the question: difference from what? This can actually end up by reifying existing patterns of Norm/Other which privilege the white, the male, the middle class, the heterosexual, and lock discussion back into a Hegelian reduction of difference to identity. Differences, plural, are not so reducible. Differences are excessive, and cannot be contained.

Differences, plurality, multiplicity: these are features which lay out a landscape of much greater texture than can or does identity politics.[3] This is a thick account of the world. We can add fluidity to this set. If the logic of equity does not proceed from reduction to essentializing categories, nor does it posit categories as fixed and stable. Against sameness and fixity is set multiplicity and fluidity. The logic of equity is, then, one which invites flux rather than strives to contain it, order it, control it. The logic of equity, in this respect, offers a thoroughly shifting and unstable framework for theorizing. This is not so, however, in all respects. A stress on differences can actually leave a political agenda bereft, for one step forward from this is into an ethical abyss which sees a collapse from acknowledgement of differences into sociopolitical indifference. This, perhaps, may be a different logic from that of identity, but it could scarcely be one congruent with a feminist perspective. If differences and flux are the terrain in which the logic of equity is positioned, emancipation is the direction towards which it points. The *ekklesia* is thoroughly ethical in constitution. The logic of equity in which the *ekklesia* constitutes itself is *both* multiple, shifting and fluid *and* ethically oriented.

Within this unstable landscape, how might we conceive of the gendered subject? Let us consider the category 'women'. The task is to avoid both essentializing and neutralizing accounts of gender. The first point to draw attention to is that we speak of the category 'women', not 'woman'. The latter lends itself to an essentializing account of femaleness in a way which the former can potentially resist. Yet if we refuse an essentialist account of femaleness, this does not mean that we must in consequence ignore, negate or transcend sexed bodiliness. If we do not suppose that 'biology is destiny' or that being a woman necessarily entails this or that particular sociopolitical situation or personality structure or sexuality, then being a woman is to live from a category which is neither universal nor essential. Being a woman can be seen as a biologically constituted condition – noting that biology does not fall outside of the realm of discourse – which in current sociopolitical structures (kyriarchy) is scored by a certain contingent commonality: the rendering as Other to man, played out in myriad ways in the realms of language, production, reproduction, metaphysics and so on. However, this is only a *certain* commonality, since it has been suggested already that subjectivity is mapped not in gender-dualistic terms but by a whole set of co-ordinates which are themselves culturally shifting and various.

We have, then, rejected conceptions of gendered identity based on sameness – signalled, indeed, by our preference for speaking of identity as gendered rather than of gender-identity. At the same time we have already indicated that, given the kyriarchal ordering of current conditions, it is expedient to recognize commonalities in the position of women within this system as a basis for political action. This could be deemed a form of 'strategic essentialism', for it appears to accept the kyriarchal projection of women into a culturally consistent grouping – however, in fact, it operates in a different key: it recognizes commonalities in the causes of women which are not reducible one to another but which nevertheless offer a basis for a shared but differentiated ground for speaking. This model mirrors that of the *ekklesia* itself, as a knotwork of differences which are nevertheless loosely woven together. This 'knotting together' is an important move because it disrupts and dislodges the dominant order by letting one of its repressed others 'speak', which might allow space for an equitable order to emerge. That, of course, is the ultimate goal of the *ekklesia*.

The Ekklesia *and Ethics*

It should be clear that the *ekklesia* is a profoundly ethical construct. Indeed, a commitment to equity and to justice within a counter-kyriarchal logic are the defining characteristics of the *ekklesia* as laid out here. However, a commitment to respecting differences, within a metaphysical worldview which denies sure foundations from which to speak, poses certain questions of the ethical constitution of the *ekklesia*. Namely, the *ekklesia* is certainly not relativist; how, then, do we theorize this such that it is consistent with a rejection of epistemological warrants grounded outside of the discursive site?

One response would take its cues from Habermas. Certainly, this would seem to be a logical move: Habermas, in his formulation of discourse ethics, utilizes the notion of an ideal speech community which surely resonates with an understanding of the *ekklesia* as an ideal rhetorical site from which to speak. Habermas

famously adheres to the metanarratives of modernity as an unfinished project; observing the fragmented conditions of late
modernity, his answer is not to turn to postmodernist gestures,
but to reinvigorate the liberal post-Enlightenment emancipatory
impulses. The principle on which Habermas sees ethics proceeding is communicative action. This supposes that the goal of
rational dialogue is to seek agreement; and the regulative centre
for ethics is therefore an ideal speech situation; truth and justice
become discursively oriented but not relativist. Critical philosophy should be guided by emancipatory interest, with the objective
of exposing the socioeconomic private interests and forces which
distort communication.[4] Norms and values can then be established intersubjectively in a compulsion-free speech situation by
rational consensus, in which the only force is that of the better
argument, and in which no argument should be excluded. This is
the ideal speech situation. It depends on a distinction between
distorted and undistorted communication and the premise that
norms and values in fact can be decided by rational consensus.

Habermas recognizes the contextuality of communication and
reflection but developed the theory of universal pragmatics to
justify the possibility of genuine intersubjective communication.
This aims to demonstrate that meaningful communication
presupposes certain conditions held in common: linguistic com-
prehensibility, propositional truth, intentional veracity, and
appropriateness. Discourse is the meta-communicative level at
which criteria for truth and value are decided. While all meaningful communicative action depends on the four validity-claims
above, the rational decidability of truth and norms is presupposed
at the level of discourse. The belief that norms and values can be
rationally discussed is, for Habermas, justified within a framework
of communicative ethics, in which only those interests which are
universalizable and generalizable survive.

Clearly, the discursive theorization of truth and justice in
Habermas' work also, like the idea of an ideal speech situation,
points to a certain common ground between his framework and
this one. Yet despite these obvious affinities, Habermas may in the
end not be so useful a resource as one might initially suppose.
Feminist philosopher Seyla Benhabib notes three distinct difficulties with Habermas' proposals (Benhabib, 1982). The first springs
from the goal of his ideal speech situation, which is to deliberate

rationally on generalizable interests: these, indeed, could *only* be articulated in the ideal speech situation, for only in such a context could interests be agreed as generalizable (Habermas, 1975, pp. 111–17). Yet, given that we inevitably speak from particular contexts, how could we actually formulate and judge such claims? Benhabib considers that there is a gulf in the positing of an ideal speech situation between 'the ideal and the actual, the normative and the empirical' which cannot be bridged. Furthermore, even if ideal speech conditions could be established, that does not in fact guarantee that rational intersubjective communication will take place, only that participants would have equitable access to the advancement of claims. This, then, is her second criticism: if the ideal speech situation depends on the rationality of arguments and evaluation, what is rational must be decided *a priori*. And thirdly, from whence would come the universal standards necessary to determine the validity of given communicative acts which are the basis for the discursive positing of generalizable norms? By homing in on the generalizable rather than the particular, there is another *a priori* distinction between legitimate and illegitimate interest claims, between distorted and undistorted communication, which imports the ideal of impartial decision-making into a contextually based forum proceeding from the assumption that reason is, by nature, interested.

In effect, the argument is that Habermas' discourse ethics runs aground on its failure to let go of the ideal of universalism. Beginning from a recognition that there is no guaranteed ground for making judgements, he nevertheless seeks to establish objectively valid and universalizable norms on the basis of communicative reason. This leads him to the positing of the ideal speech situation, as the only forum in which such principles could be impartially established. Yet the conditions for the ideal speech situation founder fatally on empirical inequitabilities in discursive practices, and on what basis could one critique the non-ideal speech situation if the basis for universalizable critique is an ideal speech situation?

Therefore, the ethical constitution of the *ekklesia* as outlined here shares Habermas' commitment to an ideal rhetorical speech situation and to the discursive formation of truth and justice, but takes leave of his communicative ethics in several crucial respects. The most important of these is an abandonment of the ideal

speech situation as the ground of ethical procedure, and its relocation as, rather, the goal. This means that we must look
elsewhere for the ethical grounds of the *ekklesia*, and it also means
that the nature of the ideal speech situation changes in key
respects which follow from a foregrounding of the fact that it is
unrealized. We shall see how this articulates in the discussion
below.

First, though, it is important to establish a distinction between
stating that norms are historical and contingent and stating that
norms are arbitrary. The two do not equate. The charge of relativism is often brought against worldviews proceeding from
postmodern rejection of absolutes and universal foundations.
This is an error which conflates the recognition that truth and
values are formulated in specific contexts and from specific
interests, rather than from the hypothetical 'Archimedean point',
with a belief that all values and truth-claims are thereby of equal
worth. Ethical viewpoints may be ultimately ungrounded, but that
does not make them groundless. Merely the grounds are themselves contingent. This leads to the protestation that it then
becomes impossible to justify one set of values and practices
rather than another. On the contrary, it does not become impossible: it becomes a matter of profound importance, which is,
however, a site of contestation. This introduces nothing new into
the practice of ethical discourse, which is historically anything but
monolithic.

It is necessary to ground feminist ethics in contingency because
of the potential epistemological crisis which arises from the destabilization and historicization of the subject. Under the impact
of anti-foundationalist philosophies, appeals cannot simply be
made to unmediated truths located externally to subjects.
However the 'subject' is itself a shaky foundation for theorizing.
Selves understood to be contextually anchored cannot occupy the
transcendent subject site of Kantian ethical theory. Selves which
are fluid and non-unified sites of conflict cannot act as a foundation for self-transparent ethical theorizing. Selves which do not
form part of stable and unified categories such as 'woman' cannot
ground ethics in appeals to privileged corporate standpoints such
as 'women's experience'. The instabilities inherent in individual
and communal constitution render identity politics of any sort a
problematic starting point for ethics. We need, therefore, to set

forth the non-arbitrary but contingent bases from which the ethics of the *ekklesia* can proceed.

Linda Hogan has offered some helpful principles for a feminist ethic which takes seriously the instability of 'woman' as subject and category. Praxis remains a central feature, understood as a noetic characteristic, as does 'women's experience'. However, she also observes that methodological consistency requires that 'one would be reluctant to make any claims apart from the radical historicity and diversity of women's experience and praxis. The social and historical character of feminist ethics' primary resources makes the language of certitude impossible to retain'(Hogan, 1993, p. 89). Hence, there is a danger of impotence in the ethical realm which she seeks to overcome. The crucial move is to resist both universalism and relativism. This is achieved in her articulation of provisional prolegomena to the development of a feminist ethical theory.

The limitation of ethical appeal to pragmatic rather than onto-logical foundations plays a central role in her account. Such pragmatic grounds in a feminist ethic would be based on the posi-tionality of women in networks of shifting power relations (see Alcoff, 1988). This enables a critical ethical voice to be raised which is rooted in women's locations within and outside of ideolo-gies and institutions, validated by the nature of commitment and values inspired (Hogan, 1993, p. 92). The risk of a subjectivism which would not allow for arbitration between perspectives and experiences is combated by the centralization of community. This reflects a commitment to dialogue as epistemological context. It might seem that here relativism has simply been displaced from the personal to the social; Hogan concedes that at one level this is 'inevitable', but points out that the community, as centre of 'enquiry, debate and dialogue' is not the individual 'writ large' (Hogan, 1993, p. 94). A bulwark against relativism is introduced by Carol Christ's notion of 'embodied thinking' (Christ, 1989), which unsettles a polarization between 'truth' and 'contextuality': 'We should think of our "truth claims" as the product of embodied thinking not as eternally or universally valid thought' (Christ, 1989, p. 15; Hogan, 1993, p. 96). This resources the advocacy of one worldview rather than another with reference to experience, praxis and embodied being; while all universal truth claims are culturally relative, not all truth claims are thereby deemed equal. Injustice is validly denounced because of particular experiences of injustice. This may suggest that no transcontextual critique could be offered, and that we could have nothing to say to injustices perpetrated on others and not ourselves. That possibility is warded off by insisting, with Sharon Welch, that to express our resistance to injustice in its multiple formations what we need is a concept of universal *accountability*; this begins from the particular, but is attentive to the particular experiences of others and the impact of our own practices upon them (Welch, 1985, p. 81; Hogan, 1993, p. 97).

Hogan's sketch leaves us with four preliminary principles for an adequate feminist ethics: pragmatic foundations, the centrality of community, embodied thinking, and accountability. In this articulation, the *ekklesia* clearly occupies the central site of community, as a community of feminist communities. This is the feminist rhetorical space of debate and disagreement. We can now begin to perceive some of the ways in which the *ekklesia*, as centre of feminist ethics, differs from the ideal speech situation as central to Habermas' discourse ethics. Accountability means that the *ekklesia* is not only concerned with interests which are generalizable, but with the particularities of others' experiences and articulations of the world. Indeed, if thinking is embodied, then it is the particular and not the general which excites orientation towards the other in the ethical imagination. 'Rational argument' is displaced from a position of primacy, to be replaced by the articulations of 'communities of resistance and solidarity' which are rooted in experiences of oppression. This does not, of course, exclude or marginalize 'rational' ethical debate; rather, it broadens the kind of discourse which the *ekklesia* hosts. The *ekklesia* proceeds from the assumption that the speech situation is not ideal. If the speech situation were ideal, then conditions of equity would already have been established. The *ekklesia* is an ethically oriented speech space lodged in profoundly inequitable sociopolitical discursive orderings. It seeks to establish an ideal speech situation in its commitment to polyphonic and open enquiry and dialogue, but it does not aim monolithically to solicit agreement and consensus. Such would be, as Benhabib terms it, a 'transcendental illusion' requiring the elimination of plurality and human differentiation into a 'self-identical collectivity' (Benhabib, 1982, p. 71). It is also a frankly *a priori* justice-seeking community of communities, constituted by a feminist emancipatory interest, pragmatically grounded in particular embodied experiences, praxis and thinking.

Conclusion

Feminism should not disdain its liberal heritage. Liberal ideals of freedom, equality and justice; of openness, of value for pluralism and diversity; liberal emphasis on dialogue, on questioning given truths and authorities: these should continue to resonate with feminist agendas. It is true, as we have seen, that liberalism and liberal feminism have both generated criticisms of some weight. But liberalism, if it is to be true to its own philosophies, cannot be cast in stone as an unchanging dogma, forever entrapped in the flaws of the past. Rather, feminists, and others sympathetic to liberal ideas, should move to reclaim liberalism, to refashion it more appropriately for their purposes. What could be more liberal than such a self-reconstitution in the light of contemporary needs and concerns?

Much of this chapter worked towards just such a refashioning and recontextualization of liberalism in the light of feminism and postmodernism.[5] The structural analysis of critical feminist theologies of liberation became a crucial part of the framework, the more adequately to incorporate diverse oppressions. The liberal subject, the neutral individual preceding society, became positioned within shifting social configurations. This subject does not transcend its own locations, including that of its own bodiliness: but nor, in the non-essentialist framework espoused, is it determined by them. Reason and experience remain key criteria, but within a framework attentive to the contextuality of knowledge. Liberal individualism transmutes into a concern for specificity and particularity within community: this was theoretically conceived through development of Fiorenza's notion of the *ekklesia*, an imagined community of communities, hospitable towards differences within a shared ethical perspective set counter to that of kyriarchal formations. Lastly, the question of warrants for these emancipatory narratives was addressed. The argument took shape in counterpoint to Habermas' attempt to rescue the unfinished project of liberal modernity and with reference to Hogan's work (1993); it was put forward that feminist ethics could be grounded appropriately in pragmatism, community and contextuality. Such ethics could not claim a universal foundation but ought properly to be universally accountable.

This set of suggestions is undoubtedly one of many which might be formulated. The point is that liberalism has never been static and we should not be afraid to robustly reclaim those key tenets of liberalism which we wish to continue to affirm. Liberal feminism may have fallen into disrepute. Some may say that liberal theology is a dying relic of the nineteenth century. But the conversation between liberalism, feminism and theology has not had its day.

Notes

1 Fiorenza uses the term wo/men because she wants to transcend the sex/gender polarity. She uses it in order to destabilize the category 'women' so that it may refer to all women and also marginalized men.

2 The conceptual origins of the term are with Edouard Glissant. For further elaboration of the themes in the remainder of the chapter, see Jobling (1999).

3 I use 'identity politics' here to signify sociopolitical frameworks ordered according to particular identity categories, whether understood as constructed or pre-discursive. The connection between identity politics in this sense and the logic of identity should be plain. This is a necessary clarification, because the phrase is variously utilized: Linda Alcoff uses it in a quite different sense, to denote the construction of identity by political action (Alcoff, 1988, p. 432).

4 Habermas argues that all knowledge is constituted by interest, identifying three broad categories of human inquiry. The first is empirical–analytical and reflects a technical interest which objectifies the object of study in order to produce general laws of prediction with respect to it and to manipulate it. This is an instrumental reason. The second is historical–hermeneutical and springs from a practical interest in understanding human communication and action. The third is critical sciences and philosophies, which demonstrate an emancipatory interest as exemplified by ideological critique or psychoanalysis. See *Knowledge and Human Interests*, Beacon, Boston, 1971.

5 Inevitably, given constraints of space, this discussion is notable for its limitations. For a further expansion of the nature of the *ekklesia* and gendered subject, see Jobling, J., *Restless Readings*. PhD thesis, unpub., 1999. For an expansion of the argument into the realms of theological doctrines, see the forthcoming work of Hannah Bacon on the trinity within a liberal–postmodern framework.

References

Alcoff, L., 'Cultural Feminism vs Post-Structuralist Feminism: the Identity Crisis in Feminist Theory', *Signs*, 13.3, 1988, pp. 405–36.

Benhabib, S., 'The Methodological Illusions of Modern Political Theory: The Case of Rawls and Habermas', *Neue hefte fur philosophie*, 21 (Spring), 1982, pp. 47–74.

Bible and Culture Collective, *The Postmodern Bible*, Yale University Press, New Haven and London, 1995.

Chopp, R., 'Latin American Liberation Theology', in Ford, D. (ed.), *The Modern Theologians: An Introduction to Christian Thought in the Twentieth Century*, Blackwell, Massachusetts and Oxford, 1997.

Christ, C., 'Embodied Thinking: Reflections on Feminist Theological Method', *Journal of Feminist Studies in Religion*, Spring, 1989, pp. 7–15.

Damico, A. J., *Liberals on Liberalism*, Rowman and Littlefield Publishers, New Jersey, 1986.

Eisenstein, Z. R., *Feminism and Sexual Equality*, Monthly Review Press, New York, 1984.

Fiorenza, E. S., 'G*d at Work in our Midst: From a Politics of Identity to a Politics of Struggle', *Feminist Theology*, 13, 1996, pp. 47–72.

Friedan, B., *The Feminine Mystique*, Victor Gollancz Ltd, London, 1965.

Habermas, J., *Legitimation Crisis*, Beacon, Boston, 1975.

Hogan, L. 'Resources For a Feminist Ethic: Women's Experience and Praxis', *Feminist Theology*, 3, 1993, pp. 82–99.

Murray, J., 'Liberation for Communion in the Soteriology of Gustavo Gutierrez', *Theological Studies*, 59, 1, 1998, pp. 51–9.

Nash, K., *Universal Difference*, Macmillan Press, London, 1998.

Niebuhr, H. R., *Theology, History, and Culture,* Johnson, W. S. (ed.), Yale University Press, New Haven and London, 1996.

Pena, M., 'Feminist Christian Women in Latin America: Other Voices, Other Visions', *Journal of Feminist Studies in Religion*, 11, 1, 1995, pp. 81–94.

Schleiermacher, F., *On Religion: Speeches to its Cultural Despisers*. Trans. Oman, J., Harper and Row Publishers, New York, 1958.

Welch, S., *Communities of Resistance and Solidarity*, Orbis Books, Maryknoll, 1985.

Wollstonecraft, M., *A Vindication of the Rights of Women*, printed for J. Johnson, London, 1792.

CHAPTER EIGHT

Reluctant Communion: On Sacrificing Purity

Martyn Percy

If we had more humility we should probably have much fewer difficulties to encounter than we have [. . .] And that we may not be otherwise, do not let us hastily set ourselves up to condemn any of these systems and those who propound them. Our consciences, I believe, have told us from time to time that there is something in each of them which we ought not to reject. Let us not reject it. But we may find, that there is a divine harmony, of which the living principle in each of these systems forms one note, of which the systems themselves are a disturbance and violation. (Maurice, 1837, p. 308)

How does the proverb go? 'The first casualty in war is truth.' So, Anglicans ought to be doubly concerned when wars, rumours of wars, along with talk of legitimized schisms and rifts start to surface within the mother church of the Anglican Communion – the Church of England. Standing as we are, on the shoreline of the Third Millennium, it is still not difficult to forget some of the ugly scenes that took place at the Lambeth Conference at Canterbury during the summer of 1998. On matters of sexuality in particular, the talk was of irrational fears, of a new strident conservatism, of an old and dominant liberalism, of traditionalism, homophobia or homosexuality, and of a split between North and South – reminiscent of the first Great Schism of over a thousand years ago, between the East and West. It seems to be the usual story. In spite of the many good and excellent things that were going on at Lambeth, the public were nevertheless presented with a picture of a Communion that was unravelling, unable to keep itself together any more, agree on common services, ordination, consecration, and its own future. Things are falling apart: the centre, as Yeats says, cannot hold.

At that Conference, it was Rowan Williams, the Bishop of Monmouth, who won the dubious award – gifted by Andrew Brown, a Religious Affairs Correspondent who writes for a number of newspapers – of having 'the most interesting failure' of the Conference. Dr Williams gave a keynote address on making moral decisions. It was a lecture of considerable subtlety and some substance, which, for all the effect it had, Brown noted that 'he might as well have delivered it in a motorway service station'. After the lecture, Brown states that Williams commented: 'Wittgenstein said that the most important thing a philosopher can say to another is "give yourself time". The question is whether we can, in some sense, bear to keep talking to each other.'

Well, can we? It would seem that when we get to issues such as the Act of Synod, women bishops, Third Provinces, Theologies of Reception, anthropologies of purity, and then, of course, the inevitable talk of schism, Anglicans have indeed lost the art of talking to one another. So, the central questions I wish to concern myself with are these. Can Anglicans re-learn the art of talking to one another in a fractured Communion? Second, is there anything that liberalism can particularly contribute to this art and practice? Third, if the first casualty of war is indeed truth, then what is liberalism supposed to do in order to rehabilitate it? All of these questions are part of the background in determining how liberals in the Church of England engage in debate, relating to women bishops.

Before any of these questions can be addressed, it is important to identify the context in which the questions are set. There can be no doubt that the Church of England has always had its 'wings'. Characteristically these have been enormously important to the Church, tilting it this way or that. The Evangelical and Catholic wings of the Church have hardly ever, except for a few brief periods in Anglican history, regarded themselves as being 'central' (either of occupancy or constitution): in short, they have understood that their identity and role is comprised through influencing but not inhabiting the centre.

In this respect, T. S. Eliot is right – Anglicanism is a *via media* (Eliot, 1928, p. 14). As every schoolchild knows, a fall-out with the Pope doesn't equate to a true Reformation – and this has been the

English situation for almost 500 years. Catholics proclaim the priority of sacraments, a threefold order of ministry and the priority of bishops. But this version of ecclesiology is rather snookered by the fact that many of the key decisions in the Church of England are ultimately taken by the House of Laity, also known as the House of Commons. Synodical government, moreover, stands somewhere between this; and ultimate authority lies with the Crown. In short, the English Church is the people's church, and the historical mistrust of the Catholicism within its ranks is matched in equal measure by suspicion of Evangelicalism – just look at the treatment meted out to John Bunyan. The English are not a people of particular excess, but of liberal breadth.

I am conscious that this is a contestable thesis. Nevertheless, I think that in speaking of the two wings of a church, some kind of centre is implied, and that this is still a pretty good 'map' of what the Church of England is. How does David Martin put it? 'I see the English Church primarily as some rather beautiful 16th and 17th century bottles, cracked by some rather dubious evangelical and Anglo-catholic wine' (Martin, 1967, p. 110). The political, social, theological and cultural centre of the Church of England has always been characteristically 'broad', but in a very gentle-liberal kind of way – embodying qualities of mellowness, openness, dialogue, tolerance and the like. In turn, this places enormous responsibility on those in the centre, since it becomes absolutely imperative that the centre does not lose these wings. Another way of expressing this would be to paraphrase another remark of T. S. Eliot: we are against the tail wagging the dog, but equally, against cutting the tail off. And so to those questions.

Can Anglicans Re-learn the Art of Talking to One Another?

According to Peter Kevern (Kevern, 1999), there is a reciprocal relationship between ecclesiology and practice in the Church of England. Logical arguments are invoked in support of a given course of action; conversely, pragmatic positions adopted by the Church eventually find expression as ecclesiological arguments. The debate on women's ordination represents an anomalous instance of this process, because it has resulted in two parallel 'integrities'. Each integrity has separate beliefs about the wisdom of such ordinations, backed up in both cases by a range of internally coherent ecclesiological positions. Those of the opponents of women's ordination are, on the whole, less widely noted, and less lucidly expressed.

Partly due to the fragile nature of the Communion at present, and also to a rather odd enclave mentality, the practical beliefs of the two integrities are mutually exclusive. Of course, these ecclesiologies have far more in common than is immediately apparent. As I have argued before, Anglicanism is carried in a kind of kinship – a sort of familial morphology in which mutual recognition is often quickly discerned (Percy, 1998b, pp. 163ff). There is initial evidence for this, in the fact that of those opposing the ordination of women, few have abandoned the Church of England, despite losing the debate.[1] Oddly, both sides profess to share a structured way of thinking about the Church, a meta-ecclesiology if you will, in which both wings and the centre recognize something of the other, even if they are so far not giving formal expression to it.

Naturally, there are deeper issues behind the ordination of women which proscribe against a fully cohering worshipping Communion. There is disagreement on weighty matters such as the nature of ecclesiastical authority, the relation between the Holy Spirit and the Church, and the function and duties of the Church of England within the wider ecumenical milieu. This all sounds very serious on one level, yet it pays to recall James Gordon Melton's sociological treatment of churches in terms of 'families'. For all the protestations of Forward in Faith, or proponents of Third Provinces, it is simply not very easy for your average Anglo-Catholic to feel 'at home' in Roman Catholicism (Melton, 1978).

In some of my conversations with Anglican theologians, as well as church historians, I have become struck by how much of the coherence of Anglicanism depends on good manners. This sounds, at face value, like an extraordinarily elitist statement. It is clearly not meant to be that. What I mean by manners is learning to speak well, behave well, and to be able to conduct yourself with integrity in the midst of an argument. At the risk of introducing another proverb (and turning it), it isn't so much a case of 'manners maketh man', but 'manners maketh communion'. Reading some of the recent contributions from liberal theologians to debates on the nature of the Church and its authority, I have been struck by how the authentic voice of liberalism has been a kind of plea for old-fashioned Anglican manners to be restored to their rightful place. It is often the case, that in Anglicans' disputes about doctrine, order or faith, it is actually the means that matter far more than the ends. Because Anglicanism is a *via media*, there is an unwritten expectation that there will be very few ends that we actually arrive at – which places all the more importance on the means of not quite getting there. Therefore, politeness, integrity, restraint, diplomacy, patience, a willingness to listen, and above all, not to be ill-mannered – these are things that enable the Anglican Communion to cohere, as it continues in its pilgrimage for truth (Percy, 2000).

There is ample enough evidence of this approach to ecclesiology in the works of Richard Hooker, the sermons of Launcelot Andrewes, and many others who hail from the Caroline period. Hooker is a model of engaging, polite, passionate and persuasive polemic. Hooker and Andrewes could demolish their opponents in sermons with a well-turned phrase, but what is more remarkable about the texts of theirs that we have inherited, is the combination of restraint and passion, rather than any attempt to launch a full-blooded assault. They understood that in 'winning' an argument prematurely, communion was impaired; truth was comprehended, but necessarily delayed. It is these people who are the architects of Anglicanism, and we would do well to heed their example (Percy, 1998a).

Can Liberals Contribute to the Coherence and Practice of Communion?

In a recent essay for the *Church Times*, Peter Selby notes that part of the cost of belonging to a church is 'sacrificing a straightforward confidence in our own purity' (Selby, 1999, p. 11). Communion is something that is necessarily shared; and correspondingly we are all touched by one another's failures, and the necessary incompleteness of what constitutes church life. Selby's essay leans on the parable of the wheat and tares and presents a characteristically systematic and passionate plea for living together in tension, rather than trying to pre-empt the refining fire of God by building a pure church on this side of the Parousia.

As he notes, situating the Church in that context, is not 'a plea for
flaccid tolerance, let alone indifference on the matters of
profound importance'. It is, on the other hand, a plea to try to
work together as much as possible for the widest common good.

Liberals, and all those who might claim the 'broad' title,
continue to occupy much of the central space in the Church, and
therefore have particular responsibilities to bear at this point. It is
not in the character of liberalism to walk away from dialogue, or
to behave in a sectarian manner. As Selby notes again, 'the structures of our church hold open the possibility of truth discovered
in taking risks'. Equally, on the other hand, they 'hold open to us
the possibility of shared decisions, or truth to be discovered when
we take risks with and for each other. The frustrations and
tensions, and the loss of purity involved might turn out to be a
price worth paying, despite all the apparent advantages of
guarding our individual consciences' (Selby, 1999, p. 11).

In this respect, Selby holds to a classic Anglican liberal line. To
paraphrase a writer from an earlier generation, Alec Vidler, the
liberal vocation, faithfully exercised, is not only humbling, but
also reconciling. It has the effect of showing that no party, or
school of thought, or phase of orthodoxy, is ever as right as its pro-
tagonists are inclined to suppose, and that [men], including
Christian men, have much more in common both of frailty and
strength, both of falsehood and truth, than the makers of systems
and sects acknowledge. As a true English liberal, Vidler proscribes
liberalism in the very act of preaching for it.

In Vidler's *Essays in Liberality* (1970), he suggests that the patron
saint of theologians ought to be the person who is tolerant; not
because they regard all opinions as doubtful, but because they
know that God alone is true. The person who is ready to learn
from all people, not because he or she has no creed of their own,
but because their creed assures them that God is teaching and
chastening all people, the man who has plumbed the meaning for
the human intellect of the great New Testament word about
having nothing and yet possessing all things; that person who can
at once rigorously doubt and sincerely believe epitomizes the true
spirit of liberalism. In short, the person who has discovered that it
is not only the sinner, but the doubter, who is justified by faith. For
Vidler, this is the liberal heart of Christianity, and the making of
its patron saint.

Behind Vidler stands the deeper liberalism of scholars such as Isaiah Berlin. Berlin is conscious of the tension between liberty and equality, which is frequently at the heart of liberal dilemmas (Berlin, 1991, pp. 12–18). Equality may demand the restraint of liberty. Equally, liberty may prevent degrees of equality: in liberalism, there is always a collision of values, which reflects the very essence of what we are as individual human beings, and as collective peoples – or a communion. Berlin is clear that the primary task of pursuing the ideal of liberalism is to avoid extremes, particularly extremes of suffering. Yet in order to do that, Berlin states that it becomes necessary to live with tensions. Of course, one does not opt for intolerable choices – but one is often left with a precarious equilibrium. 'A certain humility in matters is very necessary', he writes. Moreover, he goes on to point out that 'out of the crooked timber of humanity, no straight thing was ever made'. And because of this, liberals need to be particularly wary of fortifying a centre in the Church that somehow will be alienating or sectarian. The first task of liberalism therefore must be to maintain a kind of peaceful openness, which will be the foundation of a true communion. The very idea of church and communion rests upon this. Churches are places of education, among other things, where one can learn to live in fellowship and love with those we disagree with strongly, and yet still share in the life and liberty of the body of Christ (Berlin, 1991, p. 17).

Is the Truth Suffering?

The honest answer to this question is 'Yes'. But I have phrased the question in a deliberately ambiguous way in order to highlight the double bind that is at the heart of the obligation of belonging to and believing in communion. Yes, of course, we strive for the truth – yet it is beyond us. And so, the truth does indeed suffer, for what we now have is imperfect. And even when we have grasped, in Tolstoy's phrase, 'the truth has been, is, and will be beautiful', we know that however that is carried in communion, it will be imperfect. On the other hand, truth is therefore suffering – that is an existential statement that precisely clarifies our present situation, and yet strangely carries us forward.

Campaigning liberals, at this point, could rightly feel rather nervous about a liberalism that, in one sense, apparently accepts the *status quo*. I want to make it clear that I am not advocating that. I am quite clearly and plainly in favour of women bishops, as I indeed campaigned before for women priests. And yet to belong to a church, which I recognize as not having the whole truth (yet striving for it), I want to say that the very conditions of communion have to bear tensions within them in order for the communion to adequately flourish.

To return to my earlier analogies about families, manners, behaviour and language; we can see this at work in almost any issue that threatens to divide the Church. For example, if journalists had one pound for every bishop that said they 'held to the statements published in the report *Issues in Human Sexuality*, on the issue of homosexuality, there'd be, well – they would have about a hundred pounds by now. Because journalists are interested in truth, they know that 'holding' to a statement can mean many different things. Journalists also know that very few Church of England bishops believe that the report, in addressing homosexuality, is now the last word on the subject. It is clearly not a definitive statement that can now be sewn into the canon of Scripture. Rather, it is some kind of linguistic attempt to hold things together with a degree of civility. Clearly, not everybody is blessed by this; but neither is everybody hurt by it. As we noted from Berlin earlier, liberty and equality are actually competitive, even within the most coherent communions.

The apparently defensive rhetoric of 'holding' to a statement – a comment that is designed to deflect questions – may satisfy anxious churchgoers, but it does not throw a good journalist off the scent. 'Holding' can mean anything from 'Amen' to 'I accept it but don't really agree'; or, 'This is a temporary political settlement' to 'This is as far as we'll be going at the moment'. The problem journalists have is that few bishops will actually say any of that precisely – which is actually what they mean. The rhetoric of 'holding' is therefore rendered porous, and journalists are inclined to try to flush out the truth, rather than settle for the prevailing political patois.

But what is the truth in this matter? Actually, the Church and its bishops are not really being evasive when they use language that can be read on many levels, ranging from the literal to the subtle. Such statements are part of a long tradition in the Church that uses language as a mesh for holding together polarities, tensions and differing perceptions of the truth. Just look at the creeds. In short, telling the truth in this kind of way deliberately lacks precision as a matter of pastoral priority. To be too precise about what you mean now – on any issue, especially a sensitive and contested one – can foreclose on future options, and the Church of England does not believe that it owns the truth, but rather that it is owned by it. This means that there is often a necessary humility about its statements, which is sometimes mistakenly interpreted as blandness or woolliness, which in turn rather misreads the motives.

Finally, there is something utterly holy about such a vocation. In promoting restraint, bishops (or any other church leaders) are practising a particularly paternal role. Restraint is an important key in the coherence of familial and ecclesial bodies, and, where offered, can usually promote growth and maturity. An absence of restraint means that assertion, dogma, anger, precipitous action and passions can run riot. Restraint, in contrast, models holiness for all parties, reminding us that discipline is inseparable from love. With giving and offering, comes the spiritual responsibility of withholding and abstaining.

Conclusion

So, compromise is often preached because it really is the case that our knowledge is partial and not complete. The Church makes up its mind slowly, because it is part of that work which is 'gathering all creation into Christ'. And, of course, the Church of England is the people's church: so all harmful words are avoided where possible.

'Compromise' may appear to be a rather ugly term in connection with this debate. Why should women, or liberals for that matter, agree to compromise on the issue of women bishops? I am not of course, suggesting that they should. But I am suggesting that it is desirable and necessary for liberals to keep the interests of communion close to its heart as it debates, and not respond to sectarianism in equal style and measure. Moreover, liberals are especially obliged to find ground on which thesis and antithesis can dialogue and unite, to remain open themselves, and to recognize that it will take time for others to understand and share the vision of a church where equality and freedom flourish. This means that finding some (temporary) middle ground now may leave many on both sides unhappy. Yet the commitment to compromise is one based on the virtues of reconciliation, settlement and co-operation. Beyond that, one can trace a theological idea, in which God himself apparently compromises his divinity in order to redeem humanity. The incarnation, the initiative of God in Jesus, is an embodied risk; communion is achieved through the sacrifice of purity. Liberalism cannot afford to be less. Vladimir Lossky, the Orthodox theologian, puts it like this: 'By his birth of the Virgin, He suppressed the division of human nature into male and female' (Lossky, 1976, p. 137).[2]

Here, Lossky expresses the necessary inter-connection between sacrifice and communion, which is a vocation for all Christians, no matter how worthy their cause, or vital their truth.

For Anglican liberals, it does in the end boil down to continuing to develop proper, well-informed theological manners; yet at the same time, these should not always and automatically be observed at the expense of striving for the truth. It is surely right to push forward for sensible and just causes such as women priests and women bishops. However, as I have commented before on liberalism, the means of working for these sorts of things are just as important as the ends. Furthermore, liberals are perhaps uniquely obliged to try to hold all things together in tension, as they at the same time seek truth and equality. It is therefore imperative that any campaigning by liberals is marked by compassion, that discussions are ones that foster genuine dialogue, and that liberals remain well mannered, open and thoughtful throughout. This is the example the liberal centre can embody and offer to its wings. That, in the end, is the strength and virtue of liberalism, not its weakness. How does Vidler put it? 'A liberal-minded man is free from narrow prejudice, generous in his judgment of others, open-minded, especially to the reception of new ideas or proposals [. . .] Liberal is not the opposite of conservative, but of fanatical or bigoted or intransigent. It points to the *esprit large* away from the *idée fixe* (Vidler, 1970, p. 93).

Vidler's words remind us of some of the great liberal prophets of the twentieth century, such as Martin Luther King or Nelson Mandela. The causes and people that these men worked for cannot be doubted; neither can their commitment to equality and truth. Yet in pursuing their goal of justice, something even more lay beyond it: reconciliation. Sometime, somewhere, the torturer and the persecuted would sit down and eat together; the victor and the vanquished sup from the same cup. For liberals, beyond the horizon of justice and rights lies a vision of a reconciled communion.

Now, none of the walls that are built within churches to protect a particular purity or various integrities are capable of reaching to heaven. There, all divisions are suppressed, as they are in Christ. So liberalism, at some cost to itself, must always keep open the doors to the causes it most cherishes, to the truths it most ardently advocates, and to the teachings it sincerely insists upon. It is only by these doors remaining open that others may see, and come in. For communion to flourish, all parties must accept that the purity of their identity and beliefs will be compromised – even those of liberalism – if the Communion is to be genuine and true. Only by such generous love for the other, will liberalism be known as an expression of Christ's freedom. Only by 'bearing all things, hoping all things', can liberalism claim to embody the gospel, and lead a nervous and uncertain Church from its fragile centre, to a new future, in which all can participate.

Notes

1 The statistics are contentious. An average of 250 clergy may leave stipendiary ministry in any one year. In 1994, the year women were ordained in the Church of England, more than 400 left. Up to 2000, some 30 or more who left the Church of England over the ordination of women and were ordained into the Roman Catholic Church have since returned. At present there are 250 'Resolution C' parishes in the Church of England – several dioceses short of a Third Province.
2 Lossky is paraphrasing St Maximus the Confessor's *De Ambiguis*, P.G., 91, p. 1309.

References

Berlin, I., *The Crooked Timber of Humanity*, HarperCollins, London, 1991.
Church of England House of Bishops, *Issues in Human Sexuality*, a statement by the House of Bishops of the General Synod of the Church of England, Church House Publishing, London, December 1991.
Eliot, T. S., 'Launcelot Andrewes', in *Essays on Style and Content*, Faber, London, 1928.
Kevern, P., *Unity, Diversity and Trinity in the Rhetoric of the 1998 Lambeth Con-*

ference, PhD Thesis, University of Birmingham, 1999.

Lossky, V., *The Mystical Theology of the Eastern Church*, SVS Press, New York, 1976.

Martin, D., 'Interpreting the Figures' in Perry, M., (ed.) *Crisis for Confirmation?*, SCM, London, 1967.

Maurice, F. D., *The Kingdom of Christ: Hints on the Principles, Ordinances and Constitution of the Catholic Church*, J. M. Dent, London, 1837.

Melton, J., *Encyclopaedia of Religion in the USA*, Gale, Washington DC, 1978.

Percy, M., *Introducing Richard Hooker*, DLT, London, 1998a.

Percy, M., *Power and the Church: Ecclesiology in an Age of Transition*, Cassell, London, 1998b.

Percy, M., 'Reflections on the "Gift of Authority"', FOAG paper, 2000.

Selby, P., 'The Parable of the Wheat and the Tares', *Church Times*, 17 December 1999.

Vidler, A., *Essays In Liberality*, SCM, London, 1991.

CHAPTER NINE

Liberal Theology and Church Structures

Giles Legood

THE LIVERPOOL STATEMENT on theology in modern Britain ('A New Theological Vision') called on its readers to rise to the challenge of engagement with contemporary culture. The signatories to the Statement argued that: 'We must engage openly with our contemporary culture. We need to demonstrate that our tradition has the resources to engage in an ongoing dialogue with the social, cultural and political problems of our age.' Those who drew up the Statement and those who later assented to it further felt that this would require 'a critical openness to interdisciplinary work and the richness of much contemporary culture'. To fully engage in such a challenge as this is no easy task in any culture, let alone our own, where so many are ready to say that we now live in a post-Christian Britain where religious talk is a language game in which few can participate and in which fewer choose to participate.

However, contrary to such voices of doom predicting the end of significant religious input into our country's public life, there are signs in certain quarters of encouragement. One example of optimism is close at hand for the contributors to this book: the world of higher education. The university sector (known intimately in various ways by the contributors) is one in which the areas of theology and religious studies are not only holding their own but are at the vanguard of educational expansion and have increasing interest and influence within British universities. Departments of theology and religious studies are attracting more research students than ever before, numbers of mature students are increasing at all levels, there has been a rapid expansion of taught postgraduate courses. Indeed there are now more university departments dedicated to such study than known previously, there are approximately 400 people teaching in publicly funded departments, and there is a further tranche of people teaching in theological colleges, seminaries and Bible colleges.

If this then is the state of religion in the world of higher learning, might there be a message here for the Churches as they consider their role in the twenty-first century? Because of the plurality of religious traditions now alive in Britain and the decline of the Established Church's influence in certain spheres of public life, there are calls from some within the Church of England (and some without) for the Church to be disestablished. Such calls, together with the diminishing resources of ordained personnel within all the mainstream Christian denominations in this country, have forced the churches to re-examine what sort of ministry and mission they are undertaking in modern Britain, both nationally and locally. What has been largely missing from these deliberations, however, has been a sustained consideration of how the Church might inform public life and be informed by it in turn. Whilst admittedly debates such as how many bishops and other religious representatives might sit in a new House of Lords and what sort of oath the future King Charles III might swear at his Coronation have seized newspaper column inches (if not public imagination), what is additionally needed is further hard thinking about how the Church is to exercise its task locally as well as nationally.

The rest of this chapter will argue that, far from being pessimistic about the future of religion in Britain, the Churches, having noted the prosperous state of theology and religious studies in British universities, ought to have confidence that religion is not past its sell-by date but is (to extend the analogy) still a fresh product and is attractive to many consumers. If Christianity is to have something relevant to say to individual people's lives, the Church must engage with people in meaningful ways in situations where people spend much of their time, and in a way which will make connections between the world of work and matters of faith. In addition to thinking about the Church's national life, the mainstream Christian denominations have rightly thought about the parish or congregational systems within which they operate. What further needs to be thought about, however, is the ministry of those ordained Christians who do not primarily work in such ways. Such clergy (mostly called 'chaplains') work largely with those who do not go to church (and therefore those whom the Church claims it most wants to reach). The experiences and voices of such clergy (and others who work in their various fields) can both inform the Church about the sectors worked in and inform the sectors about the Church. This is an exciting prospect as there is the possibility of real dialogue and mutual learning.

This dialogue and mutual learning can take place in a number of different areas of interest and expertise. There are hundreds of clergy and other licensed workers employed as chaplains in a wide variety of settings in Britain. Significant numbers of these people work in large institutions such as the armed forces, hospitals, universities, schools and prisons. Others work in chaplaincies to smaller institutions or groups of people where there is not such an established historic link between the Church and the host culture. Examples of this second group include sectors such as industry, police forces, seafaring, airports and agriculture. Even those sectors with a longer established history of chaplaincy involvement have not, for the large part, had an involvement lasting hundreds of years. Most chaplaincies have arisen over the past 100 years. In this country, the Church's formal links with people's lives has mostly been based on a residential model, based on where people live, rather than an employment model, based on where they work. In order to understand the latter and to suggest how contemporary church structures may have to be remade or reinvented, it is first necessary for us to appreciate more fully the residential, parochial model of the Church's ministry.

History of the Parish System

Christianity was already well established in England before Augustine of Canterbury arrived in Kent in 597 to meet King Ethelbert who allowed him to settle and preach in his kingdom. In each of the kingdoms of the land the local bishop would first build a church and then a school at which the king and chiefs would be invited to send their sons to be educated. The bishop would send out priests from this centre on missionary journeys into the surrounding areas to teach and baptize. Accounts of such journeys and such a style of ministry are frequently recorded by Bede who writes, in summing up the work of this period,

Wherever any priest or monk paid a visit, he was joyfully welcomed by all as the servant of God. And if people met him on the road, they ran to him and bowed, eager to be signed by his hand or receive a blessing from his lips [. . .] When a priest visited a village, the people were quick to gather together to receive the word of life; for priests and clerics always came to a village solely to preach, baptise, visit the sick, and, in short to care for the souls of its people. (Bede, 1968, p. 194)

It seems that once a significant number of people in an area had been converted to Christianity the priest would arrange to make periodic visits to administer the sacraments and would hold an act of worship at a convenient place. Before churches were built, such places where the people used to gather to meet with the priest would often be marked by a cross of stone or wood, perhaps at a site previously used for ancient religious ceremonies. Some of these crosses survive today.

With the coming of Theodore (c. 602–90), however, a new chapter in English church history begins. Theodore, an Asiatic Greek (and therefore a member of the Eastern Church), arrived in around 668 having been sent by Pope Vitalian on the recommendation of Hadrian who accompanied him to Britain. In 673 he called a synod, presided over by Hlothere, King of Kent, at Hertford, which was attended by all the English bishops, with one exception, and by the kings and many of the most important members of the nobility and clergy. At this synod it was agreed by the independent national Churches to unite in an ecclesiastical province, with the Archbishop of Canterbury as its Metropolitan. Those attending also agreed that the bishops and other clergy should meet in synod twice each year. Augustine and his successors at Canterbury, although holding the titular distinction of Archbishop of Canterbury which Pope Gregory I had given them, had never been really more than bishops to the people of Kent. However, Bede tells us in his *Ecclesiastical History* that Theodore was the first Archbishop whom all the Churches of the English obeyed. This position was to give Theodore the authority which he would need to carry out the plans he had for reforming and uniting the English Church.

Theodore set about his task of reform by first breaking up some of the larger dioceses. In this he met considerable opposition, especially among those who felt that there was much to commend the idea of 'one king, one bishop'. Not only did such an existing arrangement have the advantage of established use but it also made some practical sense in that ecclesiastical organization mirrored that of political organization. Theodore, however, as Metropolitan of the new ecclesiastic province, felt that there was a desirability in having sees which could be more reasonably managed and better administered and that to do this, fragmentation was necessary. Wilfrid of York, who occupied the post of Bishop of the Northumbrian Kingdom, was opposed to his own diocese being divided into four. Surprisingly, Theodore's reform was backed by the King of Northumbria and though Wilfrid took his case to Rome and had his complaint upheld, the King, Theodore, the nobility and clergy of the area all refused to accept the judgement of the Bishop of Rome. Theodore met resistance in other areas too (Mercia and Wessex for example) but his plans were eventually enacted, even if some only came about after his death.

The annual synods which the Council at Hertford had resolved to hold became important events in the life of the English Church. Attended by kings and their councillors as well as thanes, bishops and clergy, the synods engendered a feeling of national identity and stability to the Church and thus gave a stimulus to its life and work. Although there was considerable political unrest at this time, with warring factions fighting for the thrones of the various kingdoms, ecclesiastical life enjoyed a unity that it had never felt before. The increase in the number of dioceses and a commensurate increase in the numbers of bishops brought with it closer episcopal involvement in the daily life of the Church. Subsequent to this change an obvious progression for the Church to make in ministering to the needs of its various scattered peoples was to place resident priests among the Christian communities of the dioceses. This was to be brought about by persuading landowners to first accept and then make provision for a priest to be resident in the local community, having pastoral care for all of its households and people. This innovation was the parochial system.

It is sometimes said that Theodore was the inventor of the concept of dividing church administrative districts into individual parishes. While it is true that he introduced the system to England, parochial organization already existed in other countries. For all intents and purposes Rome, for instance, was divided into 40 parishes by the end of the third century. The idea of appointing a priest to take charge of the pastoral care of all the people within a defined, small geographical area existed in Alexandria in the first half of the third century. The Emperor Justinian decreed in 541 that a person who could build an oratory and support a priest, should present a clerk to the bishop, who, finding the clerk worthy, might ordain him. The Synod of Orleans in the same year pronounced that if anyone wished to have a 'diocese' on his estate, he should allot sufficient lands for the maintenance of the church and its clerks. Gregory the Great was asked by the Bishop of Fermo to rule on whether it was permissible to have a church, newly built on an estate, consecrated. Gregory's ruling was that it was, provided that proper endowment was made for the priest. It is interesting to read that the provision consisted of a farm with its homestead and bed, a yoke of oxen, two cows, 15 sheep, the necessary tools for working a farm, and four pounds of silver as the working capital.

Throughout Europe then, as these examples and other documents such as the Canons of the Fourth Council of Toledo (633) show, at the time of Theodore the parochial system with its individual parochial endowments and legal rights was being established throughout Europe. It is fair to say, however, that it is Theodore who largely conceived the diocesan and parochial structures of the Church of England, structures which are still recognizable in our time. Before Theodore, priests and other clerics went out from monastic centres to administer the sacraments and perform other occasional ministerial tasks; after Theodore's reforms the Church in England became intimately involved in people's lives in a local and, crucially, a residential way.

Other Clergy

The Domesday Survey of 1086 makes mention of fewer than 2,000 churches (including chapels) in England. Half of these are listed as being in three counties, and in two counties no mention is made of any church at all, so we cannot with any accuracy estimate the total number of churches in England at the time. In those counties where good record is made over half of the parishes listed had their own church. The parochial system sketched out by Theodore 400 years before had significantly established itself as part of the English way of life. Theodore's plan of a parish church with a resident priest (*ibi ecclesia et presbyter*) was the reality being experienced by many. In a 1291 survey, 8,000 parishes were registered, and there is further evidence that there may have been approximately 1,500 more (Russell, 1993, p. 163). These parishes were served by as many as 23,000 clergy (not all of whom would have been priests; many would have been deacons or sub-deacons or would be in the minor orders of doorkeeper, lector, exorcist and acolyte).

In addition to parochial clergy, the Church of the Middle Ages was also served by priests working in other capacities. The bishop of a diocese retained a large number of staff around him, both to maintain the worship of his cathedral and to administer the work of the diocese. For the latter work, one person might deputize for the bishop when he was away on visitation in the diocese, another might have charge of the schools, another might have special charge of the services and yet another might be treasurer of the bishop's common fund. From such job division arose the posts of cathedral dean, chancellor, precentor and treasurer. Such became the position of the cathedrals staffed by secular clergy. Later some of these cathedral dignitaries were able to also hold one or more parochial benefices in addition to their cathedral posts. Other cathedrals were staffed by clergy who had adopted the Benedictine rule and were monasteries in which the bishop occupied, in some respects, the place of abbot, but the prior was the actual ruler. Such foundations included Canterbury and Durham, among others. A post-Norman see, Carlisle, was run by Augustinians.

The bishops soon also found it necessary to appoint one or more archdeacons to assist them in maintaining the oversight of their scattered clergy. Soon after the Norman Conquest, archdeacons had their own courts of jurisdiction which dealt with most of the minor cases of ecclesiastical discipline. The archdeacons held visitations at which they inquired as to the state of the fabric and furnishings of the church and clergy houses.

Chantries began to be founded in the late thirteenth century and over the next 300 years more than 2,000 were established.

Chantries were foundations for the maintenance of one or more priests, to offer Mass for the souls of the founder, his family and ancestors and usually an additional group of people (often other members of the foundation, such as those living in almshouses, also built by the founder). Chantry chapels were situated either as part of a parish, monastic or cathedral church or were built as chapels in their own right. Chantry priests were under no canonical obligation to assist the parish clergy, but in practice they often acted as curates or schoolmasters, as often the terms of a chantry foundation also endowed a grammar school or other school in the parish.

Thus far we have noted, albeit briefly: the division of dioceses in the eighth century and the subsequent spread of the parochial system of a priest in each manor; the foundation of monasteries (often serving as cathedrals of the dioceses) in the twelfth century; and the establishment of chantries during the thirteenth and fourteenth centuries. There were also other clergy of whom we should make mention, as their importance for our purposes lies in the fact that they were not employed in parochial tasks. Domestic chaplains, for instance, were for the large part free from parochial duties. Since Saxon times members of the nobility had often built a private chapel in their manors, served by a chaplain. In Norman times this practice continued and we have noted how many of these chapels became parish churches. In the Middle Ages almost every castle in England had a chapel in its keep-tower. Such chapels were served by chaplains. The colleges of Oxford and Cambridge, together with schools such as Eton and Winchester, also had their own chapels, although those who performed the religious duties in such chapels were employed as teachers rather than purely as chaplains. The larger medieval households contained regular garrisons of soldiers, and these would require the attention of a designated cleric to act as chaplain. Priests had accompanied kings and knights into battle: for instance, on the eve of the Battle of Crécy in 1346 the king retired to his oratory to pray and the next morning rose early to hear Mass and receive communion while his army made their confessions and prepared for battle. Chaplains were also aboard the ships of the English fleet which sailed to Cadiz in 1597 (see Smythe, 1968 and Taylor, 1978). In addition to such chaplains there were also those clerics who served as personal chaplains to bishops, often offering additional scholarship to the bishop, leading the worship in his private chapel and generally being of administrative assistance in the bishop's task of oversight of the diocese.[1]

Clergy were also concerned with the care of the sick. This happened in a number of ways: there were monastic orders dedicated to care for the sick and dying (in which places the boundaries between physical care and spiritual care were blurred); charitable foundations which made provision for chantries or almshouses may have included the care of the sick as part of their work; there were special hospitals dedicated to care for those suffering from particular afflictions, such as the Lazah Houses caring for those with leprosy. In all these institutions dedicated to caring for the sick, both priests and lay persons would have been involved in a variety of ways. Chaplains were also appointed to the newly built prisons of the late eighteenth and early nineteenth centuries, ministering to the condemned, administering the sacraments and organizing welfare and education. From these earliest days until the present time, chaplains have additionally had statutory duties to meet all prisoners on their entry and exit from prison.

The Industrial Revolution

So far in this chapter we have seen that the population of England from the time of Theodore onwards was, for the most part, ministered to by a priest who lived among them and whose own life was thus linked to theirs. Other clergy who were in existence either assisted them in this parochial task or were employed to perform a particular function for a very small section of the population. However, this connection with priest and people was to alter in a radical way in the latter half of the eighteenth century. Until the Industrial Revolution of the eighteenth century the inhabitants of England were relatively static in their life-styles. It was quite usual for a person to receive the three occasional offices of the Church, baptism, marriage and funeral (often referred to today as the so-called 'hatched, matched and dispatched') in the church of the parish in which they would be born, would work and would die. The new technology of the Industrial Revolution had a most profound effect on the ministrations of the Church and its clergy. New technology radically altered patterns of working. Not only was agricultural work mechanized, thus requiring fewer people to do the same work, but also the factories of the emerging towns and cities necessitated a population shift never before experienced in England. People began to travel in a way never previously imagined. Before the Industrial Revolution it was quite possible, indeed even quite usual, for a person not to ever travel outside a ten-mile radius of the place where they were born. As the mechanization of working the land meant the loss of traditional jobs in the countryside, it brought with it new jobs in the new factories. People now not only travelled outside their local parochial environment in search of work, they also left it to reside elsewhere when that work was found.

This movement by individuals, together with the cumulative effect of urbanization created by the massive population shift from the countryside, weakened the link between the Church and the general population of England for ever. The nature of the parish system in which all the significant rites of passage of a person's life were marked at the local parish church, the church which in all probability had also witnessed the same rites of their forebears, was radically altered. The Church's influence among the general population of England before the Industrial Revolution is often under-estimated. Politically and economically the Church exerted enormous influence over almost all of a person's life. The influence was made apparent both nationally and locally. In addition to this virtual hegemony, the Church's local representatives, its priests, also were at the very centre of people's lives. Parishes were much smaller numerically than today, with population numbers being measured in parishes by hundreds rather than by thousands (George Herbert's benefice of Fugglestone and Bemerton, for example, had a population of 400 in the 1630s; today it is 8,000). This size, together with the cultural position the Church enjoyed, allowed a parish priest to know his parishioners in an intimate way. Although divisions of class often separated the clergyman socially from many in his spiritual care, all parishioners throughout their lives nevertheless turned to him. His level of education, however basic, was vastly superior to most and this gave him additional standing and influence. One church historian looking at this time, which is sometimes called that of 'Merrie England', has written of the local parson: 'He was often much, very much to the society around him. When communication was so difficult and infrequent he filled a place in the country life of England which no-one else could fill. He was often the patriarch of his parish, its ruler, its doctor, its lawyer, its magistrate, as well as its teacher, before whom vice trembled and rebellion dared not show itself' (quoted in Russell, 1993, p. 2).

It can be seen from such an account just how extensive the Church's grasp was on the lives of those who lived under the parochial system (and of course every square inch of the country was, and still is, in some particular parish, for which some particular named person has responsibility). The Church's loss of influence was great indeed because of the Industrial Revolution. However, the decline only began at this time, as the two succeeding centuries which bring us up to our own time were to bring further losses. It is to this subsequent decline, set in motion by the Industrial Revolution, that we now turn.

Nineteenth- and Twentieth-Century Influences

It would be wrong to give the impression from the above that because of the Industrial Revolution, England went from peasant society to industrial nation in one rapid movement. Even before the urbanization and mechanization brought about by the Industrial Revolution, farmers and their families, as well as craftsmen, did enjoy some degree of mobility. The economic position of some small landowners also meant that there was a significant number of waged labourers who were hired and fired (and therefore had to seek work elsewhere) as market forces dictated the actions of their employers. The Industrial Revolution acted as a catalyst for the changes that were already taking place in English society.

The changes gathered pace from the end of the eighteenth century onwards. An examination of parish registers from the early nineteenth century shows that marriage partners were drawn from a much wider area than had hitherto been the case. Villages were drawn into regional and then later national economic systems. Even when the Industrial Revolution had taken root, the industries it created were still closely linked to the work of the countryside and its population. At the end of the eighteenth century, when 80 per cent of the population still lived in the countryside, many of the new factories and industries closed at harvest in order to allow their workers to go 'home' to the villages for the period to bring in the crops. The newly emerging towns and cities, as well as being the focus for industrial activity, were also the places where markets were held. Such a blurring of town and country had important ramifications for the Church. Those who formerly lived in the villages but who now lived and worked in towns and cities still looked to their old community as the place where they truly belonged. While they still connected with the Church for their rites of passage (held in the church of the community where they once lived) their daily working lives now had little to link them with either the Church generally or its local representative, the parish priest. For those in such situations, encounters with a member of the clergy became infrequent and the hold exercised by the Church over their lives generally also loosened. As the nineteenth century moved on, England gradually changed from being a predominantly rural society to being a predominantly urban one. As new generations were born in towns and cities rather than villages, the link with a particular church and its clergy changed to a greater degree. Despite concerted efforts in urban areas by the Church both corporately and locally, in the nineteenth century attachment to the Church diminished still further.

The nineteenth century saw the Church lose influence in a whole host of areas of people's lives. Charity for the poor moved from being the responsibility of parish vestries to being that of local government. Trades unions and employers' associations replaced the Christian Guilds of craftsmen and other masters of the Middle Ages. The trades unions also often saw the Church as an instrument of the ruling classes (which it often was). The improved education which came about in the nineteenth century (led in no small way by the Church) allowed people to develop critical faculties and opened up new vistas of knowledge. Such knowledge exposed the Church's denial or suppression of scientific discoveries and potential advancements. All this added to the growing secularization.

The experiences of the First World War (1914–18), felt both by those who fought and those who remained at home, profoundly affected the religious mood of the country. At the outbreak of the war a feeling of patriotism was high. The Church contributed to the notion of it being a just war and a war that was likely to be over quickly. The Bishop of London, Winnington-Ingram, tapped into this feeling when he said of killing the Germans, 'Kill them not for the sake of killing, but to save the world.' However, such a mood of optimism quickly evaporated. Stories and pictures of the massacres in the trenches brought the reality and the horror of warfare home to the whole country. Many felt that God had either abandoned the soldiers or did not care about them. Nevertheless the experience of many of the troops of the various religious representatives involved in the conflict in France particularly was good. Chaplains had been heavily recruited some months into the war to aid morale and to give medical and other assistance when required. Although many thought that the 'God-botherers' had no place in the trenches, the ministries of the vast majority of chaplains, notably those of Philip 'Tubby' Clayton and Geoffrey Studdart-Kennedy (known as 'Woodbine Willie' because of his distributing cigarettes to the troops) were well received and the chaplains themselves held in high esteem.

During the period between the end of the First World War and the outbreak of the Second World War the armed forces of Britain made a considerable effort to build up the chaplaincies to the Royal Navy, Army and Royal Air Force. The three services had come to recognize the need for permanent provision to meet the needs of the military community. When peace was declared in 1945, many had become used to having chaplains involved in every aspect of military life and felt that a similar experience might be replicated elsewhere. In the early 1950s therefore, 'padres' began visiting factories in order to engage with people in their own working environment. The ground-breaking work of Ted Wickham in the steelworks of Sheffield, becoming involved in counselling and education and training, set a model which others copied in other industrial settings. The concept of clergy working as chaplains in full-time, paid posts which were not centred on the residential, parochial model, gained support in other sectors too. With the expansion of higher education in the last 50 years university chaplains are now to be found in every university in Britain. As well as in hospitals, prisons, the armed services, industry, universities and schools there are also chaplains working in agriculture, airports, arts and recreation, police forces, the retail trade and commercial seafaring.[2]

The Church's Response to the Challenge

In this chapter we have sketched the genesis and establishment of the parochial system as found in this country and have looked at some of the responses which the Church has made to its changing circumstances. It is clear that not only is the society which the Church serves today vastly different from that of 1,000 years ago but that it is also substantially different from that of 50 years ago. The Church today faces the issues of multiculturalism which it largely did not have to face, or was able not to have to face, 50 years ago. Not only have questions raised by living alongside other faith communities of necessity forced the Church to look at its own expression and form of belief, but the development of ecumenism has engaged individual churches over the same period. Against such developments has been the increased feeling of secularization trumpeted by many. Whilst these voices have said that religion is in its death throes in Britain, others have said that the spirit of the age is not so much anti-religious but anti-church in its tone. Such external events have profoundly affected the ministry of the Church. Internally the Church has had to face the financial problems raised by declining weekly attendance and diminishment of its historic resources. Not only has the Church had to try to maintain its presence with fewer church buildings, but it has also had to do this with fewer clergy too. The contemporary Christian scene in Britain is, from such a perspective, bleak.

However, as we noted at the outset of this chapter in regard to higher education, there is a marked interest in religious issues and a considerable desire to know more about the life and witness of faith communities. From this other perspective, the contemporary religious scene is potentially rosy. The Church of England, and other Christian denominations in Britain, should grasp the opportunities which the interest such as this presents. We suggest that the residential parochial model of ministry which the Church has maintained so faithfully for so long is no longer fully adequate to take the Church into the twenty-first century. While the basic parochial structure should be maintained, chaplaincies should be further established in order for the Church to continue the Church's link with people's working and leisure lives, not just their residential lives. Writing nearly 40 years ago Leslie Paul concluded that 'One conclusion presses itself: the inflexibility that exists in parochial systems is an impediment to the exercise of the Church's pastoral ministry' (Paul, 1964). Changes in residential models of ministry have been made since these words were written, especially in regard to clergy working in groups or teams; the Church's action in regard to chaplaincies, however, has been somewhat different. Too often, chaplaincy posts have been the first to be cut as the Church faces financial hardship. We suggest, however, that far from reducing such posts, the Church ought to be increasing them. If there is such interest in religion as our rosy perspective suggests, such posts could be financed in partnership with the sectors in which the chaplains will work. There is a danger of the Church becoming unhealthily self-regarding and self-serving unless it is confronted by more than the experiences of its worshipping congregations.

Chaplaincies maintain the link between the Church and the wider world, a link historically maintained by a residential parochial system. Chaplaincies force the Church to take seriously the challenges of the society it seeks to serve as it ensures that it is enmeshed in them. This inclusiveness of attitude is not something of which the Churches should be afraid, for if the Church is to be taken seriously by the world at large, its clergy must be seen to be involved in more than ministering to the needs of particular congregations. In order for the Church to have something relevant to say about the forces at work in society, the Church must have a ministry to the social structures that shape life today. Education, industry, agriculture, prisons, airports, retail trade, health care, police and armed forces: all present issues to which the Church should both respond and help set the agenda. To minister in the midst of such settings through formal chaplaincies, the Churches would be concurring with the words of the Liverpool Statement with which this chapter began: 'We must engage openly with our contemporary culture. We need to demonstrate that our tradition has the resources to engage in an ongoing dialogue with the social, cultural and political problems and achievements of our age.'

Notes

1 See the chapter 'The Episcopal Chaplain' in Gibson, W., *A Social History of the Domestic Chaplain 1530–1840*, SPCK, London, 1993, p. 2.
2 For an introduction to all the ministries listed here, together with analysis of the theological, sociological and professional issues of chaplaincy, see Legood, G. (ed.), *Chaplaincy: the Church's Sector Ministries*, Cassell, London, 1999.

References

Bede, *A History of the English Church and People*, Book Three, chapter 26, Penguin, Harmondsworth, 1968, p. 194.

Paul, L., *The Deployment and Payment of the Clergy*, Church Information Office, London, 1964.

Russell, A., *The Country Parson*, SPCK, London, 1993, p. 163.

Smythe, J., *In This Sign Conquer – a Story of the Army Chaplains*, Mowbray, London, 1968.

Taylor, G., *The Sea Chaplains – a History of the Chaplains of the Royal Navy*, Oxford Illustrated Press, Oxford, 1978.

CHAPTER TEN

Structures for Theological Conversation

Shannon Ledbetter and Ian Markham

QUESTIONS OF STRUCTURE in theology are an integral part of the current debate surrounding the way in which theological conversation is conducted. By 'structure' we mean the framework that enables theological discussion to be progressed. Liberation and feminist theologians have constantly stressed the need for the structures to ensure inclusivity, especially of the poor and oppressed; while many theologians believe that the central structure needs to be the tradition of the Church. This, after all, is the believing community founded upon the revelation of God in Christ. However, although these points are often made, the precise components of these structures for academic theology are subject to much less reflection.

Academic Theology as a discipline has its own set of complicating factors that heighten the issue of structures considerably. Theology within higher education has many masters and several conflicting agendas. In the United States, publicly funded institutions have a constitutional obligation to make sure that theology is taught in such a way that it does not interfere with the separation of Church and State. Theology as an academic discipline hosts students from a variety of faiths or none. The structures needed to progress theological conversation in this setting must be given considerable thought.

In this chapter, we will begin by examining the displacement of the Church in academic theology. Now some would imagine that theological liberals will delight in such a development. This chapter will argue that this is not, and ought not to be, the case. After a brief comparison of the structures for academic conversation in the United States with those in the United Kingdom, we shall then argue that there are three areas in which British

Theology needs significant restructuring. First, the churches need to take an interest and responsibility for academic theology; second, the Church colleges within the UK need to become the impetus and resource for thoughtful theological research; and on academic societies – as suggested in the Liverpool Statement itself – British Theology would benefit from a British version of the 'American Academy of Religion'. Before we detail the arguments of these three points, we will briefly describe the history of academic theological conversation in both the United States and Britain.

However, at this point we ought to declare an interest: we are both Christians, members of the Church of England, committed to the Church College sector. It is precisely our location that provokes the heart of this argument.

Academic Conversation in the United States and Britain

Historically, theology was written within an ecclesiological context. The Church's theologians were priests, monks and nuns. They perceived their work to be part of their vocational commitment to the Christian community.

The academy in both Britain and America has emerged out of Church-founded institutions. Duke University was explicitly established 'to assert a faith in the eternal union of knowledge and religion set forth in the teachings and character of Jesus Christ, the Son of God (Marsden & Longfield, 1992, p. 3). Others saw a strong link between faith and the academy. For example, in 1924, both Yale and Princeton had compulsory chapel attendance for students. The religious roots of Oxford and Cambridge Universities are well known, but less well known are the religious foundations of other institutions. One such institution is King's College, London, which was founded in the nineteenth century to oppose the overtly secular institutions such as University College, London. Naturally, given their links to the Church, the study of theology was an important element of their curriculum.

From 1850 to the present day, the situation has changed dramatically. Bebbington notes how, in 1850 at Oxford, all heads of house except one were in the Anglican ministry; virtually all tutors were clergymen; and about 80 per cent of undergraduates were intending to pursue a clerical career. Students had to subscribe to the Thirty-Nine Articles of the Church of England on admission to the University; they took an obligatory test in the Greek New Testament and attended compulsory college chapel (Bebbington, 1992, p. 259). Meanwhile, in the United States at the same time:

> the first class on Monday morning for all students at the University of Michigan was Greek New Testament. This was intended not only to teach the Scriptures but also 'to keep the students from violating the Sabbath by pursuing secular studies.' [. . .] At mid-century Wisconsin, Michigan, and Indiana required such courses as Natural Theology, Moral Philosophy, and Evidences of Christianity, and prayer before class – no matter what the subject – was not uncommon. (Longfield, 1992, p. 48)

Today this overtly Christian culture has all but disappeared. On both sides of the Atlantic, religion is relatively unimportant within academic institutions. A significant exception to this phenomenon are the publicly funded Church Colleges in the United Kingdom, which we believe to be a significant resource that the churches should make more use of. This we shall return to later in the chapter.

As the academy became increasingly secular, so the child turned on the parent. Instead of Theology shaping the institution, Theology became a sub-section of the humanities. Indeed, as time passed, American universities especially, but also some in Britain, became attracted to Religious Studies. Theology, it was argued, assumed the truth of the Christian narrative: Religious Studies promised greater fairness and neutrality. With Professor Ninian Smart in Lancaster, and Wilfred Cantwell Smith influencing developments in the States, a new subject emerged, which took seriously all the major religions of the world.

Up through the 1950s, Theology continued to operate in both the academy and the Church. Most English Theology was dominated by the Church of England: many Departments of Theology had a high percentage of clergy within them. However, the situation was in the midst of change. Academic Theology wanted to distance itself from Confessional Theology: those who adhered to the former were happy to organize themselves in the same way as other subjects in the academy. The academic theologians did not want the interference (perhaps) or discipline (from the perspective of those who subscribed to a strict faith framework) emerging from the Church. This shift in emphasis resulted in two very distinct camps.

It is at this point that the structure for reading Theology becomes dominated by academic societies. Once the Church no longer exclusively provided a home for the subject, there emerged a proliferation of subject societies to progress the conversation between the plethora of specialists. But as we shall later discover, the precise form of the academic society was quite different in the United States from that formed in the United Kingdom.

The Church and Academic Theology

Although Theology remains a perfectly good skills-based training for graduates in the employment market, this is a very attenuated view of the discipline. For Christians, the subject matter of Theology is an exploration of the relationship of God to the world. These issues are of ultimate importance. If the Church desires more substantial theologians, its members need to take a more interventionist and supportive interest in academic theology.

The link between Church and theology needs to be established at two levels. At the first level there is simply the pragmatic consideration that theology is ultimately of interest to Christians. In the marketplace of subjects to study, each must find their niche. Whether we like it or not, the Bible, the history of the Church, the nature of doctrines, are topics that matter to the Church.

The situation facing Biblical Studies in British universities illustrates the problem. There was a time when a number of higher education institutions offered their own distinctive Biblical Studies degree. While Biblical Studies remains one of the strongest research areas in the United Kingdom, in the marketplace of the liberal arts' subjects, the discipline recruits badly. As a result, all Biblical Studies degree programmes are struggling. The reason is simple: the Bible has become less significant for people. The Scriptures do not warrant three years sustained critical attention. However, scriptural studies do remain crucial to the Church. For Biblical Studies to survive it needs the participation and support of the churches. The same is true of Theology.

However, on the second, more theoretical level, Theology ought to be the bridge between the Church and the world. Liberal Theology should not be confused with secularism. Although theologians have much to learn from the Enlightenment and the 'secular values' that it gave birth to, we are in the business of demonstrating how faith can survive in the modern age. Yet at the same time we do not want theology confined to those who participate in Christian communities: the possible danger of those sympathetic to Radical Orthodoxy. The academy is the home of intellectual enquiry in the universe of different disciplines: theology should be both located in faith traditions and reaching out to learn from and engage with the other disciplines in the academy. Religious Studies, which justifies its role in an entirely different way from Theology, is one such subject that theology must engage with and learn from.

The churches' contribution to theology remains mixed. Most denominations have 'official theologians' or a committee dedicated to academic theology. The Church of England, for example, has produced good work within the Doctrine Commission. However, what is needed is a combination of resources and organization among the denominations to underpin substantial theological reflection. Theological training for priests and readers ought to have, as a significant portion of their study, theological research. However, it is not only those who are committed to a vocation within church-related areas for whom the Church should resource and account for, but the advancement of theological reflection in general. This is where the unique nature and role of the Church College could potentially become pivotal.

Academic Theology and Secular Universities and Church Colleges

One of the good things about Britain is that we allow our Christianity to be interwined with our publicly funded institutions in a way that the Americans would find deeply puzzling. Bishops from the Church of England will probably survive in the revised second chamber in our parliament; compulsory Religious Education and school assemblies continue in our schools; and strong confessional Christianity is propagated in our secular universities.

In the United States, no religion is entitled to be privileged. So the state high schools and universities are all very careful to insist that it is the 'objective' study of religion that they provide: the privately funded institutions can teach from whatever vantage point they choose, but taxpayers' money should be carefully controlled.

It is important for the theological community to reflect on how we justify the use of public funds to support strongly confessional Theology. Religious Studies has no problem: they are providing 'cultural studies' and are often anthropologists or sociologists at heart. But what of theology? Consider if a Departmental Head running a strong Department of Theology in a secular British university became a fundamentalist and decided, by making various appointments, to turn the Department into a US-type 'fundamentalist' Bible College, then most of us would consider this inappropriate. It is, we would suggest, important that, at our secular universities, Theology is open to all faiths and beliefs and taught by a faculty representing a range of perspectives.

Secular universities, we suggest, have an obligation to the theologically diverse and committed to critical thinking. Bible Colleges have an obligation to be a community committed to formation and perhaps a particular approach and at the same time committed to critical thinking. Church Colleges are in a different situation. Church Colleges occupy a unique place within the academy. These higher education institutions in Britain, often awarding degrees from the prevailing regional, prestigious university, continue to have Governing Councils dominated by nuns, priests and bishops. Many of these institutions were originally set up to provide teacher training for women when women were denied higher education. Intrinsic to the Church College mission remains a system of values that implies risk (reaching out to educate those thought to be unsuitable) and formation (encouraging reflection on personal belief systems). Alongside the seriousness with which values are taken, equal respect is paid to scholarly study. The juxtaposition of the purely academic study of Theology with that of one motivated by belief necessitates conversation.

Many denominations have higher education institutions which are sympathetic to this mission: among these are Heythrop College, London (Roman Catholic) and Christ

Church Canterbury University College (Church of England). It is worth noting that the loss of Westminster College, Oxford to the secular Oxford Brookes University has been a significant blow to Methodism.

Once again, the argument for the churches thinking more strategically about Church Colleges operates at two levels. These institutions are entitled to operate inbetween secular universities and Bible Colleges. They are committed to the intrinsic value of the subject; they are grounded in particular faith communities (often, particular denominations) and yet committed to critical thinking. On the pragmatic level, the Church does have a vested interested in cultivating institutions serious about the academic study of Theology. Secular institutions will close Theology the moment the market indicates that there is not the demand: Church Colleges see a bigger picture. On the theoretical level, the Church can use the Church Colleges as direct routes to engage with the other subjects in the academy and therefore culture in general. They are, perhaps, the ideal venue for ministerial formation, especially of non-stipendiary ministers.

These Church Colleges, towards the latter part of the millennium, combined to fund a programme called 'Engaging the Curriculum: A Theological Programme' which explored the ways in which religion informed and enriched different academic disciplines in the modern academy.[1] However, the project, which highlighted religious distinctiveness, remains a small glimmer of light in an otherwise largely secular scene. It must be mentioned at this point that the American scene and the British one remain quite different. While the British academic structure allows for an entity such as the Church College, in America it has all but vanished. However, what is striking and important about structures in the United States is the emergence of a forum for all those interested in theological and biblical studies to converge: the American Academy of Religion and the Society of Biblical Literature.

Academic Societies

It was David Lodge who captured rather well the differences between UK and US conferences. For those going to a UK conference, the participants, explains Lodge, are put into student accommodation which is often unpleasant:

To veterans of conferences held in British provincial universities, these were familiar discomforts and, up to a point, stoically accepted; as was the rather inferior sherry served at the reception; as was the dinner which awaited them afterwards – tomato soup, roast beef and two vegetables, jam tart with custard – from every item of which all trace of flavour had been conscientiously removed by prolonged cooking at high temperatures. But the real source of depression, as the conferees gathered for the sherry, and squinted at the little white cardboard lapel badges on which each person's name, and university, were neatly printed, was the paucity and, it must be said, the generally undistinguished quality of their numbers. (Lodge, 1984, pp. 3–4)

Meanwhile, in the United States, Lodge describes the conference scene thus:

[it] is the Big Daddy of conferences. A megaconference. [. . .] This year it is meeting in New York, in two adjacent skyscraper hotels, the Hilton and the Americana, which, enormous as they are, cannot actually sleep all the delegates, who spill over into neighbouring hotels, or beg accommodation from their friends in the big city. Imagine ten thousand highly-educated, articulate, ambitious, competitive men and women converging on mid-Manhattan . . . , to meet and to lecture and to question and to discuss and to gossip and to plot and to philander and to party and to hire and to be hired. [. . .] There are no less than six hundred separate sessions listed in the official programme, which is as thick as the telephone directory of a small town, and at least thirty to choose from at any hour of the day from 8.30 a.m. to 10.15 p.m., some of them catering to small groups of devoted specialists, others, featuring the biggest names in academic life, attracting enough auditors to fill the hotels' biggest ballrooms. (Lodge, 1984, pp. 313–4)

In feel, style and approach, the two are completely different. The British have a separate conference for each area of the discipline. The philosophers meet at the British Philosophy of Religion Society; the ethicists have a Society for Christian Ethics;

the systematicians meet at Easter in the Society for the Study of Theology; our Old Testament colleagues enjoy the Society for Old Testament Studies; our New Testament colleagues converge at the Society for New Testament Studies; and there are even conferences for Pastoral Theology, Sociology of Religion, Patristics, Liturgy, as well as many others besides.

The strength of these British conferences is also their drawback. They are specialist conferences: the conversation therefore can be technical and detailed while a particular theme may be traced through the three or four days. At their best they can provide a real illumination of the issues surrounding a particular area.

The American Academy of Religion and the Society for Biblical Literature Annual meeting (henceforth AAR for short), on the other hand, is a complete contrast. Seven thousand scholars of religion converge on some of the finest hotels in an American city. At any one time there are numerous papers being delivered. For a visitor on his or her own the conference can be a lonely experience: by virtue of its size, it is virtually impossible to strike up casual conversations. The quality of the sessions can be very uneven: papers range from the muddled to the insightful. Some of those who have a thorough knowledge of the AAR best are the strongest opponents of the creation of a comparable organization this side of the Atlantic.

Having pointed out some of the weaknesses of the AAR, we must acknowledge the other side. The AAR hosts a wide range of conversations that makes the British conference scene appear limited. Sessions on interdisciplinary issues abound: feminism is taken seriously and the topical can be slotted into the programme with ease. At the same time, some of the small-dedicated groups do some appropriately intensive study. For example, The Society of Biblical Literature has had groups looking at the Dead Sea Scrolls, which has provided a forum for more concentrated study on this particular issue than even its equivalent UK conference. This is due to the fact that scholars from all over the world attend the AAR.

Perhaps most importantly, the AAR provides a showpiece for our subject which is not available in Britain. British Theology suffers from the lack of a forum from which to promote the field. Given the fragmentation of our subject into different conferences, no one particular conference can claim to be representative.

Given the government's need to have a representative body for the subject, all Departments of Theology and Religious Studies have formed themselves into AUDTRS (Association of University Departments of Theology and Religious Studies), yet this body's agenda is entirely set by the government which insists on a very narrow remit. Under the recent leadership of Professor John Hinnells,[2] AUDTRS has done some fine work in areas directly linked to the development of our subject, but, for example, declined to link up with a journal dedicated to the *Teaching of Religion and Theology*.[3] The quantity of conferences and the disparate conversations can be confusing for the professional, much less the lay person wanting to get a feel for the subject. On the opposite side of the spectrum is the showpiece aspect of AAR: the impressive bookroom that accompanies each conference. Each academic publisher that produces publications in Theology and Religious Studies in the English-speaking world is represented. It is essential browsing for those who want to gain a sense of the books that have been written during the past year, and a stroll around the bookroom is the quickest way to get that sense. Unlike the maximum of two or three publishers who are represented at a UK subject specialist conference, at least 100 publishers are represented at the AAR meeting.

There is yet another vital component of the opportunity afforded by the sheer size of the AAR meeting; that is, the employment opportunities. The vast majority of US institutions use the AAR meeting as a stage on their search for an appropriately qualified academic. As a result, one finds a high representation among research students who attend the meeting.

So to start bringing the threads of the argument together: the British theological scene is primarily served by numerous small, subject-specific conferences and societies. These societies all offer intimate and often quite concentrated discussions within a narrow remit. The body representing the subject to Government and Research Councils is AUDTRS. Each Department of Theology and Religious Studies who offers higher degrees is represented and each has one vote.

Although there are difficulties with the American Academy of Religion, the advantages of such a gathering outweigh the drawbacks. Concentrated discussions of particular detailed topics are still possible: small groups can be convened to progress a conversation in a particular area. In addition, interdisciplinary conversation is overtly encouraged. Those of us who straddle a range of fields do not find ourselves attending five or six conferences during the course of a year. Each individual may have several interests which he or she may choose to enhance. For example, for a person whose areas include Christian Ethics, Philosophy of Religion, Systematic Theology, and Christianity and Other Religions – in the UK there are at least three UK subject conferences he or she might attend as well as a need to start a fourth to accommodate his or her interest in Christianity and other religions. The AAR is able to accommodate most interests in the same programme book. An individual is able to move from a conversation in Systematic Theology and then to join a conversation in Philosophical Theology simply by walking down the corridor.

The Liverpool Statement was not the first attempt to put such an idea on the agenda. In the late 1980s many of the societies which make up Theology and Religious Studies in Britain were approached to consider meeting for the same week in different Cambridge (or Oxford) colleges. The idea was simple: each society would be housed in a different college and each society's meetings would be open to all other societies. In this way the structure would retain the delight of sitting down to breakfast with the undisputed authority in any given field while enabling those with wider interests to engage with other societies. This suggestion was met with little enthusiasm and even less initiative to offer alternative proposals from the various subject societies. The idea of an 'Oxbridge AAR' seems to have faded into the sunset.

The Way Forward

One manifest problem with British Theology is that there is no mechanism for progressing such ideas. It is difficult to even provoke a substantive discussion with the various societies on matters of structure. There remains no clear network of contact between members of different societies nor any one individual who is responsible for overseeing their activities. Perhaps one way forward is the creation of a society that every theologian and religious studies specialist would feel obliged to join. Britain is in need of a professional body that would carry authority. The UK model for such societies in other subject areas is a 'Royal Society'. The Royal Societies, with their distinguished Fellows, provide a forum that shapes, develops and organizes their subjects. Unfortunately, Royal Societies are not easily started overnight and much careful thought would be needed to begin such a society for Theology and Religious Studies.

It is the aim of this chapter to put forward two valuable resources which could strengthen and enrich the practice of academic Theology: first, the Church (including the laity), and second, the Church Colleges. In addition, we have argued for a British form of the AAR. It is our opinion that the resources currently available in Britain, namely the Church and its members, are being under-utilized to the point of neglect – while the fragmentation caused by numerous academic societies weakens the voice of faith and religiously inspired ethics in the political and social spheres. It is hoped that the Liverpool Statement will encourage conversation and an impetus to discover ways in which all those involved in Theology and Religious Studies may mutually benefit from each other, as well as the wider Church and community.

Notes

1 Engaging the Curriculum Project organized a journal of that name and has produced three substantial studies, namely, A. Thatcher (ed.) *Curriculum and Spirituality* (Cassell, 1999), L. Gearon (ed.) *Curriculum and English Literature* (Cassell, 1999) and L. Frances (ed.) *Curriculum and Sociology* (Cassell, 1999).

2 It is worth noting the interest and commitment that Professor Hinnells has shown to questions that preoccupy this chapter. Our subject interests have been served extremely well by his leadership of AUDTRS.

3 Both the AAR and SBL linked up with the journal precisely because they appreciated the importance of encouraging high quality research into pedagogy in Theology and Religious Studies in higher education. Despite Professor Hinnells' support for AUDTRS to make a similar move, two arguments seemed to persuade the committee against. The first was a sense that an independent body such as AUDTRS should not be seen to support a particular journal published by Blackwells. The second was the suggested link between Blair's managerial style, coupled with Blackwells' commitment to mass textbook publishing, could lead to the imposition of a national curriculum in higher

education, which could be damaging to academic freedom. For the record, Ian Markham must express his personal interest in this issue as he is the UK Associate Editor of the journal and it was he who presented the case to AUDTRS.

References

Bebbington, in Marsden, G. and Longfield, B. (eds), *The Secularisation of the Academy,* Oxford University Press, Oxford, 1992.

Lodge, D., *Small World,* Penguin Books, New York, 1984.

Longfield, B., in Marsden., G. and Longfield, B. (eds), *The Secularisation of the Academy*, Oxford University Press, Oxford, 1992.

Marsden, G. and Longfield B. (eds), *The Secularisation of the Academy*, Oxford University Press, Oxford, 1992.

CHAPTER ELEVEN

Beyond Orthodoxy and Liberalism: A Crossbench Response

Paul Avis

I HAVE BEEN ASKED to draw the threads of the various contributions together, to try to place the arguments in a common perspective, and to offer a kind of dialectical response to the overall thrust of the book, assuming that there is one. I must say that I regard it as a mark of true liberality on the part of the Editors of this volume to invite me to take this role! Perhaps it seemed to them that I would fit a liberal manifesto; if so, I find that rather worrying! I wonder what grounds I have given for such an assumption. It is true that my early book on ecumenical theology carried the subtitle 'The Elusiveness of Doctrine', but that was really an 'apophatic', not a liberal ecclesiology, and was classically Anglican in its use of the notion of probability. My study of feminist theology did indeed take a stance of critical solidarity with feminism and critiqued the patriarchy and androcentrism of the biblical tradition, but it was unwaveringly incarnational in its attempted reply to post-Christian feminists. In my work on authority I have certainly argued for an open-textured, dispersed and self-critical understanding of authority, but I have done so precisely in the cause of true authority and not in the interests of radical private judgement (Avis, 1986a, 1989b, 1992). So, whatever the perceptions of others, I do not see myself as a liberal theologian and I am not sympathetic to any push for a stronger liberal agenda in church-related theology. However, if that were the end of the matter, my contribution to this volume could stop right here.

The Elusiveness of 'Liberalism'

Defining liberalism in general, or liberal theology in particular, is not straightforward and it is not at all clear what a liberal agenda entails. A liberal manifesto – which is, I understand, what this symposium sets out to be – needs to be clearer about what is meant by liberalism (Berlin, 1969, especially pp. 8ff). Are we talking about the classical, rational liberalism of the Enlightenment, which believed that freedom of thought, untrammelled by ecclesiastical dogma, would arrive at the answer to every human dilemma? Or do we mean the nineteenth-century Gladstonian and Nonconformist type of liberalism: the ideal of the freedom to be virtuous, the reduction of inherited privileges, and the reform of historic institutions (i.e. the monarchy, the established Church and Parliament)? Or, finally, are we being reduced to the view of liberalism-as-liberty exemplified magnificently by the late Isaiah Berlin: the sceptical intellectual outlook, pervaded by historical relativism, that has lost its faith in absolutes and simply celebrates the diversity of human creativity while insisting that all values are culture-specific and ultimately incommensurable? (Berlin, 1994, pp. 167ff; cf. Gray, 1994).

Stephen Sykes defined a theological liberalism with teeth in 1971. In all its manifestations, he wrote, liberalism in theology is 'the mood or cast of mind which is prepared to accept that some discovery of reason may count against the authority of a traditional affirmation in the body of Christian theology'. Sykes continued: 'One is a liberal theologian if one allows autonomously functioning reason to supply arguments against traditional belief and if one's reformulation of Christian belief provides evidence that one has ceased to believe what has been traditionally believed by Christians' (Sykes, 1971, p. 12).[1] Is this how the Liverpool liberals understand liberal theology – as an approach that leads to piecemeal subtraction from the deposit of Christian faith?

Though Sykes immediately notes the distinction between repudiation and reinterpretation, his definition has a strongly propositional ring. Published 30 years ago, it speaks from the Cambridge theological climate of the 1960s and reflects particularly the challenge of analytical philosophy. Where the intellectual climate is more hospitable to the metaphorical and symbolic constitution of truth and its matrix in Wittgensteinian sociocultural forms of life, as it undoubtedly is today, doctrine can be more resilient and reason less of a blunt instrument. The quest for truth in theology becomes less analytical and more hermeneutical (see Avis, 1999).

These ambiguities and complexities of liberalism are barely discussed in this symposium. But they will, I think, at least enable me to offer a dialectical response and, in the process, to make common cause with some of its concerns.

First, let me put one or two cards on the table. I approach this question as an ecclesiologist, more than anything, and moreover as an ecclesiologist working in ecumenical theology and ecumenical relations. So I warmly welcome the assertion here that it is time for the Church to regain ownership of theological discourse within the academy. Like Karl Rahner, I believe that Christian theology needs to be pursued 'in the bosom of the Church' (Rahner, 1988, p. 101).[2] Even in a secular institution, that condition can be achieved, to some extent, when individual theologians and teachers retain their own private commitment to a branch of the Christian Church. But there the location of theology in the Church remains at the discretion (sometimes at the whim) of individuals. The Church can be the *locus* of theology in a much more corporate way, with richer interaction and greater accountability, when the institution itself is a church foundation. Its ecclesial trust deed and its ecclesial forms of oversight commit it more purposefully and directionally to the study of theology in the service of the Church.

It interests me very much that Liverpool Hope University College is an ecumenical – Anglican/Roman Catholic – institution. I wonder what kind of stated ecclesiology, if any, undergirds that union? What shared understanding of the nature of the Church of Christ enables these two traditions to work together in many ways and to have a common life and a shared purpose? How do Roman Catholics and Anglicans at Hope come to terms with the fact that their traditions remain not only distinct but separate – separate in oversight and separate at the Eucharist? How do they understand that separation in unity? To take a concrete example: how do they respond, institutionally, to the teaching document of the Roman Catholic bishops of these islands on eucharistic theology and the rules for eucharistic hospitality: *One Bread One Body?* (1998).

An Ecclesiology Driven by Mission

Frankly, I am convinced that much of the weakness of the churches' role in civil society today – though it undoubtedly has complex causes – is at least partly attributable to a watering down of the Christian gospel in the cause of accommodation to contemporary culture. Distinctive voices receive a hearing. They make an impact and evoke a response. Muted, tentative voices are lost; they do not prevail. I think that the Church of England is already liberal enough. I would view the prospect of a liberal hegemony in the counsels (synodical and episcopal) of the Church – which some consider exists already – with alarm. Approaching this issue ecclesiologically, as I do, I remain to be persuaded that self-styled liberals are really interested in the doctrine of the Church. Ecclesiology concerns the theological question of the place of the Church of Christ in the saving purposes of God (*missio Dei*). Is there – can there ever be – a coherent liberal ecclesiology?

To translate this into political terms for a moment: like Ledbetter and Markham, I would dearly like to see an enhanced role, within the theological resources of the churches, for the Church Colleges. The Church of England colleges of higher education, especially the university colleges and Church of England universities that are beginning to emerge, have untapped potential for theological education and research. There is a growing realization that the vision of their trust deeds needs to be recovered. Their pastoral base and liturgical life is often strong. Much could be built on this foundation. The Church nationally and in the dioceses would enjoy stronger resources; the colleges themselves could benefit from an enlarged constituency for theological education at all academic levels. But what some of my fellow contributors apparently fail to realize is that branding an institution 'liberal', in the way that this present symposium attempts to brand Liverpool Hope, will not commend it to the churches. Probably it is the most effective conceivable 'turn off' for the General Synod, the House of Bishops and the Archbishops' Council and equally unpalatable to the Roman Catholic Bishops' Conference. It is massively politically counterproductive. That effect is not a function of the ethical values of integrity, truth-seeking, and mutual respect that many self-styled liberals commendably want to promote. It is largely a problem created by the label 'liberal' and its unwelcome connotations that have historical causes.

Like several contributors to this book (especially Gareth Jones), I deplore the paucity of day-to-day, church-based, church-serving theology. However, I do not attribute this to excessive conservatism, to a lack of liberal concern for 'engagement'. As an exponent myself of working church-theology, I trace the dearth of this vital commodity to a weakness that is primarily ecclesiological – to a loss of direction and motivation that comes from not being properly 'plugged in' to the primary sources of Christian theology: Scripture and tradition. It is the Scriptures, regarded as witnesses to divine revelation, and tradition, as the hermeneutic of the witness to revelation, that must hold their place in Christianity as the primary and determinative sources for theological reflection and for official teaching. Tradition can be seen most helpfully in inextricable connection with Scripture as the living history of the exegesis, interpretation and application of biblical revelation to changing circumstances and cultures. A jealous methodological concentration on Scripture-tradition is simply unavoidable in a religion that is grounded in particular, unique events and persons, where the relation of God and the world comes into definitive focus and makes a decisive difference 'once for all', and is then perpetuated in a living, ordered community that extends through history.

I simply do not share the avowed aspiration of the Liverpool Statement and of some contributors to the present volume that we should become more 'open' (what does that mean?), more tolerant (of everything?), and more inclusive (on what grounds?). My overriding concern is ecclesiological: get the ecclesiology right and other things will fall into place. I think we should strive, as theologians, to recover the sense of the Church of Christ, in its historical embodiment, as a moral community, grounded in uniquely determinative events, sustained by distinctive God-given values, upholding key revealed truths, ordered by divinely commissioned authority, and united by common bonds of communion that are Christ's gift to the Church.

However, to hold that view of the Church dear is not at all the same, in my book, as advocating an ecclesiology of the gathered Church, or one that needs to draw membership lines that individuals cannot be left to draw for themselves, or one that revels in its

difference from the surrounding society. That approach, identified with the writings of Stanley Hauerwas, I find deeply
antipathetic. It stands at the opposite pole to what I am advocating. I regard it as profoundly misguided and counterproductive
for the Church's mission. And yet I am not promoting a liberal
solution! I am arguing for that elusive notion of a church that
glorifies God and fulfils its divine commission by being a church
for the whole community, both local and national. What might
this church look like?[3]

Such a church will make it its first priority to be present and
available, to all who will receive it, by maintaining a ministry in
every significant community of the land. The Christian ministry is
a ministry of the word in preaching and teaching; a ministry of the
sacraments of baptism and Eucharist, together with confirmation,
marriage and funeral rites; a ministry of pastoral care, support
and oversight. Such a church will recognize the imaginative
power of sacred symbols and ensure that it has its places as well as
its persons (that is, its churches as well as its clergy) comprehensively deployed. Its aim will be to provide publicly identifiable
points of access to its message and its ministrations. It will put substantial resources into ministries that complement the historic
territorial structures, above all, sector ministries or chaplaincies
(see Legood in this volume), but also diocesan evangelists and
children's and youth workers.

At the same time, such a church will value those arrangements
and structures (often a form of 'establishment') that provide it
with a platform, a voice and a recognized means of input into
great national issues. This kind of church makes an effective contribution to public doctrine, undergirded by confidence in the
credentials of its message as 'public truth'. It will be committed to
a nation-wide ministry of the gospel, combined with a nation-wide
service to the community, especially to the poor, the sick, the
bereaved and the underprivileged.

The conventional label for this ecclesiology is 'a national
church'. Both the Church of England and the Church of Scotland
tend to describe themselves as national churches. While they are
both 'established' churches, maintaining a territorial ministry,
they are not the only churches that aspire to a national witness.
The Methodist Church rejoiced in the national profile that it
once enjoyed. Now somewhat diminished, its place on the

national stage has been largely taken, one could say, by the Roman Catholic Church in England and Wales and in Scotland. The term 'national church' is still helpful and probably irreplaceable, provided that connotations of nationalism (the church supports the nation, right or wrong) or exclusivism (as the national church we have a stronger right or legitimation than other churches) are excised.[4]

What I am wanting to develop at this point, then, is an ecclesiology driven by mission. The marks of such an ecclesiology will become clearer shortly. Now any ecclesiology, as a necessarily theological discipline, requires the input of theologians and looks to institutions dedicated to theological research, teaching and reflection. Moreover, a church that reflects critically on its ecclesiology will honour theologians, support them and use their services. But an ecclesiology specifically driven by mission will need theologians (and, for that matter, practitioners of other disciplines) to resource its engagement with human pastoral needs, dynamic cultural shifts, changing social structures, and significant political and economic developments. Since its essential task is to connect – to bring the Christian gospel into effective, creative engagement with human existence at a given moment – it will need theologians with acutely sensitive antennae to the signals of transcendence, the indicators of hunger for God, in any given context (cf. Berger, 1971; Kerr, 1997).

The Liverpool Statement and its Targets

What stance does this suggest with regard to the Liverpool Statement of January 1997? Clearly, I am committed to its central agenda of engagement with contemporary culture, including dialogue with other faiths. But there is absolutely nothing controversial about this thesis. As a recent article precisely hammering liberal theology has stated: 'Christian theology has always been conducted in dialogue with the prevailing culture' (Hannaford, 2000, p. 93). I cannot think of a reputable theologian who did not or does not so engage. Open engagement is either a truism or means something more than it says.

Whom have the Liverpool liberals in mind here? Presumably, a key target is Karl Barth and the so-called 'Barthians' because of Barth's methodological concentration on divine revelation, his attack on natural theology and his contempt for apologetics. I have been as critical as anyone of these aspects of Barth's thought (Avis, 1986c, Chapter 3: 'Karl Barth – The Reluctant Virtuoso'). I now think, however, that we should make a greater allowance for the kind of person, the kind of genius, that Barth was. We should allow for the fact that Barth was a truculent character with a mischievous sense of humour. No doubt he sometimes had his tongue in his cheek. He was a virtuoso who disclaimed all such pretensions. This humble exponent of divine revelation was at the same time a highly rhetorical writer who brought all the tricks of the trade to bear on winning an argument.

However we come to terms with some of the more extreme aspects of Barth's theology, there can be no question that Barth was one of the most profoundly cultured of all modern theologians. Everyone knows of his love affair with Mozart's music. Barth's *Protestant Theology in the Nineteenth Century* begins with a protracted, sympathetic review of modern European culture. Of course, Barth then proceeds to demolish all his predecessor theologians (sometimes blatantly unfairly, as in the celebrated cases of Schleiermacher and Ritschl). Barth attacks them, not for engaging with culture, but for engaging with culture on the wrong terms and drawing the wrong conclusions. Basically, he indicts German Protestant theology in the previous century for a failure of theological method (Barth, 1972).

Thomas F. Torrance, the leading English-speaking exponent of Barth, might be another example of the kind of theologian whom the Liverpool Statement has in its sights. Torrance is famous (or infamous, depending on your point of view) for his concentration on theological method. Torrance's is fundamentally the Barthian method that takes divine revelation, given unsurpassably in Jesus Christ as he is known in the Scriptures and in the tradition of the Church, as its sole datum. While Barth developed a massive exposition of Christian doctrine out of the datum 'Jesus Christ', Torrance has proved himself perhaps even more wide ranging and versatile. His theological energy and intellectual appetite are outstanding. His own engagement with contemporary culture largely took the form of dialogue with the philosophy of physical science. This aspect of Torrance's *oeuvre* (which is very far from being the bulk of it: his patristic theology is also substantial) has not won general support. It raises crucial methodological and hermeneutical questions, above all about the commensurability of the data of physical science and the data of theology. I am afraid that the image of the Procrustean Bed is never far from one's thoughts when reading Torrance. His work has provided, however, valuable stimulus and momentum to reflection on theological method and on the relation of theology to the physical sciences. No one can take away from Torrance his achievement in sheer *engagement* (Torrance, 1969, 1980, 1985).

In succession, within the Reformed tradition, from Barth and Torrance stands Colin Gunton who has cultivated a reputation for scorning liberal theology and is widely perceived to have used his (deserved) influence in the Society for the Study of Theology to favour conservative, evangelical, or broadly Barthian theology. Gunton himself has made a notable contribution to doctrinal theology, notably in the areas of Christology and the understanding of the theology of revelation and creation. He has also reflected on method in systematic theology and has applied more rigour to this than many of his critics. What no one can deny to Gunton is the extent and quality of his *engagement* with modern culture. Both *Enlightenment and Alienation* and *The One, the Three and the Many* are precisely studies that proceed by engagement – critical engagement of course – with modern culture (Gunton, 1985, 1993).

Today, and more prominently than when the Liverpool Statement was first drafted, the most salient group of anti-liberal (some would say illiberal) theologians is one linked with the slogan Radical Orthodoxy. This rather hazily defined group annoyingly combines outstanding brainpower and creativity with what seems wilful obscurity and an unhelpful tendency to polarize arguments. Its two most typical members are probably John Milbank and Catherine Pickstock (Graham Ward having, it seems, 'gone native' in his work on postmodernity [Ward, 1997]). Whatever the merits of the theology these two have produced, no one can accuse them of lack of engagement with culture, ancient and modern. Milbank's programme of practising a theology without metaphysics and without social science may smack perversely of the cultivated paradox. Pickstock's nostalgia for the Roman Rite as the paradigm of all proper speech about God may be a touch too romantic. But of the sheer fact of their *engagement* with Western culture there can be no dispute. Milbank's method is to move forward through dialogue with benchmark theologians (like Augustine) and to bring them into dialogical relation with facets of modern thought, usually to the latter's disadvantage. The size and scope of the writers he engages with is impressive. Milbank's doctorate was on the first modern philosopher of history, Giambattista Vico. Anyway, who can disagree with his fundamental goal? Milbank sets out to reclaim and uphold the central Christian mystery (the Christian *mythos*) over and above the babel of godless voices in today's world (Milbank, 1990, 1997).

Pickstock's *After Writing* comprises a sweeping reinterpretation of the Western tradition of philosophy and theology, a devastating critique of modern and postmodern culture equally, and a new direction for theological endeavour in harness with a renewal of liturgy and prayer. Its target is the complex of broadly rationalistic and secularist ideas and practices that began to emerge in the late medieval period, were reinforced in the Reformation, acquired momentum in seventeenth-century empiricism, and received ideological form in the instrumentalism of aspects of the Enlightenment. They are dominant in technological modernity and finally run into the sand in the fragmentation and nihilism of postmodernism. For Pickstock, our increasingly information-based culture represents the nemesis of the domination of the world by the alienated analytical intellect, in which an original whole and integrated vision of the world is chopped up into discrete data, spread out and moved around, commodified, packaged and manipulated. Who can quarrel with an agenda like this? (Pickstock, 1998).

I think we can see from a brief review of the likely targets for the Liverpool liberal agenda, that it is not cultural or philosophical engagement as such that is the issue, but rather the theological method underlying and determining that engagement.

'Orthodoxy' and 'Liberalism' Weighed in the Balance

There is a method espoused by orthodoxy (Barthian or other) that believes that it is empowered by divine revelation (which it is confident it has got right) to more or less sit in judgement on everything else. It does not believe that it needs any help from other disciplines in understanding revelation. Revealed truth has its own integrity and authority. Here orthodoxy has a point. As

Ayres irrefutably says in this volume, it would be immoral for Christian theology, with its central revealed truth of the free creation of the world by a triune God, not to 'privilege' its account of reality. Perhaps orthodoxy's failure is in recognizing how much in the Christian understanding of freedom, creation, transcendence and Trinity has come about through engagement with ideas that did not originate in the bosom of the Church.

Orthodoxy's strength is that it robustly affirms the full orbit of Christian truth. It sees it steady and it sees it whole! It is mastered by the Christian *mythos*. Its motto is: 'He who is not with us is against us.' Orthodoxy's Achilles' heel, on the other hand, is the impression it creates (no doubt unjustly on the whole) of a take-it-or-leave-it mentality, one that smacks of intellectual arrogance. One suspects self-conscious Radical Orthodoxy of revelling, just for fun, in political incorrectness, defiance of fashion, and downright fogeyism. However, I do not believe that the serious agenda – its desire to be captive to the revealed word – in orthodox theology should be obscured by such incidentals.

Then there is a method typical of liberal theology that is much more receptive to culture and is prepared to accommodate itself to it. There are valid theological reasons for this. Liberal theology believes that revelation is to be found 'out there' in the world as well as 'in here' in the Church. For liberal theologians, the subject matter of theology is an exploration of the relationship of God to the world.' Rather than sit in judgement, liberal theology wants to get alongside, to trace connections and to find common ground. It sees elements of the good and the true even in murky ideological situations. Its sympathies are quickly kindled. It wants to reclaim as much as it can from a world drifting from God. Its motto is: 'He who is not against us is for us.'

Once again, Isaiah Berlin is something of an exemplar. His biographer, Michael Ignatieff, has suggested that, for Berlin, empathy was the core liberal attitude – 'the capacity to be open, receptive, unafraid in the face of opinions, temperaments, passions alien to one's own'. Empathy, Ignatieff continues, summarizing Berlin, 'committed you to leave the stockades of liberal reason itself in order to understand reason's limited purchase on a world propelled by passionate conviction and radical intensity' (Ignatieff, 2000, pp. 256f). In this privileging of empathy we find the secret of Berlin's attraction to the thought of Giambattista

Vico (1668–1744) (Berlin, 1976, 1981). The founder of the method of historical reconstruction through a combination of empirical knowledge and strenuous imaginative empathy, Vico believed that it was possible to understand the mind of primitive humanity, immersed as it was in the earthiness of passion and fear, and to discern there the dawning of incipient reason, manifested in rudimentary sacred rites of passage, basic moral scruples and emerging social order (Avis, 1986b).

Unfortunately, this admirable empathetic attitude can get muddled up, in liberal theology, with something a lot less robust and courageous than Berlin's intellectual vision – a loosening of the moorings, a vagueness about doctrine, a tentativeness about what you believe, a disposition to feel a lot more secure in your faith once some prestigious secular thinker has said that there might be something in it after all. All too often, liberal theology is distorted by rampant political correctness. Sometimes it can degenerate into the kind of abdication typified in the notorious World Council of Churches' slogan from the 1960s, 'Let the world set the agenda.'

At its best, however, liberal theology has a different kind of vision, infused with a passion for justice, equality and love. The world is God's world still, and we find God in it. Rather than claiming to see the full orbit of Christian truth, liberal theology will be more attracted to the essence of Christianity project. It will ask, what is crucial in Christianity amid the cultural flux? Is there an enduring centre that we should hold on to if other things have to go? Where is the rock of ages in the quicksands of criticism?

As this already suggests, the nemesis of liberal theology is the relativism that has given up the possibility of 'objective' conceptual truth and 'objective' ethical value. To Anglican traditionalists today, liberalism is a provocative word, a red rag to a bull. It was the spectre of relativism that made Newman condemn liberalism as though it were the antichrist (see Thomas, 1992). (Ironically, Newman's own thinking had done much to foster scepticism about truth [see Nicholls and Kerr, 1991].) Robert Hannaford's attack on the legacy of liberal Anglican theology targets relativistic thinking, typified for him in the Doctrine Commission report *Christian Believing* and the symposium *The Myth of God Incarnate* (Hannaford, 2000). Hannaford's is rather a selective target: there is more to liberal theology than that. The serious agenda in liberal theology should not be obscured by an artificially narrow focus.

The discussion so far suggests to me that 'liberalism' and 'orthodoxy' in current theological debate are artificial constructs that are fraught with ambiguity. Orthodoxy is far too pretentious a word for that loyalty to biblical revelation and its embedding in tradition that is not exclusively reserved for card-carrying traditionalists. Many who do not claim the distinction of being 'orthodox' or 'traditionalist' also aspire to this faithfulness: it is a basic Christian virtue. To boast of orthodoxy inevitably seems to imply that others are less than fully orthodox or even heterodox. That can be named: it is bigotry.

On the other hand, liberalism is far too vague a term for the theological values that its devotees advocate. For Anglicans it is loaded with explosive historical baggage from past controversies, such as *Essays and Reviews* (1860), *Ecce Homo* (1865), *Lux Mundi* (1889), *Foundations* (1912), the Girton Conference of the Modern Churchman's Union (1921), and *Honest to God* (1963), to come no closer to home. In Martyn Percy's contribution to this volume, it seems to me that liberalism proves to be an inadequate vehicle for the ethical values of the disinterested pursuit of truth, integrity in the theological task, and respect for partners in dialogue that he wants to advocate. The gift of divine charity should not be hitched to the wagon of theological liberalism. To claim the label 'liberal' for oneself inevitably implies that others are illiberal. Liberalism can be as intolerant and smug as orthodoxy can be.

Both 'liberalism' and 'orthodoxy' have turned out to be slippery, inadequate and invidious terms in which to conduct a debate about the public task of Christian theology. I want now to try to put this whole problematic on a more constructive basis by exploring three absolutely essential characteristics of a truly Christian theology. Any Christian theology worthy of the name must be identifiably catholic, evangelical and reasonable. That is to say, it must be rooted in tradition, welded to the gospel and marked by intellectual integrity. But, such a theology can only be realized when it is pursued in the bosom of the Church (to repeat Rahner's phrase) – a church that itself is professedly catholic, evangelical and committed to theological discussion by public canons of reasoned argument.

Towards an Evangelical Catholicism with Intellectual Integrity

It is the Creed itself that commits us to catholicity. Both the Apostles' Creed and the Nicene (Niceno–Constantinopolitan) Creed affirm the Catholic Church. No one doubts the Roman Catholic Church's adherence to the Creeds. Anglicanism also uses both Creeds a great deal: the Apostles' in Morning and Evening Prayer; the Nicene in the Eucharist. Thus there is no act of Anglican common prayer in which we do not profess our belief in the Catholic Church. The Creeds are also given a central place of authority in both the Thirty-nine Articles of Religion and the Chicago–Lambeth Quadrilateral. There the catholicity of the Church is seen, not only in adherence to the Creeds, but also in terms of its loyalty to the Holy Scriptures, the dominical sacraments, and a ministry linked to the historic episcopate.

Its catholicity is not, however, the first thing that should be said about the Christian Church. The very first thing of all is that it is the Church of Jesus Christ, his mystical body, bride and temple. The Church is essentially a mystery hidden with Christ in God (Colossians 3.3) and must be understood primarily in a christo-logical sense. The Church is founded on the gospel of God that tells of Jesus Christ's coming into the world, of his ministry, passion, death, resurrection, ascension and glorification for us humans and for our salvation. The Second Vatican Council states that Christ founded the Church by preaching the gospel (*Lumen Gentium* 5: Abbott, 1996). The Church is born of salvation history and belongs in the realm of grace.

But catholicity and the gospel are not opposed: far from it. It is precisely the gospel that leads us to affirm the catholicity of the Church. To look at the Church christologically is to look at it incarnationally. The incarnation is manifestly an historical, this-worldly event, carved out of our real human nature, so to speak. The view of the Church as the mystical body of the incarnate Jesus Christ already implies that the Christian Church is a visible, his-torical, continuous community. The catholicity of the Church is entailed in the incarnation: some earlier Anglican theologians spoke of the Church as the continuation of the incarnation. The catholicity or universality of the Church cannot satisfactorily be invisible or intangible, nor can it be expressed in ways other than the social and historical.

Hans Küng has suggested that catholicity has to do with fullness and completeness. Catholicity denotes an integrity that belongs to the Church by nature because it is grounded in the unity of the Church with Christ.

That integrity enlarges the hospitality of the Church to all humanity (Küng, 1971, p. 303). The aspiration towards fullness, completeness and integrity is expressed in the Church as a visible community, a divinely commissioned, though highly imperfect society.

It is important to stress that catholicity is concerned with completeness, universality and hospitality, because of all the notes of the Church it is the one that has been most prone to being hijacked for sectarian purposes, not least within Anglicanism. It is not long since the word 'catholic' was appropriated by one strand of Anglicanism, and others, it seems, were content to let it go. Owen Chadwick remarked in his Bishop Gore Memorial Lecture that 'catholic' was a word easy to misappropriate, 'to stuff into your waistcoat' and treat like a piece of private property, 'like a sixpence in your trousers pocket' (Chadwick, 1973, p. 173). But catholicity cannot be allowed to become the private prerogative of any one part of the Church: by definition it has to do with the whole.

In essence, Catholicism understands the Church of Christ to be a continuous historical community, commissioned by the risen Christ, a universal divine society in which Christ dwells through the Holy Spirit, and which communicates the saving and sanctifying grace of God through ordered means and structures, notably sacraments and a ministry based on the principle of transmitted authority.

It is clear that this is how the Roman Catholic Church understands itself: it is well known as a *societas perfecta*, a society complete in itself. But how does Anglicanism match up to this definition? What is catholic about Anglicanism? Anglicans certainly believe that the Church is a visible universal society, of which their particular Communion is a part, portion or branch. In Anglicanism, the dominically instituted sacraments of baptism and the Eucharist are fundamental, though confirmation, ordination, marriage, confession and extreme unction also have sacramental status for many Anglicans. Transmitted authority is mediated through the historic episcopate which is affirmed (for example in the Lambeth Quadrilateral 1888) as an essential component of the structural unity of the Church, though its rationale is not defined and there is disagreement among Anglicans on the question of whether unity of order in the historic episcopate is a condition of any degree of structural intercommunion, involving interchange-ability of ministries, with other churches.

To insist on its catholicity is, however, only the first step in iden-tifying the nature of Anglicanism: it does not tell what it is like to be an Anglican; it does not indicate the ethos of Anglicanism. So we need to ask further, what is the character of Anglican catholic-ity? In answer to that question, Anglicans would generally assert (the sense if not the words) that Anglicanism is an evangelical expression of Catholicism, renewed at the Reformation in the light of the rediscovery of the gospel of the free, unmerited grace of God bringing forgiveness and new life. Its evangelical quality stems from the emphasis on personal faith in Christ and the cen-trality of the Bible in worship, preaching and doctrine. But even that is not enough: in Anglicanism the evangelical dynamic is modulated by a tenor of thinking and a structural way of handling issues of authority that has been variously identified as conciliarity or dispersed authority or liberality.

What is clear is that the qualifier 'liberal' will no longer do. The language of liberal Anglicanism makes most Anglicans uneasy today. Some are more than happy to call themselves evangelical, and others readily identify themselves as catholic. Neither group sits comfortably with the qualifier 'liberal'. It has become a pejora-tive term and almost unusable. Bishops John Selby Spong, formerly of Newark, New Jersey, and David Jenkins, formerly of Durham, are liberal, and some people, bishop or theologian, may be nervous of being too closely identified with them!

However, it was not always thus. It is salutary to recall that Bishop Charles Gore, that bastion of orthodoxy who died in 1932, rejoiced in the designation 'liberal catholic' and the term came to distinguish the school which produced *Lux Mundi* in 1889 and opened a new chapter in Anglican theology with its synthesis between doctrinal orthodoxy and openness to new movements in science, philosophy and social thought. Gore described 'liberal Catholicism' as the 'maintenance of the ancient tradition and the ancient system which insists at the same time on expecting the individual member to do much for himself, which curbs the excesses of sacerdotalism and authority, which is scriptural and historical and a religion for free men' (Gore, 1918, p. 94).[5]

It appears that the word 'liberal' was already attracting pejorative overtones as long ago as the First World War. John Neville Figgis of the Community of the Resurrection (founded by Gore), preaching in 1917 in Grosvenor Chapel, Mayfair, London (where Gore would later have a regular ministry after his retirement) exhorted his congregation of upper-class Anglo-Catholics: 'Let us not be afraid to claim for ourselves as Catholic Christians the name of liberal.' The term 'liberal', Figgis points out, is not the exclusive property of persons with negative and heterodox views like the egregious Bishop Hoadly in the eighteenth century (Figgis, 1919, p. 10).

It seems that world wars concentrate the mind on the issue of liberalism. Writing in the aftermath of the Second World War, Alec Vidler acknowledged that liberalism in the nineteenth-century sense – the liberalism of which John Morley, the biographer of Voltaire and Gladstone and who resigned from the Cabinet when Britain declared war in 1914, was a pre-eminent exponent – had had its day. The liberal agenda with its lofty tolerance, its exaltation of conscience above all external authorities, whether of Scripture or Church, its faith in the ideal of a principled but by no means equal society was not, Vidler asserted, what was needed now. What the world needed to hear from the Church was the voice of prophecy and a message of full conviction. 'Freedom to believe and say what you think has been won; nobody minds what you believe or say; we are no longer shocked. In such a world the Liberal has lost his bearings. Original and independent minds are no longer attracted to his ranks. For Liberalism has ceased to be original. We can be as independent as we please' (Vidler, 1957, p. 18).

But if liberalism as an ideology was defunct, the liberal qualities of mind and character – Vidler prefers to call it liberality – were needed more than ever: The word 'liberal' denotes not a creed or a set of philosophical assumptions or any 'ism', but a frame of mind, a quality of character, which it is easier no doubt to discern than to define. A liberal-minded man is free from narrow prejudice, generous in his judgement of others, open-minded, especially to the reception of new ideas or proposals for reform.

'Liberal' is the opposite not of 'conservative' but of fanatical or bigoted or intransigent. It points to the *esprit large* and away from the *idée fixe* (Vidler, 1957, pp. 21f).

The need for liberality in Vidler's sense has more recently been argued by the (then) Archbishop of York, John Habgood, who adopts the stance of a 'conservative liberal'. 'Liberal', he observes, is used by some as a term of abuse: 'The General Synod has heard liberalism described as "a cancer in the Church of England", and there are those who seem to imagine that any faith short of fundamentalism is really a form of apostasy.' But for Habgood the word 'liberal' represents an openness in the search for truth which is essential to the health of religion. 'We grow in knowledge only insofar as we are prepared to criticise what we think we know already. True knowledge is tested knowledge [. . .] That is why an illiberal faith must in the end be untrue to a gospel which promises abundant life and growth' (Habgood, 1988, p. 2).

The evangelical and reasonable character of Anglicanism – its appeal to the principles of the Reformation and to reasoned enquiry – means that it aims at an evangelical Catholicism that is reformed in the light of sound learning: principally biblical scholarship and its theological interpretation and evaluation. And the well-founded conclusions of theological scholarship are allowed to act critically upon ecclesiastical tradition. With whatever admixture of less worthy motives – political, economic and personal – that was certainly the essence of the Reformers' approach both in England and on the Continent. It is an ideal that has been reiterated and reinforced by such modern interpreters of Anglicanism as Mandell Creighton, Charles Gore, Hensley Henson and William Temple. Though this interpretation of Anglicanism may seem to invite a good deal of qualification, and may even seem provocative to some, my central point is that Anglicanism is a particular form or expression of Catholicism, one that brings together the biblical gospel, the historical catholicity of the divinely constituted society, and reasoned theological enquiry and debate.[6]

In conclusion: neither 'liberalism' nor 'orthodoxy' will do as manifesto mastheads. What is called for is something more complex and more nuanced. Michael Ramsey identified it as the gospel, the Catholic Church, and sound learning (Ramsey, 1936). Certainly we are looking at a threefold theological allegiance, first to the Catholic Church rooted in the spirituality and theology of the Apostles, the Fathers, the Martyrs, the Councils of the early Church and continuously unfolding through history; second, to the gospel of God's free grace in Christ, rediscovered by the Reformers and revived in the evangelical movement both inside and outside the established Church; and third, to the conditions that promote the virtues of mutual respect, willingness to listen to and to be convinced by others, openness to criticism and reasonableness and charity in handling disagreement.

Notes

1 See also now Sykes' sophisticated discussion in '"Orthodoxy" and "Liberalism"' in Ford, D. F. and Stamps, D. L. (eds), *Essentials of Christian Community: Essays for Daniel W. Hardy*, T&T Clark, Edinburgh, 1996, pp. 76–90, where Sykes protests against the polarization of the two terms.

2 'Theology is a science of faith in the bosom of the Church' (Rahner, 1998, p. 101). Notwithstanding that statement, it is hard to think of a modern theologian who has been so fully open and engaged, both methodologically and substantively, with the broad currents of society, culture and the sciences.

3 These ideas are developed in my forthcoming book on mission and ministry in post-modernity.

4 See my *Church, State and Establishment*, SPCK, London, 2001, and in brief 'Establishment and the Mission of a National Church', *Theology*, SPCK, London, January 2000, pp. 3–12.

5 On Gore's Liberal Catholicism see Carpenter, J., *Gore: A Study in Liberal Catholic Thought*, Faith Press, London, 1960; Avis, P., *Gore: Construction and Conflict*, Churchman, Worthing, 1988.

6 On the character of Anglicanism see Avis, P., *Anglicanism and the Christian Church*, T&T Clark, Edinburgh, and Fortress Press, Philadelphia, 1989 (revised and expanded edition forthcoming); *The Anglican Understanding of the Church*, SPCK, London, 2000.

References

Abbott, W. M. (ed.), *The Documents of Vatican II*, Geoffrey Chapman, London and Dublin, 1966.

Avis, P., *Ecumenical Theology and the Elusiveness of Doctrine*, SPCK, London, 1986a.

Avis, P., *From Machiavelli to Vico: Foundations of Modern Historical Thought*, Croom Helm, London, 1986b.

Avis, P., *The Methods of Modern Theology*, Marshall Pickering, Basingstoke, 1986c.

Avis, P., *Gore: Construction and Conflict*, Churchman, Worthing, 1988.
Avis, P., *Anglicanism and the Christian Church*, T&T Clark, Edinburgh, and Fortress Press, Philadelphia, 1989a (revised and expanded edition forthcoming).
Avis, P., *Eros and the Sacred*, SPCK, London, 1989b.
Avis, P., *Authority, Leadership and Conflict in the Church*, Mowbray, London, 1992.
Avis, P., *God and the Creative Imagination: Metaphor, Symbol and Myth in Religion and Theology*, Routledge, London and New York, 1999.
Avis, P., *The Anglican Understanding of the Church*, SPCK, London, 2000.
Barth, K., *Protestant Theology in the Nineteenth Century*, SCM, London, 1972.
Berger, P., *A Rumour of Angels*, Penguin, Harmondsworth, 1971.
Berlin, I., 'Political Ideas in the Twentieth Century' and 'Two Concepts of Liberty' in *Four Essays on Liberty*, OUP, Oxford, 1969.
Berlin, I., *Vico and Herder*, Hogarth Press, London, 1976.
Berlin, I., 'Vico's Concept of Knowledge' and 'Vico and the Enlightenment', in *Against the Current: Essays in the History of Ideas*, OUP, Oxford, 1981.
Carpenter, J., *Gore: A Study in Liberal Catholic Thought*, Faith Press, London, 1960.
Chadwick, O., 'Catholicism', *Theology*, SPCK, London, 76 (1973).
Figgis, J. N., *Hopes for English Religion*, Longmans, Green & Co., London, 1919.
Gore, C., (ed.), *Lux Mundi: a Series of Studies in the Religion of the Incarnation*, J. Murray, London, 1890.
Gore, C., *Dominant Ideas and Corrective Principles*, Mowbray, London, 1918.
Gray, J., *Isaiah Berlin*, HarperCollins, London, 1994.
Gunton, C. E., *Enlightenment and Alienation*, Marshall Pickering, Basingstoke, 1985.
Gunton, G. E., *The One, the Three and the Many: Bampton Lectures 1992*, CUP, Cambridge, 1993.
Habgood, J., *Confessions of a Conservative Liberal*, SPCK, London, 1988.
Hannaford, R., 'The Legacy of Liberal Anglican Theology', *Theology*, SPCK, London, March 2000.
Ignatieff, M., *Isaiah Berlin: A Life*, Vintage, London, 2000.
Kerr, F., *Immortal Longings: Visions of Transcending Humanity*, SPCK, London, 1997.
Küng, H., *The Church*, Search Press, London, 1971.
Milbank, J., *Theology and Social Theory: Beyond Secular Reason*, Blackwell, Oxford, 1990.
Milbank, J., *The Word Made Strange: Theology, Language, Culture*, Blackwell, Oxford, 1997.
Nicholls, D. and Kerr, F. (eds), *John Henry Newman: Reason, Rhetoric and Romanticism*, The Bristol Press, Bristol, 1991.
One Bread One Body, Catholic Bishops' Conferences of England and

Wales, Ireland and Scotland, CTS, London, and Veritas, Dublin, 1998.

Nietzsche, F., *Ecce Homo: How One Becomes What One Is*. Trans. R. J. Hollingdale, Penguin, Harmondsworth, 1979.

Pickstock, C., *After Writing: On the Liturgical Consummation of Philosophy*, Blackwell, Oxford, 1998.

Rahner, K., *Theological Investigations*, vol. XXI, Darton, Longman & Todd, London, 1988.

Ramsey, A. M., *The Gospel and the Catholic Church*, Longmans, London, 1936.

Robinson, J., *Honest to God*, SCM Press, London, 1963.

Seeley, J., *Ecce Homo*, London, 1865.

Streeter, B. H. *et al.*, *Foundations: A Statement of Christian Belief in Terms of Modern Thought*, Macmillan, London, 1912.

Sykes, S. W., *Christian Theology Today*, Mowbray, London and Oxford, 1971.

Sykes, S. W., in Ford, D. F. and Stamps, D. L. (eds), *Essentials of Christian Community: Essays for Daniel W. Hardy*, T&T Clark, Edinburgh, 1996.

Temple, F., *et al.*, *Essays and Reviews*, J. W. Parker & Son, London, 1860.

Thomas, S., *Newman and Heresy*, CUP, Cambridge, 1992.

Torrance, T. F., *Reality and Scientific Theology*, Scottish Academic Press, Edinburgh, 1985.

Torrance, T. F., *Theological Science*, OUP, Oxford, 1969.

Torrance, T. F., *The Ground and Grammar of Theology*, Christian Journals Ltd, Belfast, 1980.

Vidler, A., *Essays in Liberality*, SCM, London, 1957.

Ward, G. (ed.), *The Post-modern God: A Theological Reader*, Blackwell, Oxford, 1997.

The Liverpool Statement:
An Overview

Rachael Penketh

Introduction

The argument of the Statement is simple: Markham *et al.* seek to make theology more relevant both to society and to culture by establishing something similar to the American Academy of Religion, and at the same time, venerating modern liberal society and the values it holds to be true. For those opposed to the Statement, who in the United Kingdom academy are probably in the majority, the Statement is representative of 'an utterly secularized theology and worse, suspect of having made academic theology its own, self-sufficient religion' (Loughlin, 1998, p. 12). Modern liberal society on which the Statement is parasitic is to be condemned and undermined 'for it is a form of death masquerading as life, in which post-modern carnival [. . .] enjoins difference in order to maintain homogeneity all the more securely' (Loughlin, 1998, p. 12).

The purpose of this short appendix is to outline the genesis of the Liverpool Statement and offer a tentative evaluation of its impact. For all the limitations of the Statement, I shall show that the debate it has generated is worthwhile. In addition, I shall argue that the Statement's methodological concern with certain 'conservative' theologies is entirely justified.

Genesis of the Statement

Underpinning the Statement was a research project, which was co-ordinated by Christopher Williams (a research student at Liverpool Hope University College). During the period August to September 1997, 340 questionnaires were sent to various individuals in the United States of America, all of whom were university-based, and many of whom had professional status (see Williams, unpub.). All were carefully selected from the American Academy of Religion and the Society of Biblical Literature Membership Directory that lists those working in the area of theology/religious studies. The questionnaire had been commissioned by Ian Markham, the aim of which was 'to investigate the, apparently, widely held view that American theologians know little of and so do not value the work of British theologians' (Williams, unpub., p. 1). The results were quite startling. Thirty-three per cent thought that there was nothing significant about British theology; 22 per cent could not name someone whom they thought was the most important British theologian; arguably, 60 per cent saw British theological trends to be irrelevant to their work; and overall, the impression was that British theology is 'insular', and 'staid' (Williams, unpub., p. 4, p. 5, p. 7, p. 8). It would appear that the 'widely held view' that 'American theologians know little about British theology and so do not use it', was justified.

Given the results of this questionnaire, and his views of contemporary British theology, it was perhaps no surprise that Markham was one of the two major players behind the Liverpool Statement, the other being Gareth Jones. They invited Jim Byrne (St Mary's University College, Strawberry Hill), Mark Chapman (Ripon College, Oxford), David Horrell (University of Exeter), David Law (University of Manchester), Shannon Ledbetter (Liverpool Hope University College), Clive Marsh (University College of Ripon and York St John), George Newlands (University of Glasgow), Kenneth Newport (Liverpool Hope University College), Martyn Percy (The Lincoln Theological Institute for the Study of Religion and Society, University of Sheffield), and Linda Woodhead (University of Lancaster) to join a discussion on the 'state of contemporary British Theology', on the 26 and 27 September 1997 (Badham *et al.*, 1998, p. 11; Markham, interview, 1999). Markham was the host and set the agenda for this meeting; he was also responsible for the first draft of the Statement (Markham, interview, 1999).

The group rejected this initial attempt at the Statement. The overall impression that the first draft of the Statement gives is polemic running to diatribe (See 'The State of British Theology', unpub.). David Law apparently dismissed it as 'pompous, pretentious, and presumptuous'. This draft starts as it means to go on: 'We believe that current trends in British systematic theology are deleterious to the place of the wider discipline of Theology in our modern University' ('The State of British Theology', unpub., p. 1). The Barthians are accused of being insular and so placing the future of theology in danger in the modern university; the Radical Orthodox of dismissing the concept of university completely, instead arguing that theology has to 'out-narrate' other disciplines. 'The Barthians and the Radical Orthodox often sound as if they believe that theology has nothing to say to the wider culture of Britain or indeed to Christians who seek to express their faith along other lines' ('The State of British Theology', unpub., p. 3).

It is perhaps no wonder that this original Statement was rejected. If the aim of the Statement was to alienate those who signed the Statement from the rest of the British theological world then it would have succeeded with disastrous consequences. The Statement was modified and agreed upon,[1] and then circulated to the heads of department of all academic institutions with a Theology/Religious Studies Department to gather further signatures,[2] and in January 1998, the Statement was released to the press (Markham, interview, 1999).

The revised Statement begins by describing very briefly past trends in theology, and the tribalism and insularity of theology today (see Badham *et al.*, p. 11f.). It declares that the future should be free from both conservative and liberal approaches to theology, for there are problems with both, and instead theology must learn from this past, and look to the future. 'A future theology must learn from the past failures of both liberal and conservative approaches. For the Christian message to flourish a clear vision of the theological task is required, a vision that uses the tradition creatively yet critically to engage with our modern age. We need to encourage a positive, open view of theology in the hope that it might once again influence the public sphere' (Badham *et al.*, 1998, p. 11f.).

To enable this to happen, five changes to British theology were considered necessary.

1 'We must engage openly with our contemporary culture' (Badham *et al.*, 1998, p. 12). There is a call for theology to show that it is still able to involve itself with the social, cultural and political problems and achievements of the present time; in the academy this will mean interaction with other disciplines and with contemporary culture. Theology is seen to be largely irrelevant to the man in the street, yet at the dawn of a new millennium there has been an upsurge of interest in 'spirituality', but instead of filling the churches of this country, individuals turn to 'New Age' religions and cults. For those who actively reject the Church, theology could have an important role to play exploring different ways of understanding key doctrines and beliefs.

2 'We need to be much more international in our vision' (Badham *et al.*, 1998, p. 12). Theological insularity in the past has been to the detriment of British theology, thus British theology has to look to

the rest of the world and explore different theological options. As was demonstrated by the results of the British Theology Questionnaire, only British theologians are interested in British theology. The results reflect a perceived snobbishness on the part of British theologians. ' . . . [T]he British don't seem to take much notice of American trends, nor do they come to our professional meetings much [. . .] a tone of condescension toward American scholarship is, to say the least, off-putting' (anon. cited in Williams, unpub., p. 9). In the 'global village', British theologians will find themselves increasingly marginalized if such introversion continues.

3 'The neglect of other faiths is wilful' (Badham *et al.*, 1998, p. 12). In a multicultural, multi-faith society, it is thought that the neglect of other religious traditions demonstrates a lack of responsibility. University and college students reflect the make-up of society and that society is multicultural and, therefore, also multireligious. As such, to concentrate on Christianity and Christian theology could lead to charges of institutionalized racism. Furthermore, the study of religious studies encourages an openness and tolerance towards other people and other faiths.

4 'A plurality of approaches in theological method and formulation needs to be encouraged, in order that, in a time of undeniable change, the better may stand out from the worse' (Badham *et al.*, 1998, p. 12). Staff in university departments of theology and religious studies ought to reflect a plurality of approaches, for to be able to accept plurality and difference demonstrates strength. Indeed, it could be argued that lecturers have a moral obligation to undertake such an approach; universities are not seminaries: they are financed by central government revenue.

5 'There is need for structural change' (Badham *et al.*, 1998, p. 12). The tribalism rife in British theology's past and present needs to be replaced with an open forum, 'The Forum for Religion and Theology', which will encourage change in those areas mentioned above. An attempt at this approach is central for the future of British theology, for without it the impasse will continue.

For those who supported the Statement, and with whom there has been correspondence, it was this need for more unity and communication in British theology that was the major factor in their willingness to offer this support. Their hope was for 'open conversation between branches of theology', 'a greater awareness of the impasse theology has come to in the UK and the will to creatively respond to it', ' . . . that the theological world in Britain [. . .] recognizes there is a strong tradition of openness and tolerance in British theology', and to 'let in some fresh air' (pers. comm., 1999).

The *Liverpool Echo* (9 January 1998), *The Tablet* (24 January 1998, 7 February 1998), the *Church Times* (30 January 1998, 6 February 1998 [letters]), *The Independent* (31 January 1998), the *Catholic Pictorial* (1 February 1998), the *Methodist Recorder* (5 March 1998), and *The Guardian* (14 March 1998), all ran stories or editorials on the release of the Statement. The majority were very positive, but it has to be noted that Markham had his hand in more than one of them! The most negative coverage was to be found in the *Church Times*. Here, the Statement was charged with 'sweeping inaccuracy', of being 'less than informed, failing to do justice to the transformations going on in the field, and attempting to issue a broad call without having engaged first with the major players' (Ashworth, 1998, p. 7). Both Markham and Clive Marsh rebutted these criticisms in the letters page of the next issue. This aside, in general the Statement was widely welcomed in the press, even if as one correspondent put it, 'I think that the people who might have been swayed by the statement [sic] would probably have been amenable to it anyway – preaching to the converted. those [sic] who are not amenable probably simply ignored it' (pers. comm., 1999). The fact that the majority of correspondents recognize the impact of the Statement to be 'fairly limited', 'relatively small', and 'rather little' backs up this observation (pers. comm., 1999).

In September 1998, a second meeting was held. Some of those who attended the original meeting were unavailable, and it was decided that critics of the Statement should also be invited (see Markham, interview, 1999). Those who attended who were for the Statement were: Jim Byrne, Mark Chapman, David Law, Shannon Ledbetter, Clive Marsh, Martyn Percy, and Alison Webster. Those opposed to the Statement were: Lewis Ayres (Trinity College, Dublin), who presented a paper; and Stephen Moss (St Stephens House, Oxford) who chaired a discussion. Paul Murray was probably somewhere inbetween (a signatory who is not a liberal). Independent observers were: Ruth McCurry (publisher) and Bill Beaver (Communications Director of the Church of England). The aim of this meeting was to thrash out the disagreements between those for and against the Statement, and this is where advancement of the Statement has been left. Markham has noted that one of the points of the group was that they did not want to start yet another theological society, but what the group did want for the future remained undecided. It could be (tentatively) suggested that the outcome of the Statement was not quite as expected, and so the group found itself back-pedalling; certainly there seemed to be no clear way forward. As one correspondent put it, ' . . . it was clear at the last meeting that there was a lack of consensus about what should happen next' (pers. comm., 1999). Perhaps the tribalism within British theology has become so ingrained that it is inescapable, and yet despite these difficulties, the debate continues and this volume of essays is the next contribution to it.

Analysis of the Statement

The only individual who has actively voiced opposition to the Statement is Lewis Ayres. However, it can be safely assumed that there is wide opposition to its assumptions and to its aims. This opposition is not voiced because those with whom it was concerned largely treated the Statement with indifference. It is not perceived as a threat to the current dominant conservative trend, purely, it is suspected, because of the numbers involved. Thirty-five individuals felt strong enough about the issues to sign the Statement, yet there are a large number of people employed in a professional capacity in the area of theology and religious studies in this country. Furthermore, would-be critics, such as John Milbank and others do not see the need to respond, not only because of a complete indifference to the Statement, but because they argue that the position they take is just another discourse within postmodernism, neither right, nor wrong, just different.

In his opposition to the Statement, Ayres has two criticisms. First, he argues that the Liverpool Statement was neither 'clear' nor 'straight-forward' as had been posited by Gareth Jones in an earlier article (see Ayres, in this volume; see Jones, in this volume). Ayres' problem was with the word 'engage'. ' . . . while we are told that theology must "engage" with the "modern age" and "contemporary culture" in a "positive" and "open" way, and while we must engage in an "ongoing dialogue", we are nowhere told what sort of practices "engaging" involves' (Ayres, internal reference).

The use of this word is, according to Ayres, too vague. It fails to do justice to the multiplicity of styles in theology, or it acts as a 'rhetorical ploy reliant on an unexpressed and possibly [. . .] unthought-out set of assumptions' (Ayres, internal reference). Despite these criticisms, Ayres, at a later point in this paper, himself uses the word 'engage', in a similar way to the Statement, and so although it may well be a 'rhetorical ploy', it is obviously one Ayres himself is familiar with.

The second objection raised by Ayres surrounds the concept of privileging. Underlying all the aims of the Statement is the need for openness and a plurality of approaches in British theology opposed to the tribalism rife today. Jones made this point more explicit thus:

> When a theological movement seeks to privilege its access to reality, or to claim that genuine reality is distinct from social reality, or worst of all, to state that there is something immoral about not privileging theology's access to reality, then I think we are on the slippery slope towards prejudice and discrimination. (Jones, internal reference.)

Ayres, on the other hand, argues that theological movements should, and do, privilege their access to reality, including liberal theological movements, and that not to do so is immoral. Traditional Christian theology always has privileged an account of reality in order to bring people closer to God, and this, according to Ayres, is social reality. The problem for Ayres is not privileging but how to privilege. By privileging their account of reality, Christians should aim to grow in the ability to privilege appropriately, and thereby recognize the immorality of the whole of humanity. To not privilege their account of reality, and the ability to know God, is to deny the incarnation and the self-revelation of God; what is required, according to Ayres, is faith.

On the basis of this, the basic problem with the Statement for Ayres, is that it claims that a plurality of perspectives is a good in itself. For Ayres, what is needed is a limited plurality of perspectives, based upon the principles of Christian thought.

In reply to Lewis Ayres' objections, five points need to be made. First, no one can claim access to the reality of God (Jones, 1998a, p. 88f.; internal reference). God is the 'other', 'beyond our comprehension and ineffable' (Markham, 1998c, p. 21). As such, Ayres and those who agree with him, cannot claim that their account of reality, that is the conservative theologian's account of reality, is true or right: it is an unknown. It may well be a matter of faith, but it is not a certainty, and should not be asserted as such. Their God, if he or she exists, created the world to include difference and diversity in many things including religion and theology (see Markham, 1998c, p. 21). This begs the question that if Christianity is the one, true faith, why do other faiths exist to lead the majority of the world's population astray and into eternal hell and damnation? There would appear to be a huge theodicy problem if this position is pursued. The Statement does call for plurality, and yes, it probably does need some clarification; but what is clear from the first draft of the Statement, and indeed from the Statement itself that is available to all, is that underlying this is the want to break down the tribalism inherent in

British theology. Indeed, Ayres betrays his own tribal preferences by assuming that only Christians, who should then privilege their account of reality, do theology. Whether theology should only be done by Christians is not the issue; the fact is that in universities and colleges it is done by individuals who do not ascribe to the Christian faith, and such institutions are funded by public money: therefore theology, when taught and 'done' in these institutions, should not privilege any account of reality.

Finally, it is important to note that theology has practical as well as theoretical consequences. As Paul Vallely notes, 'the road which begins in Dublin with a theological "sham" ends with a bullet in the head in Belfast' (Vallely, 1998, p. 161). The root of this bullet is the privileging of one access to reality over another, and it is not just in Ireland where this is relevant. It can be seen in the roots of the Holocaust, and in Kosovo today. It is indeed a dangerous tendency, the beginnings of a 'slippery slope', thus actively privileging any account of reality needs to be undertaken with great care (Jones, 1998a, p. 89; internal reference).

It has been left largely to Jones to pick up the ball for those who signed the Statement and run with it. Dr Jones has discussed the issues involved in an excellent article, 'After Kant: The Liverpool Statement', in *Reviews in Religion and Theology*, and expanded upon this in a paper given at The Modern Church People's Conference, in Oxford, in 1998.

In the first article, Jones, with the help of Kant, argues that 'reality' is an unknown; any claim to know reality or what is 'true' is a claim based purely in the realm of the subjective (see Jones, 1998a, p. 89; internal reference). Therefore, theology cannot be privileged over any other subject, and nor can one theological point of view be privileged over another. Jones makes the point in the paper 'Liberalism and the Vexed Future of British Theology', that whereas knowledge of God cannot, and is not, to be had, the Christ event enables the individual to participate in the mystery of God (see Jones, 1998b, p. 2f., p. 6f.; internal reference). As such, the point of theology is to look at faith in terms of what is, and can, be known, and thus theologians are enabled to recognize theology as one discourse among many. Theology only becomes distinct when no judgements are made with regard to its truth; but that, as Jones notes, is the job of the priest, not the theologian. 'Christian uniqueness can be celebrated, it cannot be reasoned' (see Jones, 1998b, p. 8; internal reference). Kant has enabled Christian discourse to be recognized as discourse, one among many; only from a faith perspective does this change.

It is interesting to note that on the point of faith, Markham and

Jones differ somewhat. For Jones, Christian theology is concerned with mystery, and the 'truth' of it can only be partly revealed through faith; reason does not come into it (see Jones, 1998b, p. 8; internal reference). For Markham, faith is knowledge based on reason. Markham, in *Truth and the Reality of God*, argues that if the concept of truth is understood in a certain way, then the world must ultimately be explicable; this is a 'logical necessity' that Markham calls 'God' (see Markham, 1998a). However, as Jones notes, faith defines what is true, and it is the work of theology to mediate between this definition and the world (see Jones, 1999, p. 31). Furthermore, surely to base an argument on a particular definition of anything is to open oneself up to criticism.

This aside, in 'Liberalism and the Vexed Future of British Theology', Jones goes on to argue that theories of ignorance, or limited knowledge, are linked to what individuals should do in their proscribed worlds (see Jones, 1998b). The world is immoral and yet academics are not interested in addressing it; Christian faith has been/is being reduced to a commodity and the Church of England has become impotent and so cannot deal with such issues. This is the world that the Liverpool Statement was set to address. The essence of the Statement is that theology has to make itself more relevant to both society and the Church. At the moment it is relevant to neither. British theology and its theologians would appear to be divorced from the world. It has an obligation to make itself relevant and thereby open up a new world to those on both sides of the divide.

Conclusion

That the Liverpool Statement was needed has been demonstrated. The conservatives, who dominate the current British theological landscape, believe that theology can only be done from a faith perspective; there is no, or little, dialogue with those who hold otherwise. The effects of this were reflected in the results of the British Theology Questionnaire. British theology is not considered to be relevant. In turn, this is reflected in universities and colleges around the country who are not answering the basic questions that surround Christianity and are largely refusing to enter into dialogue with any other discourse. This threatens the future of British theology in such institutions. In the current climate, every university, and indeed, each department within each university, is competing for students. Universities and colleges will not and cannot sustain a course that appeals only to those who are Christians. Conservative theology, in the light of this, either has to become more open and enter into dialogue with those who hold other beliefs, or retreat into a Bible school environment. For if the conservative tradition remains closed to other ideas and also remains dominant, theology will be subjected to a long, slow death.

What was said in the Liverpool Statement needed to be said. Theology as a whole has to open itself up to both society and the Church. As was noted earlier, at the dawn of the millennium there has been an upsurge in the interest in 'spirituality'. It seems a pity that this is the celebration of Christ's appearance on earth 2,000 years ago, and yet individuals who are searching for answers look at this time not to Christianity, but to 'New Age' religions and cults. Christian theology could do so much for these individuals. Surely those with a more conservative leaning recognize their 'duty' to proselytize at least. This itself means an engagement with those with whom you disagree.

The Liverpool Statement can be looked upon as the sounding of a warning that the future of British theology is in danger. Markham claimed that the issues involved are what is important, not the fulfilment of the aims and objectives of the Statement (Markham, interview, 1999). 'The Statement challenged the consensus and brought people together' (Markham, interview, 1999). This is the bottom line. There are problems with the Statement. Some of the language does need qualifying and there would also appear to be problems with the future of the 'Forum for Religion and Theology'. But these problems can be worked out. The issues are indeed what are important. Whatever its faults, the Statement is an essential and necessary pre-requisite to safeguard the future of British theology.

Notes

1 The only parts of this initial attempt that survived into the final draft are the aims and objectives. They are to engage with contemporary culture, to be international in vision, to look to other faiths, to encourage a plurality of approaches and methods, and to change structurally.
2 It is perhaps interesting to note that one of the individuals, with whom I have corresponded on this matter, complains that it only got to their Head of Department and no further.

References

Ashworth, P., 'Theologians want more openness', *Church Times*, 30 January 1998, p. 7.

Ayres, L., 'A Lack of Theological Vision: The Liverpool Statement and the Interpretation of Reality', The Modern Church Peoples Conference, Oxford, 1998.

Badham *et al.*, 'A New Theological Vision: A Call to Join the Forum for Religion and Theology', *Reviews in Religion and Theology*, May 1998/2, pp. 11–13.

Jones, G., 'After Kant: The Liverpool Statement', *Reviews in Religion and Theology*, 1998a/3, pp. 85–91.

Jones, G., 'Liberalism and the Vexed Future of British Theology', The Modern Church Peoples Conference, Oxford, 1998b.

Jones, G., 'Within Reason's Embrace', *Times Literary Supplement*, 19 March 1999, p. 31.

Jones, J., 'A Challenge to Boring Theology', *Methodist Recorder*, 5 March 1998, p. 11.

Loughlin, G., 'Rains for a Famished Land', *Times Literary Supplement*, 10 April 1998, pp. 12–13.

Mahon, D., (ed.), 'The New Millennium Needs New Theology', *Catholic Pictorial*, 1 February 1998, p. 3.

Mahon, D., 'Merseyside Looks to Theology's Future', *Catholic Pictorial*, 1 February 1998, p. 8.

Markham, I., *Truth and the Reality of God*, T&T Clark, Edinburgh, 1998a.

Markham, I., 'Feuding Theologians Will Always Be Ignored', *The Independent*, 31 January 1998b, p. 20.

Markham, I., 'The Road to God is Paved with Disagreement', *The Guardian*, 14 March 1998c, p. 21.

Marsh, C. and Markham, I., 'New Directions in Religious Thought' (letters), *Church Times*, 6 February 1998, p. 9.

Todd, A., 'Oh Come all Ye Faithful', *Liverpool Echo*, 9 January 1998.

Vallely, P., 'Theology for the Real World', *The Tablet*, 7 February 1998, p. 161.

Williams, C., British Theology Questionnaire, Department of Theology, Liverpool Hope University College, 1997 (unpublished).

'British Theologians Outline New Approach' (un-named), *The Tablet*, 24 January 1998, p. 120.

The State of British Theology, unpub. copy provided by I. Markham.

Interviews and Correspondence
Interview with Professor Ian Markham on 30 March 1999.
Correspondence (March–April 1999) with: Dr James Alison; Rev. Dr William Beaver; Dr James Byrne; Dr Frances Knight; Dr Clive Marsh; Rev. Canon Dr Martyn Percy; Dr Tinu Ruparell.

Please note that some correspondents did not wish to be quoted, and therefore correspondence is referenced to in general terms.

After Kant: The Liverpool Statement

Gareth Jones

In a recent review in the *Times Literary Supplement* someone took Ian Markham's name in vain. Or rather, Gerard Loughlin (*TLS* 10 January 1998) wrote that Markham's brand of liberal theology was akin to New Labour's advocacy of the Millennium Dome, both wanting to position what are essentially intellectual qualities in the marketplace as commodities to be bought and sold. What price Markham as the Mandelson of British theology? It may be an idea whose time has come.

It's been a bit like this for Ian for some months now, even before the quite considerable publicity he received for the publication of his statement announcing the birth of the Forum on Religion and Theology. Articles in *The Independent* and *The Guardian,* news coverage in the *Church Times* and *The Tablet,* mentioned in dispatches in the *TLS*: no other British theologian has received this much coverage in recent years, certainly not one who as a layman has no appreciable church connections. And Ian, being a decent bloke at heart, has shared the attention around, because the Liverpool Statement was signed by a wide range of other British theologians, all of whom (presumably) share his concern for the future of a subject which, in this country, can seem dubiously parochial.

At this point I have to state a vested interest: I, too, signed the Statement. Not only that, but I also co-organized the event in Liverpool which led to it and simultaneously founded the Forum for Religion and Theology (although, in truth, Ian did nearly all of the work, for which he deserves the credit). Subsequently, however, I went on secondment to the Church of England and, as I'm not supposed to make any statements which contradict the considered positions of the General Synod (heaven forfend), took something of a back seat when it came to the Statement's publicizing.

So why am I writing this commentary now? Well, because I think the time has come to follow up on Ian's suggestions for British theology, and try to push the argument on a little. And I say as, presently, a Church of England theologian, because the Church desperately needs a vital and energetic dialogue in and with British theology, to help to invigorate its own deliberations at a time of pressing concern. That might not be one of the Statement's principal arguments, but it is one of mine, and it is something one finds, here and there, in most wings of contemporary British theology. At the risk of being highly contentious, then, what I want to do in this short piece is take up the challenge the Liverpool Statement articulates, and call for an active development of the dialogue it wishes to see.

The Statement is predicated on the claim that contemporary British theology has a recognizable shape, and that there are certain tensions in it centred upon particular institutions, groups, individuals, journals and so on. But what is that shape? It's impossible to be objective about such a thing, and most analyses are highly impressionistic. I do think, however, that one can make some fairly sound judgements which help to contextualize the Statement, and which will go a fair way towards developing Ian's basic premise. Leaving aside biblical studies, therefore, and concentrating upon contemporary British *theology* and to some extent religious studies, here is one theologian's impression of the present state of the subject in question.

Starting with the most explicitly theological centre, first, there is the Institute for Systematic Theology at King's, London, headed by Colin Gunton. This is an avowedly conservative group, in the best sense of that word: it is centrally occupied with Christian doctrine and its interpretation, particularly its Protestant interpretation. Gunton has close links with David Ford and Dan Hardy in Cambridge – explicitly through the new book series *Cambridge Studies in Christian Doctrine*[1] – and with John Webster in Oxford, who shares Gunton's general theological concerns (and who edits with him the new *International Journal of Systematic Theology*). The great strengths of the Institute are Gunton's own prolific work, which is highly respected within the discipline, and the large numbers of graduate students it educates. It is undoubtedly a key power in contemporary British theology.

Colin Gunton is a past President of the Society for the Study of Theology, which meets annually and which is the second significant area I want to mention. Recent meetings of the SST have been characterized by an increasingly Barthian agenda, evident both in seminar discussions and some of the keynote lectures (particularly the presidential addresses). This, whilst understandable, is a fairly narrow way of presenting contemporary theological questions, and I think it is valid to suggest that the SST might consider a wider spectrum of positions in its future meetings.

The third and fourth significant areas are the liberal theology of the Liverpool Statement, signed by many British theologians (both established and up-and-coming); and Radical Orthodoxy, which has not published a statement or theses, but which also has a book series (with Routledge). Radical Orthodoxy is a small group, comprising an inner sanctum of John Milbank and Catherine Pickstock, with substantial satellites in the form of Graham Ward, Gerard Loughlin and Lewis Ayres; but it is highly significant, and in John Milbank boasts undoubtedly the finest senior intellectual in contemporary British theology. Pickstock is clearly an important talent, not least in her ability to understand and communicate every nuance of Milbank's extensive agenda. To varying degrees, however, Ward, Loughlin and Ayres are all semi-detached from the Milbank–Pickstock axis: Ward, because of his thoroughgoing postmodernism; Loughlin, because of his emphasis upon contemporary ethical concerns; and Ayres, because of his focus upon the patristic and biblical origins of post-liberal theology.

There are other noteworthy areas where individuals are doing significant work, such as feminist theology, the philosophy of religion, and of course Roman Catholic thought; but the fifth and final main area is what I would call the 'theology of religions' school, if I am allowed to define 'school' so widely as to include scholars who are explicitly working in the field of religious studies. The 'theology of religions' school is pretty diffuse, but would include such significant figures as Gavin D'Costa and Keith Ward, as well as Ian Markham himself. Whilst undoubtedly far less of an identifiable entity than Radical Orthodoxy, or even the liberal Forum, the 'theology of religions' school is recognized because of its intellectual and social relevance to the present state of religion in this country.

This is far from a complete picture: recent work done by the Theological Research Initiative listed over 4,000 items of research currently under way in theology and religion in the UK, at the widest possible range of institutions (and independently, of course). My brief survey does, however, give us a working model of what's going on in contemporary British theology. It is a political analysis, certainly, and undoubtedly presumptuous and judgemental; but I have undertaken it solely to provide a frame of reference within which to try to understand both the Liverpool Statement and the tantalizing possibility it holds out for the future. I hope this will now become clearer, as I elaborate what I take to be the main issue at stake in both the Statement and contemporary British theology.

The issue is the *status* of theological discourse with respect to other discourses. Or, to put it another way: the issue is the status of theological epistemology with respect to other epistemologies. Or, to put it yet another way: how does whatever we say and do as human beings and theologians, relate to what other people say and do as human beings (and theologians, if so they be)? This last alternative tells us what's at stake: not simply an argument about methodology, nor even one about how theology is related to other disciplines, but rather a claim about the way things really are. It's not a question, therefore, of theologians and academics scrambling for praise and glory, but rather of trying to influence the way people think about their lives in general, and their religious or spiritual lives in particular. There is a strong relationship, consequently, between the theological tensions and oppositions currently in play, and ecclesial authority.

The first thing which strikes me about this is how anomalous it all is, and by comparison how straightforward the Liverpool Statement is (by 'straightforward' I simply mean 'clear'; no value judgement is implied). Very few people in contemporary British theology are involved in the day-to-day writing of church theology, particularly Church of England theology, at least at a national level (I make no judgement about local or parish involvement); believe me, I know. I think this is a terrible thing, and it's a situation which desperately needs remedying, because there's a wide range of professional theological abilities which are not being employed by the Church. But it's something which goes hand-in-hand with the fact that the majority of British theologians now work in secular academic institutions, and are therefore, at least *prima facie*, directly in communication with other disciplines/discourses/epistemologies. The Statement warmly embraces this situation, recognizing it as a potential impetus to the far greater integration of theology into the world of contemporary intellectual and social analysis/criticism.

As far as I can see, however, the Statement is the only initiative in contemporary British theology that wants to make a positive virtue of this situation, something that is both intriguing and worrying. The fact is that it is bad for the Church to become divorced from society, and it is bad for theology to do the same. When a theological movement seeks to privilege its access to reality, or to claim that genuine reality is distinct from social 'reality', or, worst of all, to state that there is something immoral about *not* privileging theology's access to reality, then I think we are on the slippery slope towards prejudice and discrimination within a supposedly academic and intellectual discipline. Of the movements that I outlined in the previous section, none are guilty of such developments, and everyone involved would protest at the notion that their work could be construed as in any way totalitarian. Nevertheless, that is the danger as soon as one starts to talk about reality, and particularly divine reality, as a proper subject in which to participate. This might be the language of ecclesial and liturgical confession, but it is hard to justify in a contemporary academic situation.

Most people will realize that I want to move on from this cautionary note, to embrace Kant's distinction between reality and appearance as being of absolutely fundamental importance for the present and future of all theology, not just British. And I do this not because I think Kant said something which nobody has said before, or because I think Kant is the greatest theologian who ever lived. I do it because I think Kant made it clear once and for all what are the implications of relating theology to *thought* rather than action or practice or spirituality, and in such a way that there is no excuse after Kant for failing to appreciate this argument. Whether one thinks Kant's definition of the noumenal is adequate or not ultimately is not the point, which is rather that reality *per se* is not something which knowledge *per accidens* can control in any final or complete manner. On the contrary, our knowledge of reality is always incomplete because there is no one viewpoint from which people can see and appropriate reality – something which applies to the world just as much as to God. It is the reason why Hayek, in his great book *The Constitution of Liberty* (1960), argued so forcibly that the foundation of liberty is ignorance; for no one knows enough to coerce anyone else.

Of course, citing Hayek is the proverbial red rag to the bull in practically any academic context in Britain (certainly in British theology), and is alone sufficient to have me branded once again as the prophet of late capitalist theology. But the point which Hayek makes, and which no one seems able to answer, is that the notion of a civil society is founded upon our predisposition to listen to one another, so that we genuinely enter dialogue with an open mind as to its outcome. Now, people might not like the language of civil society, and I might agree that to make it the be-all and end-all of one's criticism is short-sighted. In a situation such as the one contemporary British theology finds itself in, however, the ability to listen is absolutely priceless. It is necessary in educational institutions like never before, and it is necessary for a church which finds itself threatened on all sides by the ever-increasing demands on people's time and identity, as does the Church of England. I'm sorry, but I'm afraid that privileging our subject area away from engagement with others is a privilege we can no longer afford.

I'm sure that many of the people I have implicated in the previous analysis will now be shaking their heads, which of course is one of the reasons for writing this short piece. I'm equally sure that many of them will not agree with the way I've set up the question of the key issue, particularly when it comes to the relationship between appearance and reality, epistemology and ontology (and indeed semantics). Well, I'm open to persuasion, and I certainly don't want everyone to become Kantians overnight. Nevertheless, I think contemporary British theology needs to get its collective head together, and ask what it thinks it is *really* talking about, and how that relates to what other people think they're really talking about. In one sense this debate is going on all the time, through books and papers, conferences and seminars, job appointments and such like. But it remains obscured by circumstances. As Ian Markham suggests in his Statement, we need to get that debate out into the open, as soon as possible.

I would like to endorse this suggestion by a call for definite action. What we need is a meeting in which representatives of each of these major groupings come together to answer the question, 'What do we think we're really talking about?' We need the liberals to come literally face-to-face with the radical orthodox, and the evangelical conservatives, and the dogmatic theologians, and postmodernists and postliberals, and representatives of the other significant voices in contemporary British theology, and to thrash out the big questions while actually listening to what each other has to say.

As such a development will be enormously valuable for the Church as a whole, and as I am currently employed by *a* church, I am willing to try to organize such an event, to find a space where it can take place, and to do the legwork necessary to make sure it happens. If I succeed, it may be that we have something more substantial and important to report than a Statement, or some suppressed theses, or a conference. We might find we actually have a dialogue we all can share, rather than mutual suspicion and antipathy.

Note

1 'Cambridge Studies in Christian Doctrine' is a new series edited by Colin Gurton and Don Hardy, published by CUP. David Ford has a book – the first – in this series: *Self and Salvation: Being Transformed*, CUP, Cambridge, 1999.

References

Hayek, F. A., *The Constitution of Liberty*, Routledge, London, 1960.
Loughlin, G. *Times Literary Supplement*, 10 April 1998.

A Lack of Theological Vision: The Interpretation of Reality and the Future of Liberal Theology

Lewis Ayres

In his argument in favour of the of the Liverpool Statement, Gareth Jones describes the Statement as 'clear' and 'straightforward'. In this short paper I want to take on two tasks: first, arguing that the Liverpool Statement is anything but clear and straightforward: in fact it so lacks these qualities that signing up to it seems to me roughly parallel to signing a petition encouraging the government to be nice. Second, I want to take issue with some fundamental themes from just one attempt by a signatory of the Statement to set out an agenda for theology. I want to raise some questions about Gareth's own encomium in the Statement's favour. This text probably does not represent the theological approach of the signatories as a group, but it seems at least *prima facie* likely that those signatories will share some of Gareth's assumptions.

First then, the Statement itself. There is, I think, one central way in which the Liverpool Statement immediately fails the test of being 'clear' or 'straightforward': while we are told that theology must 'engage' with the 'modern age' and the 'contemporary culture' in a 'positive' and 'open' way, and while we are told that we must engage in an 'ongoing dialogue', we are nowhere told what sort of practices 'engaging' involves. Well, that is not entirely true: we are told that we must be more interdisciplinary, more international and that we must encourage a plurality of method. However, these general remarks – with the possible exception of the third, to which I will return – actually tell us remarkably little. To explain what I mean, let me take the example of two theologians, Ian Markham and John Milbank, and the example of two books, *Truth and the Reality of God* by Markham and *The Word Made Strange* by Milbank.

In the former we find an 'engagement' with MacIntyre, with a number of contemporary analytical philosophers and with a few of

194

the major Christian theologians – Augustine and Aquinas for example. There is clearly here an 'engagement'. In the case of Milbank's book, we find a use of some threads in anthropology to continue an attempted subversion of some sociological perspectives; we find some developments in hermeneutic philosophy being used to develop an alternative view of the Trinitarian relations; we find recent work in historical Patristic scholarship being used to discuss the nature of self-hood. Here, we also find an 'engagement'. In many ways the character of the 'engagement' is similar, we find patterns of argument and source reference that are part of the normal or at least ideal structure of academic life that we all know so well.

If we want to try to specify how the two styles of engagement differ, it is not much good trying to typify one as engagement and one as not; nor is it much good just adding qualifiers such as 'open' or 'positive' to try to distinguish different varieties of engagement. Milbank and Markham are clearly both open and positive towards particular aspects of their engagements and less open and positive towards others. If we want to start a discussion about the nature of these engagements in such a way that we can usefully distinguish between them, we will need to offer a much 'thicker', 'denser' description of what moves they think appropriate, what points of reference and which discriminatory tools they take to be most deserving of our attention. We will need to know both what the fundamental principles of the 'engagement' that is being encouraged are, and we will need to know how we should learn to apply those principles. Let me make clear one consequence of what I have said: calling for open and positive engagement is in itself either inadequate and imprecise as a means of distinguishing many different styles of theology, or it functions mainly as a rhetorical ploy reliant on an unexpressed and possibly (but not necessarily) unthought-out set of assumptions. Thus, the Statement is neither clear nor straightforward because it uses the terminology of engagement in a remarkably loose and unclear fashion.

Of course here I have discussed only one aspect of a document which makes five different proposals. However, I think that my identification of fundamental problems in its rhetoric of 'engagement' actually gets to the core of problems in the direction of those proposals overall. I am not much interested in the fifth proposal (the call for some sort of AAR/SBL-like body in the UK) but both the first and third proposals use the term 'engage' explicitly, while the second and fourth propose shifts that are closely related. The second encourages us to avoid insularity, while the fourth clearly attempts to encourage us to some sort of acceptance of and engagement with a variety of different perspectives. Unless the authors and signatories of the Statement are able to be considerably more precise about what they actually want theologians to do by way of 'engagement', this Statement will continue to appear either imprecise, or it will seem just a cover for the sort of British woolly liberalism in theology whose problems the Statement initially claims to recognize.

So, if the Statement is itself simply unclear, how can we take this discussion further? I suggest that one good way forward is to look at the theology of those who have signed up to the Statement and try to see if we can discern a theological programme that can be considered in a little more depth. As just one example, I propose to consider the response of Gareth Jones to the Statement. This seems a worthwhile proposition as Gareth has attempted to expand on the Statement while being closely involved in its production and publication. As promised, I will concern myself here mainly with Gareth's discussion of the Statement in *Reviews in Religion and Theology* (1998). In commenting on his *RRT* piece, I will offer no comment on his attempt to draw up a typology of current British theology, discussing only those passages that pertain to the type of practice that he takes theology to be. Gareth is here concerned, above all, with the consequences of the distinction between 'appearance' and 'reality' and with the status of theological discourse. At the heart of his exposition Gareth writes as follows: 'When a theological movement seeks to privilege its access to reality, or to claim that genuine reality is distinct from social reality, or worst of all, to state that there is something immoral about not privileging theology's access to reality, then I think we are on the slippery slope towards prejudice and discrimination . . . ' (Jones, 1998, p. 89).

These sentences seem to me to provide an excellent foundation for our discussion, and it is on them that I have focused my attention in what follows. I want to argue, first, that I think theological movements inescapably do and most certainly should privilege their access to reality, and second, I think ultimately that there is something immoral about not privileging theology's access to reality. However, before we can face these questions head-on we need also to note Gareth's comments following this passage about the difference between appearance and reality. In those comments Gareth seems to me to be saying that there is a difference between appearance and reality with the following implications:

1 There is a difference between these two such that there is a constant and unbridgeable rupture between things as they are and things as they are perceived.
2 This rupture has the consequence that theology can make no

claim to perceive the structure of reality more definitively than any other discourse.

In making these claims, Gareth is not simply arguing that there is a difference between appearance and reality. Rather, he is arguing about the nature and consequences of that distinction – he is presenting an account of how the two bare terms in this opposition are to be interpreted. In particular, Gareth is offering a particular modern liberal and post-Kantian way of enlarging on the basic rhetoric of appearance and reality. Strangely, the distinction as Gareth has raised it in this commentary is closely parallel to the sort of debased Kantian epistemology one finds in the thought of John Hick (I say 'debased Kantian' to emphasize that we are not really discussing Kant himself, but rather a particular descendant of Kantian epistemology that may be found frequently in modern liberal theology). The final and ultimate consequence of this form of the distinction between appearance and reality is that only the one who holds to this creed, to this diagnosis of the problem, is able to claim 'real' access to reality. Now, nobody here, I hope, needs me to point out the most basic problems with the semi-Kantian position of Hick: Hick is arguing in simple terms, 'You can't privilege your account of reality, because mine is simply right.' I don't know how far Gareth is actually willing to go down this particular road, and I suspect that he would be keen to put some clear blue water between his position and that of Hick. However, as his argument is here expressed, Gareth's logic seems to have started down a slip-road that pretty soon will take him onto the Hickian highway. I can put my point fairly directly: if Gareth really thinks (and if the liberal theology thinks) that appearance is such as to prevent the apprehension of reality in all cases (in such a way that my point (1) necessarily leads to my point (2), then the logical conclusion is that only a relativist creed is realistically tenable.

One very important consequence of the last few paragraphs is that we should now be able to see more clearly that liberal theological movements themselves do privilege a particular account of reality. It should also be clear that I am not condemning them for that act, it is simply unavoidable. Traditional Christian theology also, and necessarily, privileges an account of reality. A couple of fundamental and rather obvious examples deserve repeating. Christianity holds to an account of the world as the free creation of an eternal and triune God. For Christians to argue that people should actively shape an account of the world as if this is not the case would involve them in basic betrayal of Christian teaching and of the Christian tradition. Now, of course, this can get complicated: Christians may want to

argue with those who perceive this statement as intending a distinction between two objects, and they may want to argue against
accounts of God that talk as if we have to do here with a single human
person writ large. But in all such arguing, the overall strategy remains
the same: the attempt to inculcate in people a closer and closer
appreciation for and attention to the God who sustains all in
existence and yet is not simply all of existence.

This example of privileging is obvious, and there are of course
plenty of others. One more will suffice. Christians have a view of
history that also differs radically from that of those for whom there is
no God, those who privilege other accounts of reality. Accepting the
providential ordering of events towards a given end appears to me
also to be a basic thrust of traditional Christian thought down the
centuries. The calling of individuals, peoples and times towards a
mission within the overall salvific purpose of God is a basic plot
component in the stories that Christians have told about the world,
and a basic component of the Christian imagination. This has been
so despite and through the terrible events of the history of the
Christian period, despite the wars and holocausts that humanity has
horrifically and sinfully inflicted on its own. The prophetic revelation
of the consummation of history in Christ and the calling of people to
participate in God's salvific action is a fundamental structure of the
Christian drama – and a fundamental aspect of the way that Christians privilege an account of reality. There is here great room for
engagement and discussion with non-Christian theories of history,
but there is also a tradition from which to engage, some principles to
bring to bear on the discussion and which should not be lost in it.

To engage in discussions with these principles in mind is not to
privilege a particular account of reality over 'obvious' social reality – as
the quotation from Gareth's commentary seems to claim. Rather, it is
to dispute about what social reality actually is. In one of his most
important eucharistic sermons, Augustine says to the congregation
that when they receive the Eucharist they should 'receive what they
are'. The congregation should receive the eucharistic elements that
have become the mystical body and blood of Christ in such a way that
they grow in realization that through membership in the body of
Christ their very substances may be transformed through the presence
of God. Augustine is arguing here that his audience must learn to re-
think the nature of reality itself; they must learn to overcome fallen
appearance so that they may see reality in Christ: the true social reality
of a community being drawn towards life with and in God.

All this also should be painfully evident and obvious. However, now
that we have come this far we need to consider a new distinction: the

distinction between the fact that Christians do and should privilege an account of reality and the ways in which Christians should act out that privileging. What practices are appropriate and what are not? What virtues must Christians demonstrate in their privileging in order to be faithful to their creed? It seems to me that perhaps Gareth has missed the importance of this distinction. It is not the case that privileging an account of reality in and of itself leads to prejudice and discrimination. On the one hand, privileging is simply inescapable; on the other hand, those who most seem to demonstrate the discourse of claimed non-privileging may manifest excellent examples of the prejudice and discrimination at which humanity so excels. How to privilege, that is the question. Let us take an example with which the most earnest liberal will sympathize. Let us say that in the wilds of Liverpool we encounter a tribe of child sacrificers who, poor things, have never seen a TV or a Coke can. I imagine that on the one hand, the vast, vast majority of 'non-privilegers' – as I will now call those who share Gareth's position – will want to convince this tribe to put aside their child-sacrificing days: modern Western liberal values will have to be 'privileged'. However, I suspect that many of those so-called 'non-privilegers' would also argue strongly that killing one in ten child sacrificers at random or introducing a mandatory death penalty for child-sacrifice would not be a good way to privilege the modern liberal view of reality and its laws. Privileging is not the problem; how to privilege is the problem.

Similarly, privileging the Christian account of reality is something that Christians should not attempt to avoid. Indeed, trying to teach themselves both that they are Christians and that they should not privilege their account of reality sounds to me only to be a recipe for psychological trauma – let alone philosophical incoherence. However, it is of great import how Christians go about that privileging. For Christians to privilege their account of reality appropriately they must develop appropriate habits of attention, attention to the voice of tradition, to the Scriptures, to the Spirit speaking within and without their communities. I do not have time here to outline even a basic account of the sorts of habits in which Christians should be schooled, and many Christians of course fail to acquire those habits. Nevertheless there is simply no reason why Christians cannot learn to privilege an account of reality and, at the same time, learn to do so in the context of the charity, attentiveness, kindness and confession that the great theologians of the Christian tradition have always recommended.

In fact of course, the last paragraph almost makes a bad theological mistake. It is far too simple to separate the supposedly 'basic' act of privileging and the supposedly secondary 'character' of that privileging. One does not need to read too far in a theologian such as Augustine, Aquinas or even Barth to realize that the practice of Christian life, the learning of charity, has been constantly conceived as the necessary context within which one learns the nature of reality itself. 'God is "love"' is a statement which has long been taken to imply not that we may acquire through the exercise of our minds a perfectly accurate view of reality's attainable or unattainable nature which we then need to convey as nicely as possible to our sisters and brothers. Rather, the practice of love, love formed by the traditions and shape of the body of Christ, is the central focus of the partial access to reality that we may learn in this life. The Crusader who cries 'Jesus is Lord' while smashing the skulls of Saracens is not someone who has seen reality for what it is and simply privileges that account wrongly: such a Crusader does not yet see the sense of what he (for it usually was he) shouts; he has not yet progressed far down the road towards apprehension of reality.

To privilege the Christian account of reality appropriately and truly is to grow in love and to accept one's place in the salvific drama of God and the world; not to do so is to remain unperceiving of reality and mired in the fallen reality that we take to be true. Our task, if we wish to become more 'moral', more mirroring of God's love in our actions, is to grow in the ability to privilege the Christian account of reality – not to do so is, then, an act of immorality. However, in learning this appropriate privileging we come to learn that all of us are mired in immorality and that all continually lapse into practising its deceits and self-deceits. We learn also that our apprehension of reality this side of the eschaton and the beatific vision remains incomplete. Thus we learn the nature of our immorality and our ignorance best by learning to be drawn beyond it; we perceive it more clearly, the more we allow ourselves to be reformed and re-shaped within God's salvific dispensation. Within this process we are shaped to learn to listen, and we are shaped to recognize our own and others' ignorance.

We should note also that it is this conception of the discipline of Christian life that makes any parallel between some key Kantian distinctions and the Christian distinction between fallen life and the reality of God problematic and rather misguided. Underlying Gareth's argument is an attempt to parallel, on the one hand, Kantian knowledge or intuition of *noumena* with knowledge of God, and ignorance of *noumena* with Christian knowledge: that is, a knowledge which has faith in the purposes of God, but which can only know the fallen world as it appears to all. On the basis of this parallel, Gareth wishes to argue that Christians are bound by general epistemological conditions that are characteristic of humanity as a whole. The incarnation, and God's self-revelation, thus have the surprising function of demanding conformation to worldly ignorance, rather than any transcending of it. Even more problematically, this set of parallels serves to undermine some key aspects of the theology of the incarnation. This is so because Christians have traditionally claimed a certain sort of knowledge of God; it is a knowledge incomplete but real: incomplete until God is all in all; real because it is knowledge of God's saving presence adapted to our apprehension. That knowledge is, most fundamentally, inseparable from the incarnate Christ: to fallen eyes Christ remains only human; to the eyes of faith he is divine and human, two natures in one person. Through developing appropriate attention to the incarnate Christ Christians may grow in faith and hope as well as love; and faith, as Aquinas tells us, is neither knowledge (in the sense of knowledge of an object), nor simply opinion, it is a *sui generis* category that awaits final formation in the beatific vision. Christians are indeed ignorant in a way, and, yes, they cannot yet claim full knowledge of God: but they do offer a path beyond Kantian ignorance and should not be constrained by it. Kantian categories of knowledge and ignorance simply do not allow room for those developed within the Christian tradition.[1]

Looking back for a moment towards the Liverpool Statement itself, we can now identify the most basic problems with its demand that we think of the plurality of perspectives as a good in itself. On the one hand, as will be obvious already from what I said earlier, the request is simply woolly and imprecise. Very few of us want to encourage an unlimited plurality of perspectives: few of us want to work in an institution that incorporates Christians, non-Christians, child-sacrificers, rapists and kleptomaniacs. On the other hand, we need to think carefully about what sort of plurality is appropriate on the basis of the account of reality within which we operate. On the basis of the fundamental principles of Christian thought, what plurality in theology and in theological education is appropriate? The question cannot be solved by appeal to the goodness of plurality itself. To do so is simply to privilege a modern Western relativism, or sometimes it is to privilege Romantic conceptions of the universe as sites of multiple exploration. Rather, we need to see what sort of plurality and unity will deepen our mutual, grown-in attention to God, and what plurality will most help us to understand the principles through Christian action and thought.

I draw attention to this point here because the Liverpool

Statement, in making this demand, seems to operate on principles remarkably close to those Gareth espouses in his commentary. Plurality is claimed as a good in itself – perhaps because of our mutual ignorance, perhaps because it follows from a particular privileging of an account of reality – but the foundations for this account are always hidden behind a claim that this is simply how things are, that this is the most basic level at which humans may operate. In both cases a much deeper account of the nature of plurality and the basis for it is needed: for Christians this answer will need to be a theological one.

But to conclude. Gareth's account does fill out something of what the Liverpool Statement fails to do, but it does so in ways that seem to draw it – and the course of liberal theology – ever more closely towards every problem that has made liberal theology such a danger in the past. If there is a future for liberal theology that will involve it in participation in the mainstream of Christian tradition, it will both have to abandon the claim of not privileging an account of reality, and it will need to account for its own practices in detail and in detailed engagement with the practice of learned love and ignorance that is, in fact, central to traditional and non-liberal Christian thought! Of course, many liberals will not share Gareth's view of theology and the future, but I suspect that many will share his account of the virtues of 'non-privileging' and the importance of the rhetoric of open and positive engagement. However, if liberal theologians do share these principles, then it is incumbent on them to offer some detailed account of what makes this engagement and this plurality theological. Not to do so is to admit that the logic of previous British liberalism has again taken its toll on the Christian community.

Notes

1 I have tried to offer some suggestions towards an account of Christian theology that operates in awareness of this understanding of the knowledge and ignorance of faith in my 'On the Practice and Teaching of Christian Docterine', *Gregorianum* 80, 1999, pp. 33–94.

References

Jones, G., 'After Kant: "The Liverpool Statement"', *Reviews in Religion and Theology*, SCM, London, August (3), 1998.

Markham, I. S., *Truth and the Reality of God*, T&T Clark, Edinburgh, 1999.

Milbank, J., *The Word Made Strange*, Blackwells, Oxford and Cambridge MA, 1997.

Index